PRAISE FOR
RETURN TO MINDFULNESS

"This book is like sitting next to a kind teacher who guides you through the many distractions of your mind and shows you ways to return to mindfulness, to non-judging awareness. It is full of practical, playful steps to systematically integrate mindfulness into your daily life, ways that Shalini herself has learned while practicing mindfulness as teacher and governmental leader. Whether you are new to mindfulness or have been practicing for decades, you'll benefit from her guidance toward a calmer, clearer, more loving and compassionate life."

—**Mirabai Bush**, author (with Ram Dass), *Walking Each Other Home*, co-creator of Search Inside Yourself: Mindfulness-Based Emotional Intelligence at Google

"*Return to Mindfulness* is a delightful read that will open your heart and mind. Shalini Bahl shares profound yet practical wisdom that will inspire you to live with more meaning, compassion, and joy. This book is like having a wise friend gently guide you home to your best self. Shalini Bahl draws from ancient wisdom and modern science to outline eight essential mindfulness skills we can cultivate to transform our default habits and return to clarity and purpose."

—**Acharya Shunya**, author, *Sovereign Self: Claim Your Inner Joy and Freedom with the Empowering Wisdom of the Vedas, Upanishads, and Bhagavad Gita*

"Once or twice in a lifetime, you may come across a book that can change you in a most positive way. *Return* has this magic and more. I have often wondered why my mind operates like a pinball machine (monkey mind?) and what to do about it. As a teacher, scholar, and public speaker, I now recognize the multiple selves that arise from my past to hijack what I am trying to accomplish in any given moment. This volume not only helps the reader understand the process, but it also shows how to mindfully, successfully, and playfully change reactions into pro-actions that serve our individual and interpersonal needs. My plan is to use the 50 options until they become a part of who I am across situations. Of course, the process never ends, and I will revisit the eight skill chapters over and over, seeking to mine every nugget of mindfulness gold in the foreseeable future."

—**Ronald Hill**, Dean's Professor of Marketing and Public Policy, American University; Editor-in-Chief, *Responsible Research in Business and Management Honor Roll*

"*Return to Mindfulness* is a mindful companion for navigating the complexities of life. Shalini offers a refreshing and practical approach to mindfulness. Whether you're seeking clarity with the eight mindfulness skills or embarking on a systematic journey to build your capacity for real-world mindfulness, this book is your trusted guide for joyful living and empowered leadership."

—**Chade-Meng Tan,** international bestselling author of *Search Inside Yourself* and *Buddhism for All*

"Diving into *Return to Mindfulness* by Shalini Bahl, PhD., is a refreshing journey back home to inner wisdom. This elegant guidebook not only illuminates the transformative power of mindfulness in everyday life, but also shares eight practical, real-world skills to disrupt unhelpful patterns and integrate presence in any moment. Rooted in timeless Buddhist teachings and informed by modern research, Dr. Bahl's clear explanations, relatable stories, and accessible applications enliven mindfulness practice. An indispensable companion for anyone seeking to connect more deeply with life, this book embodies compassionate self-exploration and mindful leadership with authenticity and grace."

—**Rashmi Bismark**, MD, MPH, preventive medicine physician, certified yoga and mindfulness meditation teacher, and author of *Finding Om*

"With amazing openness and clarity, Shalini Bahl shares her notable personal successes and failures, bringing them together for an insightful awareness of how mindfulness can make a pragmatic difference. Her journey weaves the different aspects of herself together through mindfulness, integrating them, while neither judging nor watering down any aspect of who she is, but rather welcoming them. Shalini's skillful crafting of the process of coming together reflects much of the tensions of present-day life, showing readers how to work with the joys and difficulties inevitable in life."

—**Ted Meissner**, senior mindfulness teacher, podcast host,
Mindfulness Voyage

"*Return to Mindfulness* offers practical exercises and insights that can effortlessly be incorporated into one's day, helping to find clarity and self-awareness amid life's overwhelmingly busy moments. Shalini Bahl's expertise shines through as she demystifies the practice, making it accessible to anyone, regardless of their prior experience. This guide equipped me with the tools to lead my company and staff with greater empathy, clarity, and authenticity. By integrating mindfulness into leadership practices, *Return to Mindfulness* not only fosters personal growth but also transforms organizations and communities, creating a ripple effect of positive change on a global scale. Return is an essential companion for those seeking a more balanced, mindful, and meaningful existence. With its gentle guidance and profound insights, this book has the power to transform your life, making mindfulness not just a practice, but a way of being."

—**Caroline Aller**, founder and clinical director, Amherst Cognitive Therapy

"*Return to Mindfulness* is a wonderful book. A mix of real-life examples and practical applications. Good for both the newcomer to mindfulness as well as the person who practices daily. A reader can read straight through or skip to the different practices. I felt like Shalini was in the room leading me as I read the pages. This has been a wonderful book to read as I enter a new chapter in my life. A reminder to return to my center and take time to just breathe. A must have by your bedside or desk."

—**D. Cristi Stroud-Downey**, wife, mom, sister, and managing director,
Guardian Life

"*Return to Mindfulness* is a beautiful guide to finding moments of awareness during days filled with multiple demands and expectations. Shalini's honest reflections sharing her journey with mindfulness are relatable to all of us who struggle to pause in the moment and be with what is present. The eight mindfulness skills taught in the context of daily work and life routines will help readers further their mindfulness practice and grow as leaders bringing positive change to the world. I was fortunate to study with Shalini as I began my mindfulness journey. *Return to Mindfulness* is a lovely reminder of the compassionate and gentle guidance she provided."

—**Greg Runyan**, director, Vermont Virtual Learning Cooperative

"A *Return to Mindfulness* is what we need in this moment. Shalini offers a profoundly thoughtful guide and reminder for us to be and see one another as deeply human. The 8 mindfulness skills—awareness, compassion, curiosity, energy, appreciative joy, inner calm, focus, and equanimity—are shared with ease and clarity. This means that each of us, as leaders, can more skillfully navigate division, conflict, and competing needs, as we extend compassion and take wise action that inspires new ways of being and thinking that inform how we do what we do. *Return* calls us to co-create the conditions and solutions that help bring people together, find common ground, and flourish. The beauty of *Return* is that it applies to all that we do at home, at school, in business, in politics, and more. Everywhere we are, *Return* should be."

—**Michelle Lopes Maldonado**, Virginia state representative and founder of Lucenscia

"How many town councilors do you know who practice and teach mindfulness— and bring it into their day-to-day life? Not enough! Shalini Bahl has done just that. This book is a testament to both the practical and profound impact of the practice of mindfulness and the way of life it promotes. *Return to Mindfulness* is a rich treasury of insights, methods, and playful illustrations, and also an honest account of a real journey to openness that all of us can relate to."

—**Barry Boyce**, founding editor, *Mindful* magazine and mindful.org

"*Return to Mindfulness* masterfully articulates the barriers we all face in being mindful during our everyday lives. Whether you're a leader or seeker, this book will serve you as a wise guide—a calm, clear whisper in a noisy, distracted world."

—**Amishi Jha, Ph.D.**, neuroscientist and best-selling author of *Peak Mind*

Return

to

MINDFULNESS

Disrupting Default Habits for Personal Fulfillment,
Effective Leadership, and Global Impact

SHALINI BAHL, PH.D.

BrainTrust
INK

BrainTrust Ink
Nashville, Tennessee
www.braintrustink.com

This work is being published under the BrainTrust Ink imprint by an exclusive arrangement with BrainTrust. BrainTrust Ink and the BrainTrust logos are registered trademarks of BrainTrust. The BrainTrust Ink logo is a wholly owned trademark of BrainTrust.

Grateful acknowledgment is made to the following for permission to reproduce copyrighted material.

From "REST" from *Consolations: The Solace, Nourishment and Underlying Meaning of Everyday Words – Revised Edition*. © 2014 David Whyte. Excerpts reprinted with permission from Many Rivers Press, Langley, WA www.davidwhyte.com.

Distributed by River Grove Books

Design and composition by Greenleaf Book Group and Sheila Parr
Cover design by Greenleaf Book Group and Sheila Parr
Cover images used under license from ©iStockphoto/Marje and ©Shutterstock/pixssa

Publisher's Cataloging-in-Publication data is available.
Print ISBN: 978-1-956072-19-8
eBook ISBN: 978-1-956072-20-4
First Edition

Dedicated to—

All the teachers who've selflessly shared the wisdom of mindfulness.

My parents—Suman and Kanwar C. Bahl—whose unconditional love and support empowered me to discover and pursue a path of love, joy, and integrity.

Contents

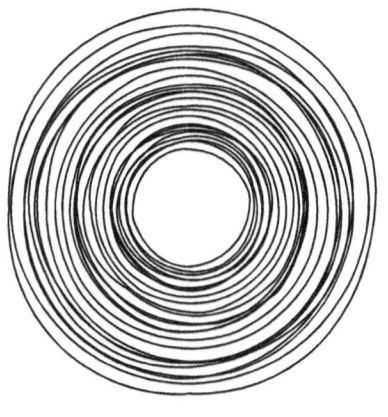

Part I

Return to Mindfulness

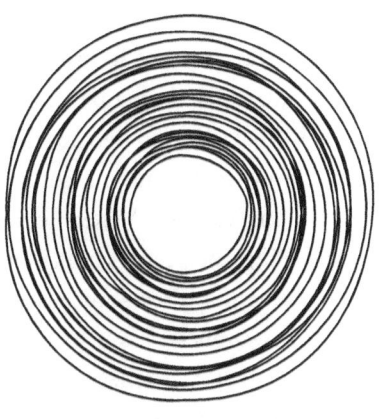

The Path to Fulfillment Begins Within

As human beings, we instinctively understand and recognize mindfulness, and each one of us has a natural ability to be mindful. But left to our own devices, our default habits get in the way, and we end up blocking ourselves from the mindfulness we seek. The key to being mindful in the real world is not more meditation but rather fostering skills that will detect and disrupt those default habits that prevent clarity and purposeful action in our daily lives.

This book is your guide for systematically (and, I hope, playfully) strengthening eight skills that will return you to mindfulness in the middle of everyday life. In this note, I offer an overview of *Return to Mindfulness* (hereafter referred to as *Return*), including why I wrote it and how I hope you will benefit from reading it.

Have you ever been delightfully lost in creating something beautiful, enjoying a phone call with a friend, or gazing at a stunning sunset? Such moments remind us that we have an innate capacity for mindfulness. We inherently know what it means to be present, connect with ourselves and each other, and make fulfilling choices. When we're connected with our inner sense of knowing, feelings of peace, vitality, clarity, and a profound sensation of ease naturally emerge. If we stray, just one intentional breath can return us to our mindful awareness.

Yet too often, what the world teaches us leads us away from our inner knowing, so much so that we forget our way back. We may catch glimpses of clarity when we're completely in the moment. But as soon as our thoughts trail off into daily chores, worries, and plans, we revert to our old ways of thinking and reacting. Much of this happens without our conscious awareness.

As adults, we may find it hard to accept that we live the majority of our lives on autopilot—without conscious choice or awareness. We think we have complete control and are making independent decisions, but often it's our default mind making the call. Our deeply ingrained habits of the mind are shaped by evolution and our environment. As such, we prioritize survival over fulfillment, efficiency over effectiveness, and validation over sustainable impact.

I'm no stranger to drifting through life unaware, disconnected from inner knowing. My Indian upbringing in Kuwait meant I learned early to rely on a world outside myself—authority figures, research, and cultural norms that proscribed women's societal role. There's nothing wrong with seeking guidance in the external world, of course. But solely relying on others can quickly alienate us from what's important to us based on our own lived experiences and unique gifts. It was only in my thirties—when I was introduced to mindfulness—that I realized the path to fulfillment begins within.

I experienced profound benefits from practicing mindfulness. It made me realize how disconnected I had been from my inner world. Mindfulness practices helped me regain clarity and confidence, especially in situations like meditation or being in nature. I was so inspired by the transformative impact it had on my life that I decided to make it my full-time career and area of research. Yet I struggled with being mindful in crucial moments, whether in the middle of difficult conversations, making complex decisions, or starting new habits. This struggle became more apparent when I entered the world of politics as an elected town councilor. I discovered that my *meditation self* could handle anything, but my *politician self* was easily hijacked by self-doubt and fear. When I got hijacked, I'd make myself small and invisible—a defense mechanism I'd mastered, which neither felt good nor led to fulfilling outcomes.

As someone who'd been studying mindfulness personally and professionally, I found myself wanting something more—a reliable path to return to mindfulness in the middle of everyday life. It turns out many of my clients were seeking the same thing. So began my journey to answer the question—how can we practice mindfulness for real-world impact?

Over the next five years, I devoted thousands of hours to reading, studying, and meditating on the original mindfulness discourse given by the Buddha—the *Satipatthana Sutta*—on which most secular programs are based. It is worth noting that the Buddha was not a religious figure during his lifetime. Born as Prince Siddhartha, he was the son of a king in ancient India (now part of Nepal). Motivated by a desire to alleviate suffering, he relinquished his kingdom and embarked on a quest for answers. At the age of thirty-five, he experienced a profound awakening to the knowledge of the human mind, which liberated him from his attachments that are the source of stress and suffering. From then on, he dedicated himself to teaching others how to tap into this innate wisdom within each of us. Intrigued by his insights into the human mind, I examined the ancient texts through the lens of science and their relevance in the modern world.

During this time, two insights profoundly shifted my practice of mindfulness as a seeker, mother, daughter, wife, politician, researcher, and mindfulness teacher. They are the bedrock of this book, as I mentioned previously. First, we have an incredible capacity within ourselves to move through the world with clarity and grace, but we let our default habits and biases get in the way, especially when we're triggered. And second, with practice (and play), we can replace our default habits with mindfulness skills that empower us to live and lead with clarity that will benefit us and others.

The promise of *Return* is simple: We can strengthen eight skills—

awareness, compassion, curiosity, energy, appreciative joy, inner calm, focus, and **equanimity**—to return to our field of inner knowing, regardless of our circumstances. *Return* offers over fifty practices and daily reminders that we can call upon in the midst of everyday life to regain a balanced perspective. The eight skills replace our default reactions with a more appropriate mindset to see clearly and choose our actions intentionally.

All the recommendations in this book are backed by scientific research and have been tested and tried by my clients and me. I encourage you to personally experiment and engage with the strategies presented here. See for yourself. Trust your inner knowing to find the best way to benefit from them. Read and explore the teachings on your own, or with loved ones, or team members—at home, school, work, and in your community. There's plenty of room to get creative about how and when you can tap into the eight skills.

As you contemplate reading this book, it's natural that your mind will conjure up numerous excuses not to invest your time in reading and trying the practices. But if you're here to truly see yourself and others, if we are here to shift the world in a positive way, together, for one another, then we have to call on ourselves to connect with this capacity within us. No matter how asleep we have become—as a people or a culture—we also have the ability to wake up!

My intention in this book is to show up fully, honestly, and joyfully and to share what I have learned to support you in returning to *your* inner knowing—so you, too, may live, love, learn, and lead with intention, integrity, and limitless joy. Whether you've been practicing for a while or are new to mindfulness, this book is here for you, like a mindful friend, to support you and celebrate you on your journey.

May you live an empowered and fulfilling life that benefits you and all *beings*.

Shalini Bahl

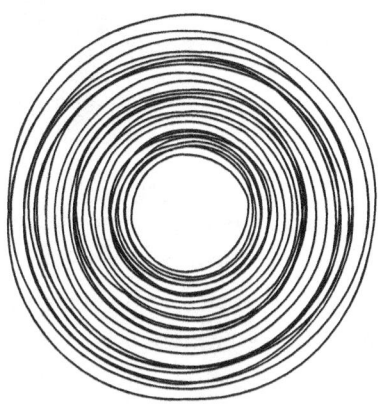

Chapter 1

A Wake-Up Call!

At all times and in any situation, how can I make mindfulness my constant habit?
—**Shantideva,** *The Way of the Bodhisattva*

Life works in mysterious ways. Just when we think everything has fallen into place—the dream job, the coveted promotion, admission to the ideal school, or the right partner—*ding*! Life serves us a wake-up call. These unexpected disruptions can be heartbreaking, challenging, or simply annoying. They can also be an invitation to discover something more, something deeper within us that we may have missed because we were distracted or disconnected from what truly matters. These disruptions are opportunities that can free us to soar higher, reach out into the world to discover what has heart and meaning for us, and be that, do that!

I had a wake-up call early in my career as a mindfulness teacher and entrepreneur. It shattered my ideas about mindfulness and my confidence to teach it . . . *and* it opened up a path that changed my life forever.

The Opportunity of a Lifetime

I stood at a crossroads in my life. After leaving my secure job as a marketing professor at a business school to relocate for family reasons, I faced the challenge of deciding my next steps. After some soul searching, I made the bold move to quit academia and pursue something more meaningful to me—research and teaching mindfulness. This new direction was a sharp detour from my comfortable and lucrative job as a marketing professor. But it wasn't entirely out of the blue: I'd experienced profound benefits from practicing mindfulness for more than a decade, and I'd found it incredibly rewarding to share the benefits of meditation with folks on campus and in my community in Salt Lake City, Utah. My research, starting with my dissertation, had focused primarily on self-awareness and mindfulness.

Quitting academia gave me the opportunity to make a true commitment to mindfulness by getting certified to become a mindfulness teacher. I was fortunate to get into the multiple-year program started by Jon Kabat-Zinn, Ph.D., at the Center for Mindfulness at the medical school at the University of Massachusetts in Worcester. My mission was clear: to make mindfulness as widely accessible as possible, with the ultimate goal of fostering thriving communities, workplaces, and schools.

At that time, I also came across the opportunity of a lifetime. I met the ideal business partner—my mindfulness teacher—and we would eventually begin our dream project together. Over the course of my training with her, we discovered an unmet need: Many mindfulness teachers with nonbusiness backgrounds struggled to market themselves. Our solution was to create a global networking platform that offered authentic marketing opportunities for mindfulness teachers. With my marketing savvy and her mindfulness mastery, we felt unstoppable! So off to the races we went, investing in a great staff, a spanking new office space, and bold plans for outreach . . . until it all came to a screeching halt.

Many start-ups fail, and there's nothing noteworthy about the fact that ours didn't take off. However, what was curious was the way we parted ways. It was highly contentious. We had to involve mediators and lawyers to avoid going to court. You know it's a real #mindfulnessfail when your accountant fires you. This was his email to us:

"I regretfully resign from working with the two of you and the LLC. . . . I can no longer let this toxicity into my life."

It's almost comical now to picture an accountant firing his clients—two mindfulness teachers who want to start a mindful business—because he found their interactions too toxic to continue working with them. Mind you, at this point, all he had to do was close the accounts of the dissolved partnership.

At the time, I was clueless about how I'd landed myself in such a predicament and how to extricate myself from it. I was also thinking of our staff and family members who had advanced us money to start the business—how could I minimize the repercussions for them? All along I thought we'd been going about our enterprise very mindfully. We had brought together an accomplished and mindful advisory board to support our inspiring vision. Every morning, we started our meetings with meditation and even invited our staff to join us. We were optimistic workers and confident in our abilities. And yet, here we were.

This unmindful ending of my mindfulness venture was a wake-up call! I had been meditating regularly. I was certified by a leading institution to teach others to be mindful. Yet, my actions (along with those of my business partner) had contributed to creating a toxic culture at work.

When it was all over, with our partnership dissolved and a no-win settlement reached, I decided to sit down to meditate on what had transpired during our years together. I made myself comfortable in my favorite spot on the porch, feeling the warm embrace of the sun and a soft summer breeze playing with the wind chimes. As I returned to my breath, moving in and out of my body, I was able to disentangle myself from my racing mind. It was full of remorse and questions. The most important was, *how could I (we), with all the mindfulness practice and training, have messed up so badly?*

As I contemplated my experience, gaps in my practice became clear, both on and off the cushion. I'd spent hours meditating on my body during my training and as a part of my regular practice. But once in the real world, I had missed all the cues when my body had tried to warn me—the clenching in my stomach, the tightening in my chest, the escalated heart rate—that something was wrong. In our race to reach the finish line, I had failed to notice that from the get-go, the heated discussions with my business partner were not just different points of view: Our values and business approaches were fundamentally different. We were misaligned from the beginning. I couldn't see it because I didn't want to accept it. I thought I could turn to positive thinking and problem-solving for what seemed like superficial issues. But by neglecting the crucial step of returning to my nonjudging awareness, I doomed the resolution of the underlying issues.

Lurking in the back of my mind was another voice. It was my *perfectionist self* posing an important question: *Can I authentically teach people mindfulness when I don't know how to be mindful in the real world?* No doubt, I was growing in some ways—more inner calm and confidence, more self-love and acceptance. However, my deep-seated ways of thinking, decision-making, and leading were not changing.

The incident devastated my confidence, but it made me pause, and in that pause was a life-changing gift.

In Failure, a Gift

My failed mindfulness venture humbled me. There was much more to mindfulness than what I thought I knew based on my secular training, but I did realize a few things: Meditating wasn't enough. Being present and thinking positively wasn't enough. If I wanted to live with clarity, courage, and integrity, I needed to be mindful in the *real* world. To achieve my goals of empowering people with mindfulness for enhanced personal fulfillment and leadership effectiveness while improving the world at large, I had to understand how mindfulness operates in everyday life. But how was I going to go about this?

The gift in my failed mindfulness venture—even though it didn't feel that way at the time—was that it launched my yearning for a deeper understanding of mindfulness. During the next five years, I devoted thousands of hours to studying, reading, and meditating on the original mindfulness teachings. I was fortunate to learn from excellent teachers of mindfulness: most notably Joseph Goldstein, Mirabai Bush, Sharon Salzberg, Jon Kabat-Zinn, and Mark Coleman. I then examined the teachings through the lens of science and its relevance in the modern world.

Further, politics pushed me to rediscover the value of mindfulness in leadership and additional challenges in walking the talk. As an elected official in my town, I had many opportunities to apply what I was learning about being mindful in the real world. There were instances where I faltered in being mindful at crucial moments. These situations allowed me to revisit my mindfulness strategies, discern my default habits that hindered clarity, and rectify—when possible—the errors made in reactive states.

Everything I learned, discovered, and experienced from this deeper dive changed my mindfulness practice and life. It became a new eight-week program that I started to teach, especially for those who wanted to deepen their practice in daily life. That program evolved into this book. There were many moments of big and small epiphanies along the way, many of which I share in this book. However, there was one aha moment in which I saw what was going on in all my failed mindfulness moments.

My Aha Moment: A Multiplicity of Selves

Dissatisfied with what I knew about secular mindfulness, I turned back once more to the original mindfulness discourse by the Buddha in Joseph Goldstein's book *Mindfulness: A Practical Guide to Awakening*. I was dumbfounded by the comprehensive framework that the Buddha had provided for all of us to understand how our minds work and how to free our minds from stress, suffering, and feeling stuck.

There was one theme I repeatedly came across in these teachings. Besides the mindfulness path and practices, there was an emphasis on different qualities of the mind that free us from our predispositions, judgments, and biases, all distorting understanding of our individual and shared human experiences. These qualities of the mind, known as mindfulness or enlightenment factors, are present in all of us but can be strengthened to become skills we can rely on to disrupt our default habits that hinder our ability to be mindful. In particular, there are eight mindfulness skills—awareness, compassion, curiosity, energy, appreciative joy, inner calm, focus, and equanimity—that act as antidotes to our biases so we may have a more accurate understanding of our reality.

I had just read about the qualities of the mind that are essential for awakening or liberation in *Mindfulness* and stepped outside for a mindful walk to contemplate these teachings. The tall trees that line the streets of our neighborhood and the vast blue sky speckled with clouds created a spacious container for me to digest what I'd just read. I was struck by how each mindfulness factor described in the book directly correlated with the qualities that mindfulness practices (like the awareness of breath, body scan, open awareness, and loving-kindness) were supposed to develop—and, indeed, I'd experienced these qualities within various meditations throughout my journey. What's more, these qualities could be integrated into my daily life . . . though admittedly only occasionally. My failed mindfulness venture was one of many situations when I couldn't bring these qualities into our day-to-day discussions and decisions. *What gives?* I wondered.

As soon as I raised that question, I saw what was going on: The *self* that sat in meditation was different from the *entrepreneur self.* The *meditating self* was calm, curious, compassionate, and had the previously mentioned qualities. In the business world, the *entrepreneur self* was in charge, conducting business as usual—checking all the boxes for a start-up, researching, paying the bills, and working super hard to make it all work.

This made complete sense. This is exactly what my dissertation work uncovered. We have a multiplicity of selves, each of which is more dominant than others in different situations.[1]

It isn't always the case that if we cultivate mindful qualities during meditation, all the selves will adopt them. For instance, my *mindfulness teacher* and *researcher self* wholeheartedly espoused mindfulness. However, my *entrepreneur self* was making decisions based on its default ways of thinking shaped by my business degrees and past experiences.

Armed with this insight, I had a new way of approaching mindfulness—all my selves were invited to practice and play with the mindfulness skills throughout the day intentionally so they could become the default habits. Much like Shantideva, an eighth-century Indian scholar, stated,

---

1   Shalini Bahl and George R. Milne. "Talking to Ourselves: A Dialogical Exploration of Consumption Experiences." *Journal of Consumer Research* 37, no. 1 (June 2010): 176–195. https ://doi.org/10.1086/650000.

"At all times and in any situation, how can I make mindfulness my constant habit?"

In essence, being mindful in the real world is a practice of returning to the present-moment experience, throughout the day, with the eight mindfulness skills that empower us to see clearly and act intentionally.

For instance, when my hand reaches out for the phone first thing in the morning, the practice is to return to mindful **awareness** to notice—with **compassion**—what my hand is doing and be **curious** about what is most nourishing at that moment, which is often to take a few conscious breaths and check in with my body, before checking my phone.

The practice reminds me to return to my senses when I drink my morning cup of coffee (or at least the first few sips) and experience **appreciative joy** for the aroma and taste of the smooth, bold coffee.

When I want to linger longer in bed, **awareness** allows me to see my resistance to getting out of my comfy bed, and **energy** disrupts my inertia so I can go outdoors for a walk or run.

In the middle of a contentious town council meeting, the practice is to return to my breath and invite **equanimity** to discern which skill is needed. I may first calm my limbic system and then bring **compassion** to understand the different perspectives in the room before acting on my judgments. And in the countless moments when I fail to be mindful, the practice is to return to the present with self-compassion, learn from my experience, and begin again.

Benefits of Disrupting Default Habits

In your daily life, have you ever noticed a gap between your intentions and your actions? On Monday morning, you might commit to start eating healthfully, but come Wednesday night, when your energy dips after work, it's ice cream for dinner! Or maybe you want to approach work conversations with more curiosity and less judgment yet find yourself getting defensive all too quickly. This is quite normal. Your different selves are at play at different times in your life—the *healthy self* versus the *exhausted professional self*, the *compassionate self* that seeks to understand and accept oneself versus the *insecure self* that automatically judges and reacts.

Return offers a path to be mindful so you—across all your selves and in all situations—can live with empowered choice. You will have access to more than fifty daily practices and reminders to strengthen the eight mindfulness skills for real-world change. You will gain agency over your responses, even in triggering situations. Here's the key benefit: It's not about being able to do more or be better, but rather learning to let go of default habits that no longer serve you. Through the following shifts in your mindset, you will develop a reliable and effortless approach to seeing clearly and aligning your actions with your intentions:

- Bring **awareness** when you find yourself automatically reacting.
- Seek to understand with **compassion** when you're feeling judgy.
- Seek new information with **curiosity** when stuck in your echo chamber.
- Tap into mindful **energy** to take actions aligned with your goals, even when it's uncomfortable to change old ways of thinking and acting.
- Choose **appreciative joy** over negativity.
- Let go of attachments to achieve **inner calm**.
- **Focus** on what is important when you feel distracted and overwhelmed.
- Respond in a balanced way with **equanimity** instead of biased impulsivity.

By embracing the eight mindfulness skills to transform your default habits, you will experience many benefits. Let's delve into three positive outcomes: (1) personal fulfillment, (2) effective leadership, and (3) global impact.

PERSONAL FULFILLMENT

Do you feel more or less in control of your world than you did five years ago?

If you answered "less," you're not alone. This question, posed by Paul Michelman, the editor in chief of *MIT Sloan Management Review*, elicited a resounding "less" from a wide range of people, including researchers, authors, and executives.[2]

The question posed by Michelman in 2019 has since become even more pertinent due to the rise of many other phenomena threatening our sense of agency—such as a global pandemic, the advent of artificial intelligence, political unrest, climate change, and other social inequities that have come to the forefront. Besides these macro issues, the pace of life has accelerated in general, leaving many feeling overwhelmed and unable to keep up with the constant flux of change. Consequently, they lack the clarity and energy to act on choices that are meaningful to them.

Even without the added pressures of a rapidly evolving world, we have an evolutionary impulse to automate our choices based on upbringing and significant life events. In the absence of awareness, we're sleepwalking through life, bumping around, unaware of our values, intentions, and potential. We may think we're free, but our minds are in cages of default thinking, judgment, and striving.

To make choices that genuinely fulfill us in our relationships, academic pursuits, career choices, and community involvement, we need to exercise our agency—the power to act intentionally in line with our values and what is meaningful. Indeed, the sense of agency is crucial not only for us to adapt to our ever-changing surroundings but also to flourish within them.[3]

The eight mindfulness skills that you will be strengthening with the practices and reminders in this book will amplify your sense of agency: the ability to disrupt your default habits with self-compassion, challenge the beliefs dictating your choices, and step out of your comfort zone. You will discover the energy in you to venture into the world to observe, learn, connect, and grow, unafraid of making mistakes and your unique creative expression.

As you journey through each chapter, explore how the practices and

---

2   Paul Michelman. "Can We End the Crisis of Agency?" *MIT Sloan Management Review*, September 18, 2019. https://sloanreview.mit.edu/article/can-we-end-the-crisis-of-agency/.

3   Christian Welzel and Ronald Inglehart. "Agency, Values, and Well-Being: A Human Development Model." *Social Indicators Research* 97, 43–63 (2010). https://doi.org/10.1007/s11205-009-9557-z.

reminders for each skill can help reclaim your agency. These skills will guide you back to your inner compass and courage to ride the waves of change with grace and discover profound meaning in this singular, extraordinary journey we call life.

EFFECTIVE LEADERSHIP

Change is inevitable. In the business world, the pace of change has accelerated significantly, with companies evolving twice as fast now compared to the 1980s.[4] As a leader or change agent, you possess the vision to see the bigger picture and understand why your organization or community needs to adapt. There will be instances where you'll be tasked with guiding your organization through challenging yet necessary transformations.

While those at the executive level might be ready for change, this mindset may not be shared throughout the entire company. More often than not, individuals resist the disruption introduced by change initiatives. This resistance stems from the fear of losing familiar daily habits, loyalties, and established ways of thinking and doing things. It's no surprise, then, that 75 percent of transformation efforts fail to deliver the anticipated results.[5]

As a leader, you've likely encountered resistance to change. The challenge lies in overcoming the temptation to either pacify or forcefully impose change. Even if you do manage to implement change, it might leave you feeling exhausted. Remember, leading change is a delicate balancing act that requires patience, understanding, and resilience.

This book offers a systematic approach for you to develop essential skills to lead with awareness and empathy. Rather than judging those who resist change, you will approach the initiative with a willingness to understand people's perspectives and challenges. Your compassion and curiosity can build

---

4   Martin Reeves and Nikhil Bhandari. "Strategy to Die Another Day: What Leaders Can Do About the Shrinking Life Expectancy of Corporations." Boston Consulting Group, September 21, 2015. https://www.bcg.com/publications/2015/strategy-die-another-day-what-leaders-can -do-about-the-shrinking-life-expectancy-of-corporations.

5   Nadya Zhexembayeva. "3 Things You're Getting Wrong About Organizational Change." *Harvard Business Review*, June 9, 2020. https://hbr.org/2020/06/3-things-youre-getting-wrong -about-organizational-change.

psychological safety within your team, encouraging members to share their ideas and ask questions without fear of reproach. Change is often difficult and time-consuming. By fostering a culture of appreciative joy—acknowledging and celebrating the good qualities in one another and the small wins along the way—you can build collective resilience, empowering your team to persevere through changes. Cultivating inner calm and focus will enable you to see clearly and allocate your resources effectively, prioritizing what matters most. Moreover, with equanimity, you will learn to care and be carefree so you listen and observe deeply what people are saying but also not be affected by the fear of failure or being disliked for your proposed changes.

The eight mindfulness skills give us the agency to live, love, and work with clarity and care. As a leader, these skills will empower you to bring real-world change without burning out or burning bridges. Delve into the practices and reminders for the skills you most need and explore how they can assist you in bringing a mindful lens to approach the good, bad, and ugly of leadership experiences. It's important to note that while sincerity in practice is important, there is room for lightheartedness and playfulness. In fact, you'll need it to sustain your practice. So, remember to maintain a sense of humor along the journey, ensuring a harmonious blend of depth and joy in your pursuit of mindful leadership.

GLOBAL IMPACT

Our world has been in great turmoil—from wars to natural disasters to gun violence and social inequities. The 2020 pandemic served as a global alarm, jolting us out of our complacency. We were forced to see our interconnectedness and discover ways that we can work together—as individuals, communities, and nations—despite our differences. António Guterres, secretary-general of the United Nations, was forceful in his virtual address that the pandemic "must be a wake-up call that prompts all political leaders to understand that our assumptions and approaches have to change, and that division is a danger to everyone."[6] The eight mindfulness skills outlined in

---

6   "Global Wake-up Call." United Nations, accessed 2023. https://www.un.org/en/coronavirus /global-wake-call.

this book are crucial not just for leaders but also for each one of us as global citizens to effectively meet our collective challenges.

The pandemic had (and continues to have) devastating effects worldwide—disruption of work, education, healthcare, economies, and relationships, with some groups impacted more negatively than others. In fact, in 2020, the American Psychological Association declared the physical and emotional stress from the virus a national mental health crisis, with dire consequences for young adults (ages thirteen to twenty-three) for years to come.[7]

Stress due to unprecedented levels of uncertainty during and in the post-lockdown period has been compounded by seemingly insurmountable challenges: political divisiveness, climate change, and racial inequities, to name a few. Our old ways of dealing with these challenges—individually and collectively—mostly offer us quick fixes, efficiencies, and strategies that favor some but not all. Many people continue to feel overwhelmed, disenfranchised, and unclear about how to move forward toward a safer, better world for all.

Even though we're striving to return to normal, the pandemic has forced us to see that normal is broken. We need a new way of thinking, working together, and finding solutions that emerge when we don't turn away from discomfort and are willing to struggle together. The eight mindfulness skills can build our individual and collective capacities to move through our resistance and return to our field of inner knowing, peace, and clarity. Here, we have the creative potential to solve any problem. Maybe not right away, but it makes the journey together worthwhile and possible.

How This Book Is Designed

The book is divided into two parts. Part I covers the basics of mindfulness, including our default habits that get in the way of being mindful and the

---

7   "Report on Stress in America: October 2020." American Psychological Association, accessed 2023. https://www.apa.org/news/press/releases/stress/2020/report-october.

eight skills to disrupt those habits and return to mindfulness for real-world change. Part II is divided into eight chapters, each dedicated to one of the eight mindfulness skills. Each of these eight chapters flows in a similar way to include the following elements:

1. A definition of the mindfulness skill and the default habit or bias that it disrupts.

2. An explanation of the mindfulness skill with stories and examples.

3. Nuances that will help you understand what each skill means, especially in the context of everyday life, and how it helps you to live and lead mindfully.

4. Where you are in the mindfulness continuum. Before you embark on this journey of strengthening your mindfulness skills, I recommend that you take the complimentary mindfulness assessment (available on my website KnowYourMind.training), which can help you to understand and reflect on your natural tendencies as they pertain to each skill. You'll also learn to recognize when the mindfulness skill is strong or weak and when that skill has been misappropriated by your default habit disguised as a mindfulness skill. Once you know where you stand vis-à-vis each mindfulness skill—no judgment— you can choose the right practices and reminders to strengthen that skill.

5. Dedicated practices to strengthen the mindfulness skills and six daily reminders (mantras) with brief practices to be mindful in real-world situations. The daily reminders are organized to provide a mindful lens to everyday experiences encompassing your body, thoughts, emotions, and social interactions. By continually applying each mindfulness skill to perceive these experiences, you will progressively enhance that particular skill and find more clarity in that moment.

Additional elements in the book that you have the option to engage with are the following:

- **Story Boxes** to understand and be inspired by key insights related to the mindfulness skills

- **See for Yourself Boxes** with simple exercises for you to experiment as you read the book and understand key concepts from your own experience

- **Geek Out Boxes** with additional scientific facts for readers who want to understand the science behind some of the concepts shared in the book

- **References** at the end of the book citing the traditional mindfulness texts and scientific research on which the many propositions and practices in the book are based

Ways to Practice and Play with the Book

My hope is that this book, like a mindful friend, will be there for you when you need it. Whether you delve into *Return* for a daily practice to strengthen a mindfulness skill, a reminder to bring a mindful lens to your situation, an insight, or an inspiration—you'll have many options to systematically nurture the eight mindfulness skills.

Because we tend to take life too seriously and turn everything into work, I invite you to practice and *play* with the offerings in this book. Find opportunities in your day to set aside your judgy mind and approach the daily practices and mantras with childlike wonder and curiosity. Have fun. Be willing to make mistakes and learn from them.

Everyone has their own unique way of learning. You know you best. Here are a few suggestions about how to benefit from this book (and the *Return to Mindfulness* cards that are also listed as an added resource). Feel free to adopt whichever approach best supports you at different times in your life:

- **An eight-week program/experiment/challenge**. If you're new to this book, I recommend approaching it like an eight-week program. Each week, focus on a specific mindfulness skill following this sequence: awareness, compassion, curiosity, energy, appreciative joy, inner calm, focus, and equanimity. Throughout your day, dedicate time to practicing and integrating one reminder for that skill, located at the end of each chapter. If you have an analytical mind like mine, you might prefer using the word *experiment* instead of *practice*.

During these eight weeks, pay attention to your default thought patterns and habits. See how they shift when you apply a mindful perspective. Try out the different skills in various situations to discover how each one can support you. It's an opportunity to observe and understand the impact of mindfulness on your life.

If competition is what drives you, consider making the strengthening of the eight mindfulness skills a competitive goal to achieve—challenge yourself to identify as many default habits in yourself as possible over the eight weeks and actively foster the corresponding mindfulness skills to transform your habitual patterns.

Alternatively, you may have a personal goal that you want to pursue—starting a new health routine, developing confidence in your first job, or leading with inner calm and clarity in a rapidly changing environment. By nurturing the eight mindfulness skills, you can discern and disrupt the defaults that are impeding your progress and take the steps (however small they may be) to move toward your goals.

You have options—read this book and practice on your own, with a partner, or colleagues at work. Sharing your experiences with others can make this journey much easier and enjoyable, allowing for mutual growth and support.

- **Open what you need most today**. Pick a mindfulness skill that is calling you. Practice and play with the meditations and reminders from that chapter for a week. If you took the mindfulness assessment or otherwise feel that you need to give your full care and attention to a particular habit of the mind, open to that chapter and explore the different ways you can develop and integrate that mindfulness skill in your life for a week or as long as you feel the need to keep going.

- **Choose randomly**. You can also use this book to randomly visit a page and see how that page is relevant to your life at that moment.

- **When you feel stuck or stressed**. If you find yourself feeling stressed or stuck in the middle of a problem at work, in school, or in a relationship, take a few moments to step back and reflect on the mindfulness skill, or skills, that will be most useful in returning you to your inner knowing and equilibrium. Try the daily practices and reminders offered for those skills and see what comes up. Use the insights to take actions that are skillful and kind.

You are the active creator of your life. The eight mindfulness skills equip you with the ability to intentionally choose your thoughts, words, and actions, thereby leading a life that not only fulfills you but also contributes positively to the world. With these skills, you'll be able to see more possibilities than a hurried mind could and make more skillful choices than you would when living on autopilot.

Let *Return* be your loving wake-up call to step into your mindful capacity—to live and lead with integrity, clarity, and grace. The more you practice and play with the eight mindfulness skills, the more you can make mindfulness your constant habit at all times and in any situation.

Let's get started!

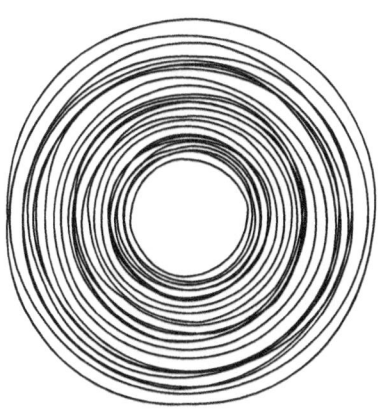

Chapter 2

Mindfulness Is Easier than You Think

Out beyond ideas of wrongdoing and rightdoing,
there is a field. I'll meet you there . . .
The breeze at dawn has secrets to tell you.
Don't go back to sleep.
You must ask for what you really want.
Don't go back to sleep.
People are going back and forth across the doorsill
where the two worlds touch.
The door is round and open.
Don't go back to sleep.

—Rumi, "The Great Wagon"

"You were not yourself," said my campaign manager after my first political debate for town council.

I remember that night in the library so clearly—the anticipation of change was palpable. More than one hundred eager citizens gathered to hear from candidates vying for seats on the city's very first town council, which would replace the town meeting. This moment marked a turning point for our city known as the Town of Amherst; residents would have to trust thirteen elected members instead of 240, as had been the case since the 1930s. Those gathered wanted answers from the six candidates running from our district. How would this new government structure address the issues that impacted them?

I was one of the town council candidates running for office. I am an Indian immigrant who had acquired US citizenship merely three years earlier, and this was my first foray into politics. I'm not going to lie—I felt really nervous standing before everyone, knowing that the other candidates knew so much more than I did about US politics and local issues.

I had been encouraged by longtime residents in Amherst to run primarily for my mindfulness skills and research background. They trusted I'd bring a fresh vantage point to bridge the rift between residents who wanted a town council form of government and those who'd resisted the change. As the only immigrant and one of two people of color running, I was committed to actively representing minority voices and bringing a balanced perspective to tackle the contentious issues that were polarizing our town.

Yet, in that moment, all I could think about was all the issues I knew so little about. My thoughts flew from one pressing issue to another. The weight of balancing budgets for crucial capital projects while preserving our natural landscape, finding solutions for affordable housing, alleviating the burden of high property taxes, revitalizing our downtown, and confronting the pressing threat of climate change overwhelmed me. Anxiety coursed through my veins, and my heart pounded like a wild drum.

My campaign manager, sensing my nervousness, reminded me, "You know mindfulness. You know what to do," and I remember thinking, *Good point! But what does it mean to be mindful at this moment?*

My mind automatically turned to my breath for comfort and grounding. As I returned to my breath, some of the unease began to dissipate. But then doubt slithered in: *I don't belong here. I've never participated in politics, and the other candidates have years of experience!* I tried to push away these negative thoughts with positive thinking and more mindful breathing. Throughout the debate, I was able to keep my composure and not fall apart while responding to the varied questions from both the moderator and residents.

Yet, I felt off. Even though I cared about the issues being discussed, my responses felt empty and superficial. Post-debate, a few attendees came to congratulate me on my performance. But I—and my campaign manager—knew that I wasn't myself. I felt disconnected from the audience and, even worse, myself.

Running for city council was a powerful—and humbling—experience. As a mindfulness teacher, I have learned over time (since my failed mindfulness venture described in Chapter 1) how to let go of my default habits and be in the moment with my clients without worrying about being liked or impressing them.

Yet as a political candidate, when faced with this new audience, I desperately wanted their approval . . . and votes. All this, of course, was happening under the radar of my conscious awareness and only became apparent the next day in meditation. *What was missing from my efforts to be mindful in that situation?* I discovered the answer to that, too, when I returned to mindfulness.

I'm sure you also have those moments when emotions cloud your judgment, despite your best intentions. Whether you're stuck in traffic, overwhelmed by a big presentation, or feeling the pressure to meet an aggressive deadline from your boss at a team meeting, it can be hard to see clearly and act intentionally in those moments.

The beauty of mindfulness is that we can return to it again and again, even after #mindfulnessfail moments. We always have an opportunity to learn, grow, and take skillful actions to undo some of the harm caused by our automatic reactions.

However, wouldn't it be spectacular if we could return to our innate capacity to see clearly in even the most nerve-racking situations—like running for election or in the middle of a difficult conversation? I am here to show you how to do exactly that—return to mindfulness in the middle of everyday life. But first, let's make sure we're on the same page about what mindfulness means. It may be easier than you think!

Mindfulness: Effortless Knowing

Mindfulness is our effortless knowing of what is present—internally and externally—without rushing, resisting, or clinging to our experiences. To put it more simply, mindfulness is our ability to see clearly and act intentionally.

When we're unmindful, it's as though we're sleepwalking through life—unconscious of and unintentional in our experiences and choices. Even when we're present, in the absence of mindfulness, we see through filters shaped by our past conditioning, and it's only a slice of reality. But we hold on to that slice as the absolute and full truth surrounding our experience.

However, when we can see ourselves, others, and our situations, free from our conditioning and automatic judgments, we clear and widen our lenses to observe more carefully what our minds on autopilot might miss. We see many more perspectives and possibilities. Mindfulness, then, can be thought of as a continuous process of updating our perceptions with new information to make them more accurate.

Let's pause here for a moment so you have a chance to see for yourself what it means to be mindful. You may be surprised that this nonjudging awareness of our inner and outer experiences requires minimal effort. Try the See for Yourself exercise on the facing page, for which we can thank Joseph Goldstein.

Were you able to return to your effortless, nonjudging knowing with this simple exercise? The main purpose of this exercise is to help us experience what it feels like to be mindful and how effortless it is. The next time you find yourself scrambling or freezing up, you can return to this ability in you to be at ease and see things as they are.

If this exercise made no sense to you, that's okay. Think of moments in your day when you feel most at ease: curling up in bed with your cat purring next to you, looking at white fluffy clouds passing by, engrossed in a captivating novel, or anything else that makes you naturally feel present and alive. The experience of ease in these instances is effortless. You don't think, *I should be present now.* You simply are. The invitation is to direct that ability to be present that's in you toward all your actions and interactions.

In moments when we can be present, free from the clutches of any kind of rushing, judging, and striving, we're at peace. We feel most at home no

See for Yourself

1. Let your right arm hang naturally at your side. Bend it at the elbow to form a ninety-degree angle, and gently swing your lower arm from side to side.

2. Do you know your arm is moving? Most likely your response would be affirmative.

3. Now, repeat this movement for a few moments, but with your eyes closed this time.

4. Were you aware that your arm was moving in spite of your closed eyes? The answer is probably yes. Did it require any effort on your part to know that your arm was moving? Likely it took no effort at all.

The exception might be if you're in pain, in which case, it can be hard to focus on the task at hand. However, assuming that you were not in pain, you should have noticed how naturally and effortlessly you were aware that your arm was moving. The essence of mindfulness lies in the ability to effortlessly see things as they are, unfettered by our default habits of rushing, resisting, and striving.

See if you can direct this ability to effortlessly see clearly toward reading this book and subsequent activities in your day. It's natural to occasionally fall back into your old habits, and the key is to continually return to mindfulness whenever you sense yourself feeling rushed or reactive. Although judging is inherent to human nature, you can transcend its limitations and choose not to act on your judgments.

matter where we are. Returning to this innate ability in us to be with things as they are is simple and effortless—all we need to do is remember to return.

However, because we've lived for so long disconnected from this kind of knowing, mindfulness can be elusive. Sometimes metaphors enable us to understand and access that which is too subtle for the thinking mind to recognize. For example, a thirteenth-century Persian poet, Rumi, invites us in his poem "The Great Wagon" to meet in a field "beyond ideas of wrongdoing and rightdoing." This field is a metaphor we can evoke to return to our field of inner awareness, which is free from judgments about how things should be or shouldn't be. This field of boundless knowing—free from any limiting thoughts shaped by our past—is available to us at all times.

When we view the world and interact with each other from this field of clear knowing, we see more, connect deeper, and gain insights into our experiences that we can't see when we're running on autopilot. However, we don't tend to stay here too long. Even when we're in touch with our nonjudging awareness, our judging mind jumps back, even if only to comment about how peaceful and calm it is to be in our spacious field of effortless knowing. Perhaps this is what Rumi meant when he wrote the following:

> People are going back and forth across the doorsill
> where the two worlds touch.
> The door is round and open.
> Don't go back to sleep.

It's as though we're going back and forth between our capacity to be mindful and mindless. Being mindful doesn't mean that we're entirely abandoning our habit of living on autopilot; however, it does mean that we're keeping the door to our inner knowing always open, and we're awake to make the choice of when to live on autopilot and when to return to mindfulness.

What Mindfulness Is Not: Thinking, Shoulding, and Efforting

As we stand at the threshold of our inner knowing, it can be easy to mistake mindfulness for one or all of these three tendencies: *thinking*, *shoulding*, and *efforting*. Let's take a look at each of these so you can clearly differentiate them from your inner knowing.

THINKING

We can't think our way back to mindfulness, just as we can't think our way to stronger muscles and stamina without exercising. Thinking helps to a certain extent—like reminding us to be mindful and inviting the right conditions of the mind to support us in being so. Thinking can bring us to the "doorsill" of our inner knowing, and then we have to let go of it to return to our present-moment awareness. Any logical or rational thinking is based on memory, not on our present-moment experience of what's alive and felt in this moment. If we want to return to our ability to see clearly, we have to find a way to let go of our usual ways of thinking, which includes judging and striving.

For instance, when I felt anxious before my first debate, I asked myself, *What does it mean to be mindful in this situation?* I heard my rational mind respond, telling me to breathe. When breathing didn't help, I tried to think positively and focus on what I needed to do. All those strategies worked well enough, but deep down, I still felt like an impostor. Engaging my default mindset—to be mindful—provided solutions, such as breathing, which is also a learned reaction based on past experiences. I couldn't see it at the time, but thinking *I need to be mindful* is different from *being mindful*, which requires letting go of thinking about being mindful.

SHOULDING

I often hear workshop participants describe being mindful as what they "should do" or how they "should" respond to life's ups and downs. However, any kind of shoulding is based on judgments about and expectations of how things ought to be and not on our present-moment experience of how things are.

If you feel that you've "tried mindfulness, but it didn't work" because you couldn't "empty the mind" or "control the thoughts," just know that these feelings are your thinking mind *shoulding* its way to mindfulness. The only way to return to mindfulness is to soften the grip of shoulds in your life, feel what's present and alive, acknowledge and accept, and listen to and trust what's emerging in your boundless field of nonjudging awareness.

EFFORTING

Mindfulness is not just a special state that we arrive at after an hour-long meditation or traveling to a peaceful spot in nature. While it's often associated with being present, aware, or peaceful, the notion of achieving this state can feel like hard work. Yet, from your own experience of moments when you're mindful, you know that mindfulness is effortless and happens naturally. But we forget, and that's okay. This book is here to remind you that mindfulness isn't another thing you have to do. It's not a should. Instead, it's an invitation to return to what is already within you. All that you need is an intention to return.

You may be wondering, *If mindfulness is an innate ability, what gets in the way of being mindful, especially when it's critical?* Let's find out!

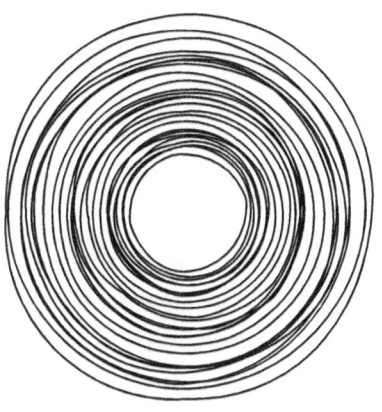

Chapter 3

What Gets in the Way Is the Way

What we call obstacles are really the way the world and
our entire experience teach us where we're stuck.

—Pema Chödrön, *When Things Fall Apart*

We're mindful beings making mindless decisions most of the time. It's a well-documented fact that we live 95 percent of our lives with little awareness or control over our impulses, reactions, and choices.[8] In our busy lives, automating decisions and routines can help us conserve valuable brainpower—our limited brain resources needed to plan, exert willpower, make decisions, and self-regulate.

---

8   John A. Bargh and Tanya L. Chartrand. "The Unbearable Automaticity of Being." *American Psychologist* 54, no. 7 (1999): 462–479. doi: 10.1037/0003-066X.54.7.462.

Our minds are incredible. We've learned to speed up the decision-making process by developing mental shortcuts shaped by our upbringing, culture, education, media, and other formative experiences, especially in our childhood. These shortcuts can be helpful in certain cases, but when it comes to those big decisions where we need more information or a better understanding of our situation before acting, these same shortcuts rob us of the freedom to make intentional choices that are fulfilling to us personally and collectively. Worse still, our minds have a ten dency to automate everything important to us, including all our actions and interactions, such as when we're with loved ones or problem-solving. The mind's automatic response system deprives us of genuine connections and creative joy.

Each of us, molded by our upbringing and personal experiences, has developed distinct patterns of automatic reactions to situational triggers. Despite these differences, one common thread binds us: We are all wired for self-preservation. Underlying our myriad reactions, three basic predispositions persist that divert us away from our inner knowing.

Wired for Survival: Three Predispositions

Buddhist psychology and Western science concur that our underlying motivations are rooted in self-preservation. While this instinct is vital to our nature, it can often hinder us in the fast-paced and ever-evolving modern world. To be more precise, there are three predispositions—pushing, pulling, and running in circles—that lie beneath our automatic reactions, obstructing our ability to see clearly and act intentionally.

PUSHING

We all have an instinctive reaction to push away things that are unfamiliar, difficult, or uncomfortable. Consider scenarios where your mind automatically resists the challenge before you: starting a new exercise routine if physical activity hasn't been a consistent part of your life; attending large networking events, especially if you're introverted; or spearheading a community-wide composting initiative, given the considerable time and effort required to alter people's habits.

Pushing away discomfort can manifest in multiple ways, such as avoidance, aversion, resistance, suppression, and dislike. If we remain unaware of this pushing instinct, we could miss the chance to do things that matter—such as discovering new opportunities to expand our world, making meaningful connections, finding meaning, and trying a new direction. Growth of any kind can be uncomfortable. If we give in to our discomfort, we lose out on the possibility of being stronger, wiser, healthier, and more fulfilled than we would be if confined to our comfort zones.

In other situations, our pushing away of discomfort can get in the way of us coming closer to our experiences and seeing clearly. An example of this was my experience during a political debate described in Chapter 2. When faced with feelings of doubt and anxiety, my automatic response was to push them away. Public speaking can be challenging, but what made that debate particularly tough was the new context—it was a political debate, different from anything I had ever done before. When we're in situations that are different, the brain goes clunk. It sees what's different as difficult. It's normal for emotions such as fear and anxiety to show up. They alert us and prepare us for the challenge. But these emotions are uncomfortable, so what do we do? We turn away from them. We avoid them with positive thinking, breathing, Netflix, chocolate, or whatever we do to ease discomfort.

In the process of avoiding discomfort, we also turn away from ourselves—from what we feel and think, including our doubts and aspirations. You know what else we're turning away from? Our passions, purpose, and the gifts we could bring to that situation. That's why I felt disconnected from myself at the debate—I was so focused on pushing away my discomfort that I forgot why I was running for office in the first place. And when we're disconnected from ourselves, we can't really connect with each other.

PULLING

Have you ever noticed how we tend to gravitate toward comfort and pleasure? Whether it's gorging on a pint of ice cream, binge-watching *Beef* with friends, or staying too long at a party because we were having so much fun—these are moments where our desire for more can get us into trouble! Pulling tendencies may be pleasurable temporarily, but if left unchecked, they pull us away from living our most intentional and fulfilling lives.

We all experience pulling in one form or another—approaching, craving, clinging, grasping, obsessing, overdoing, striving. For me, pulling showed up at the public debate as my desire for the audience to like me. My grasping for validation prevented me from seeing what was happening and what was most important—to listen to people's concerns and share ways that I would, if elected, bring my skills to address the issues impacting them. Instead, I was hooked by my desire to impress the audience. Had I acknowledged the pull of my desires, I could have softened their grip and realigned with my values and intentions.

RUNNING IN CIRCLES

If you ever feel like life is whizzing by in a blur of tasks and to-dos, it just might be that pesky tendency of our minds to wander from the present moment. Running in circles can manifest as an underlying feeling of impatience, racing thoughts, delusion, or self-doubt—all things I'm sure we're familiar with. But when we take a step back and return to this current moment, when we experience instead of constantly running between activities without pause, wonderful opportunities await us. By fully experiencing each moment instead of rushing between activities, we can see more deeply what's around us, question our assumptions, unleash our imaginations, rest up and recharge those batteries, innovate, and create . . . and, most important, realign with what matters most in each moment.

Going back to the example of my political debate, I felt like my heart and mind were running a marathon. With some intentional breathing, things started to calm me down, but only briefly. Pretty soon, those old feelings of self-doubt crept in, especially doubting my abilities to run for office and do a good job if I won. Yet, instead of facing my emotions head-on, I tried to rush past them, as if hurrying to the next moment would magically erase my doubts. I was able to compartmentalize my doubt during the debate and focus on the questions posed, but this hindered me from showing up fully and most authentically.

GEEK OUT!

How the Apple and the Tiger Shaped Our Minds

As hunter-gatherers, we used our good and bad feelings as a proxy for what enhanced our chances of survival and what threatened it. We inherited the genes from our ancestors who lived 100,000 years ago, and not much has changed in our genes or physiology since then. Going back to the Stone Age, let's say our ancestors saw an apple, ripe and juicy. The apple on the tree signaled to the brain, *Food needed for survival!* They'd approach the apple and take a bite. As soon as the sugar molecules in the juicy apple met their palate, they'd experience an explosion of pleasurable sensations.

This cycle repeated over and over again, automating the reaction that pleasurable sensations are to be approached. The initial goal of survival, which is why they approached the apple, is not relevant to the decision anymore.

Fast-forward to the modern day, and we can replace the apple with anything pleasurable such as the smell of cookies baking in the oven, Instagram likes, or the thrill of winning on a slot machine. We're hardwired to move toward what *feels* good, regardless of our intentions and goals beyond enjoying a dopamine rush—the feeling of pleasure and reward. Even though we know that all that feels good is not always good for us, we have a strong pull toward all that makes us feel good.

Figure 1 shows the original scenario with the apple. It followed these steps: See the apple → Think apple enhances survival → Approach apple and bite into it → Feels good. Over time, the original motivation for survival doesn't feature in the decision-making. We automatically approach what feels good.

Apple   Enhances Survival   Approach   Feels Good

Fig. 1. Shortcut to Approaching What Feels Good.

continued

Similarly, any negative feelings, such as the discomfort of running away from a tiger, are associated with avoiding that experience. The brain doesn't distinguish a tiger from other sources of threats—such as a threat to one's sense of self, competence, and belonging. As such, in situations—such as being shamed in a meeting for not achieving our goals, facing an angry client, and mobilizing energy to exercise—we experience a strong push to move away from, or avoid, unpleasant feelings.

Figure 2 illustrates the sequence of events when our ancestors encountered a tiger: See tiger → Think tiger threatens survival → Avoid by running away from it → Feels unpleasant to run away from a tiger. Over time, we associate anything that feels unpleasant as something to be avoided. The original motivation to avoid a threat to our survival doesn't feature in our decision-making.

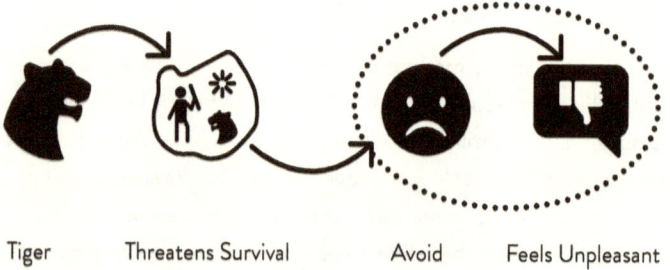

Tiger   Threatens Survival   Avoid   Feels Unpleasant

Fig. 2. Shortcut to Avoiding What's Unpleasant.

For our survival as hunter-gatherers, it was vital to stay vigilant to threats and to opportunities to find food for survival. Even now, we have a habit of continuously searching for threats and opportunities. When we intentionally allow our minds to wander, that wandering can serve as a mental rehearsal to play out future possibilities and solve problems. There's nothing wrong with that.[9] The problem is when we're unaware that our minds are wandering, especially when we need to focus. We live in a culture of "busyness" that keeps us stuck in our habitual patterns—always rushing, unable to return to mindfulness.

9 "Mind Wandering." Max Planck Institute, accessed 2023. https://www.mpg.de/11229713 /mind-wandering.

In our busy lives, it's easy to get caught up in reactions—pushing, pulling, and running in circles—that take us away from the present moment. But how often do we stop to realize that we're not fully engaged?

To determine if your predispositions are influencing you, ask yourself this: Am I pushing (avoiding discomfort), pulling (seeking comfort), or running in circles (rushing and doubting myself)? By acknowledging these tendencies, we can begin to address what hinders our mindfulness.

But the journey doesn't end there. Embracing these hindrances can lead us to profound self-discovery and a deeper understanding of the world around us. With practice, we can learn to recognize these three predispositions and their manifestations as biases, preferences, and habits of the mind that cloud our clarity. Specifically, there are eight default habits of the mind that can be roadblocks to seeing our reality in a balanced way and making fulfilling decisions.

Eight Default Habits that Hinder Real-World Mindfulness

We live most of our lives on autopilot and often don't even realize that we're acting on our default habits. Even when we're aware that we've been triggered, it's challenging to know in that moment the most skillful actions we can take. My clients confirmed what I, too, found to be a roadblock to being mindful in the real world. You may have experienced this as well: You are "aware" that you're angry, sad, resentful, or (insert any other difficult emotion here), but you don't know what to do with that emotion.

In these moments of discomfort, our instinct is often to quickly resolve it. We immediately go into a mode of pushing away our discomfort by getting defensive, justifying, analyzing, suppressing, or resorting to other habitual ways of dealing with difficult situations—all of which involve our default ways of thinking that only take us away from our inner knowing.

We are going to get into more detail about our default habits and how to disrupt them in Part II of the book. But before we delve deeper, let's take a moment to familiarize ourselves with the eight default habits and biases that we'll be addressing in this book. As you review this list, consider how these default habits could hinder your ability to make fulfilling decisions for yourself, your loved ones, your teams, and your communities:

1. Living on autopilot
2. Instantly judging everyone and everything
3. Seeking information that confirms your views—known as confirmation bias
4. Resisting change—known as status quo bias
5. Focusing on the negatives in any situation—known as negativity bias
6. Getting attached to your sense of self, including your beliefs, expectations, and how you think
7. Getting distracted by what's not important
8. Impulsively acting on your biases

We all possess the seeds of these default habits within us. Through our individual conditioning, certain habits become more dominant than others. Just as we have fortified these default habits over time, we can also foster qualities of the mind that are antidotes to these hindrances to mindfulness. We can't change our entrenched habits overnight, but we can, with practice (and play), develop a set of skills that can disrupt our default habits and provide a mindful lens to view our experiences.

Eight Skills to Disrupt Eight Default Habits

The original mindfulness texts outline specific qualities of the mind that free us from attachments and reactive tendencies. These qualities are present in all of us, but due to our upbringing and experiences, some qualities may be stronger than others. However, we can nurture these qualities of the mind into reliable skills for clear seeing and intentional actions, irrespective of our circumstances. In real-world situations where our inner knowing seems elusive, the eight mindfulness skills provide a lens to see through the fog of our default habits and reestablish our inner equilibrium and connection with our intentions. Check out the table for an overview of the eight skills and the default habits they disrupt.

Overview of the Eight Mindfulness Skills
& the Default Habits They Disrupt

	MINDFULNESS SKILLS DEFINED	DEFAULT HABIT DISRUPTED
1	**Awareness** is our capacity to observe without judgment what's happening in the outer world and the inner self, including our body, feelings, thoughts, habits of the mind, and what we value.	*Awareness disrupts our habit of living on autopilot by becoming masterful at observation.*
2	**Compassion** is our innate ability to feel, understand, and be motivated to alleviate suffering in ourselves and others when we understand our interbeing.	*Compassion disrupts our tendency to act on our automatic judgments about ourselves and others by seeking to understand.*
3	**Curiosity** is our ability to be genuinely interested and care with the purpose of understanding the situation, even when it's challenging.	*Curiosity disrupts our confirmation bias by staying open and patient in the face of uncertainty and new information.*
4	**Energy** is our vigor and vitality essential for activity and accomplishment.	*Energy disrupts the tendency to avoid the discomfort of any kind of change, also known as status quo bias, by realigning with intentions that are beneficial to all involved.*
5	**Appreciative Joy** is our innate capacity to delight in what's good in the present moment.	*Appreciative joy disrupts our negativity bias, which is the tendency to see more wrong than right in our lives, by savoring what is going well for us in our lives.*
6	**Inner Calm** is the ease that flows from letting go of attachments and reactivity when we understand impermanence—the changing nature of our thoughts, emotions, and desires.	*Inner calm disrupts our attachments to habitual hurrying, beliefs, and expectations that hinder our inner equilibrium by deepening our understanding of impermanence.*
7	**Focus** is our capacity to zero in on what matters most with a sense of ease.	*Focus disrupts our tendency to be distracted by returning to what's important in any given moment.*
8	**Equanimity** is our ability to discern which mindfulness skills are needed to accurately perceive our reality, thereby empowering us to act intentionally.	*Equanimity disrupts our impulsivity by determining the necessary mindfulness skills to apply in any given situation.*

Even though the eight skills are presented as eight distinct qualities of the mind, they are interconnected and work together to assist us in returning to mindfulness. Each skill builds upon the earlier skills, starting with awareness.

1. Let's consider a scenario where you're engaged in a conversation with someone—let's call him Tom—that unsettles you. This could occur at home or work. The first crucial skill, **awareness**, helps you recognize that you're feeling triggered. This realization might provoke judgments about Tom or even yourself.

2. The second skill, **compassion**, interrupts these judgmental thoughts by seeking to understand the causes and conditions for this situation to arise.

3. Compassion in turn sparks **curiosity**, the third skill. You then start asking questions about Tom—his viewpoint, experiences, needs, and intentions in this dialogue—and also reflect on your own needs and intentions.

4. Maintaining an open mind against default reactions can be challenging, and you need the fourth skill, **energy**, to sustain it. Stressful situations often narrow our perspectives, making us focus only on the negatives.

5. Here, the fifth skill, **appreciative joy**, comes into play, disrupting your focus on just the negative aspects of the conversation. You shift your attention to Tom's positive attributes—perhaps his reaction stems from his deep care, his proficiency in his field, or his generally kind nature. You may also want to appreciate the good qualities you're bringing to the situation.

6. The sixth skill, **inner calm**, aids in letting go of preconceived notions and beliefs about the situation, enabling you to be calm and absorb more information for a broader view.

7. Once you've gathered sufficient information, the seventh skill, **focus**, assists in directing your attention to what truly matters in this scenario.

8. The final skill, **equanimity**, empowers you to control your impulsive reactions. Your choice of words and actions aligns with your intentions, allowing you to respond with kindness and grace.

We can see from the previous example that mindfulness skills have the power to transform challenging situations into opportunities for connection, listening, and taking action from a place of deeper and broader understanding of ourselves and others. Instead of dreading difficult situations, we can view them as openings to delve deeper and gain insight into the situation. What gets in the way of being mindful can be the way to return to mindfulness.

While all eight skills are brought forth in the previous example to exemplify that mindfulness extends beyond mere awareness or presence, the relevance of each skill may vary depending on the situation. Each skill disrupts a default habit of the mind and paves the way for us to return to our natural state of equilibrium from which we can see clearly and make intentional choices.

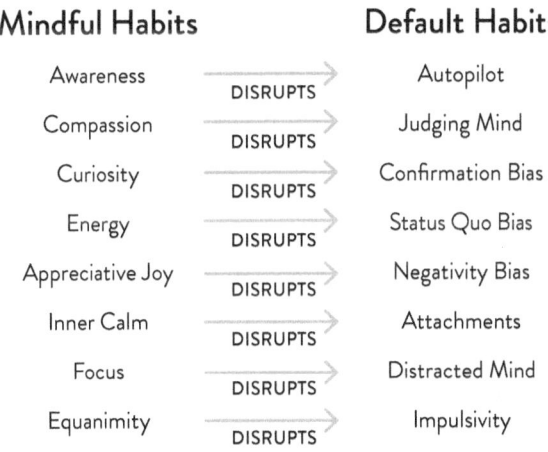

Mindful Habits   Default Habits

Mindful Habits		Default Habits
Awareness	DISRUPTS →	Autopilot
Compassion	DISRUPTS →	Judging Mind
Curiosity	DISRUPTS →	Confirmation Bias
Energy	DISRUPTS →	Status Quo Bias
Appreciative Joy	DISRUPTS →	Negativity Bias
Inner Calm	DISRUPTS →	Attachments
Focus	DISRUPTS →	Distracted Mind
Equanimity	DISRUPTS →	Impulsivity

Fig. 3. Eight Mindfulness Skills to Disrupt Default Habits.

Ever since my colossal #mindfulnessfail, I've been immersed in studying the original mindfulness teachings that led me to the eight essential skills. I meditated on these, conducted research, and even taught them over eight-week classes. Yet, it was only when I joined politics that I realized the real-world difficulty of practicing what I preached.

As an elected leader in the local government, especially during and since the pandemic, I've had many opportunities to learn how difficult it is to be mindful in the real world. For instance, I tend to be a calm and curious person in general. But, when I receive hostile emails or listen to comments in our public meetings from disgruntled residents, my default reaction in such situations is to become defensive, shut down, or try to justify and convince others rather than listen with an open mind. In the midst of difficult situations, it's a practice to remain calm, see the bigger picture, and foster curiosity about the various viewpoints present in the room.

I shared my aha moment in Chapter 1—the self that is meditating is different from the self out there in the world. While my *meditation self* can see clearly, my *politician self* is analytical but also tends to view challenging situations through a default lens of self-doubt—*I am not good enough.* Consequently, I make myself smaller and as invisible as possible. It feels safer in those moments to avoid the discomfort of difficult conversations by suppressing the self in me that is seeing more or seeking more information, only to regret it later. Can you relate? Have you ever silenced your voice of reason because it seemed easier?

It's natural for us to want to take the path of least resistance. Many of our default habits are there to protect us, so it's easy to justify acting on them. However, if we take a moment to pause and reflect, we might come to realize that our immediate reaction to a trigger is not aligned with our intentions and goals. By engaging the mindfulness skills, we can regain clarity and see things from a more empowered perspective. This allows us to take the necessary steps toward finding a solution that benefits both ourselves and others involved. In fact, we may discover that the very challenge we were reacting to has presented us with an opportunity to see the bigger picture and find even better solutions than we initially imagined.

Each of our identities is intertwined with distinct memories, expectations, and attachments. It is a practice to notice our default habits in action and use those opportunities to engage the eight mindfulness skills. Take a moment to pause, breathe, and appreciate your mind for the remarkable ways in which it allows you to engage in this world—to see, feel, listen, imagine, connect, create, evolve. In the next chapter, we will go over a practical roadmap for applying these mindfulness skills in our everyday lives.

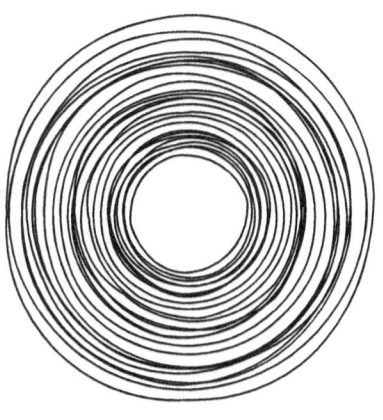

Chapter 4

A Roadmap for Real-World Mindfulness

*Within you there is a stillness and sanctuary to which
you can retreat at any time, and be yourself.*

—*Siddhartha*, **Hermann Hesse, translated by Hilda Rosner**

In the timeless masterpiece *Siddhartha* by Hermann Hesse, the author reminds us of the inherent stillness and sanctuary that resides within each of us. By simply remembering to be fully present in our experiences, we can tap into this wellspring of inner knowing and reconnect with our true selves. It's noteworthy that the original Pali term for mindfulness, *Sati*, translates to *remembering* to be present, attuned to what is before us, our intentions, and what is most beneficial for all involved. In a world that is constantly vying for our attention, mindfulness reminds us to return to what is essential.

However, as previously discussed, our predispositions—pushing, pulling, and running in circles—get in the way of being mindful. Even when we remember to be present, our default habits often hinder our ability to see things as they truly are and act intentionally in the real world. The encouraging news is that just as we've learned habits of mindlessness, we can, with diligent practice (and playfulness), also strengthen our mindfulness skills. In Part II of this book, we will delve deep into the eight skills that are essential to be mindful in the real world. Before embarking on this journey, let's first familiarize ourselves with the roadmap for practicing with the eight mindfulness skills.

The Roadmap for Practice: Return, Listen, Begin

The classic mindfulness scripture—the *Satipatthana Sutta*—offers a path to mindfulness that engages our entire being. While secular interpretations of mindfulness often emphasize meditation as the primary practice, the original teachings encompass three trainings—meditation, contemplation, and ethical behavior. Recognizing the challenges of being mindful in real-life situations, I propose a practical roadmap that leverages the power of the mindfulness skills to integrate the three trainings into our daily lives. These skills enable us to return to the present moment, attentively listen to our inner and outer worlds, and begin our actions with clarity and care. The process involves three steps:

1. **Return:** Redirect your attention back to the present-moment experience.
2. **Listen:** Cultivate the ability to deeply listen to both your inner experience and the external world.
3. **Begin:** Initiate your actions with a renewed sense of clarity and care.

These three steps work together as a continuation of one another in a cyclical manner to assist us in regaining a clear perspective. Before we go into what each of these steps entails, please take a look at Figure 4 for a visual overview of how to return to mindfulness in the real world and make decisions that benefit all involved. At our core, we have an innate ability to return to our inner knowing. All we need to do is remember to return to it. However, when we find ourselves in a situation in which one or more of the default habits is hindering our ability to see clearly, we can invite the relevant mindfulness skills to disrupt our default reactivity.

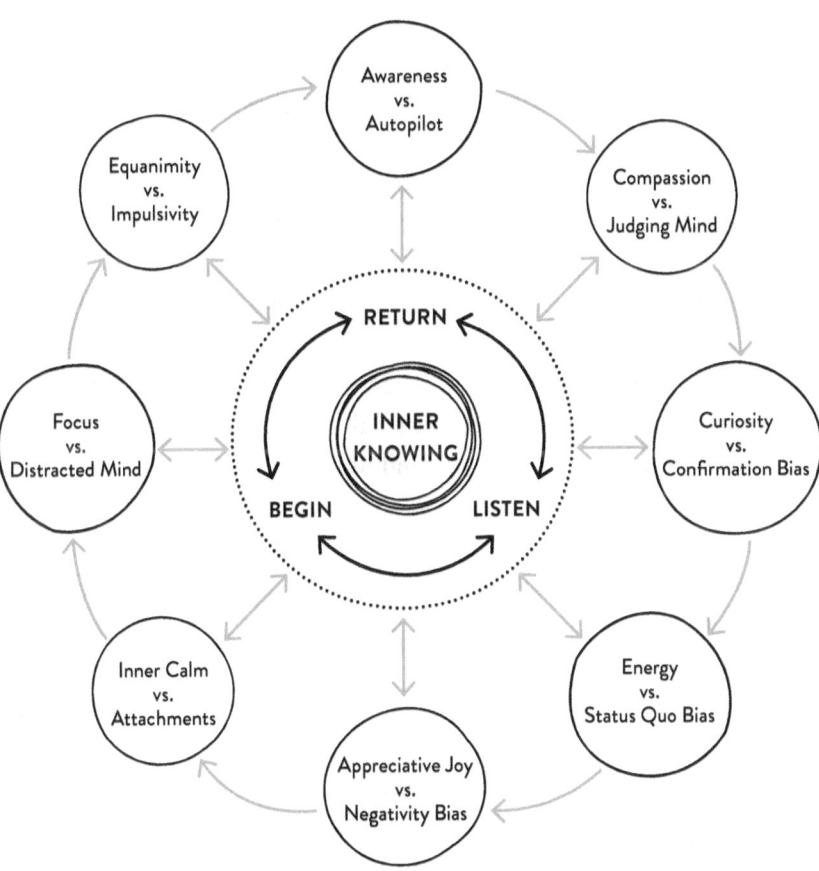

Fig. 4. The Path to Return to Mindfulness.

As we consistently cultivate the habit of returning to mindfulness in the midst of our daily lives and deeply listening to our inner selves, we will find that initiating our actions and interactions with intention becomes second nature. This practice, when nurtured over time, transforms into a way of life that liberates us from the automatic urge to rush and react. In its place, we gain the ability to make empowered choices that not only benefit our own well-being but also contribute to the greater good of all.

RETURN

An important step to take throughout each day is to remember to return to the present moment experience. In doing so, we redirect our attention to our direct experience of the body, feelings, thoughts, habits of the mind, or environmental occurrences in a particular way: intentional, effortless, and free from judgments. If we find that our default habits are getting in the way of being present, we can invite the relevant mindfulness skills to disrupt our habitual patterns and return to a nonjudging stance of observation and being.

With the right approach, the hindrances become a path to return to our inner knowing. For instance, when you realize that your mind is too busy to be present, instead of giving up on mindfulness, you have an opportunity to notice your restlessness with compassion and curiosity. Observing inwardly and outwardly from a perspective of awareness that transcends notions of "right" and "wrong," as alluded to by Rumi, paves the way to listen within to the causes and conditions for your restlessness. Once we're aware of the causes of our restlessness, we can take actions to deal with the root causes of our busy minds. The obstacle—restlessness—becomes the way to understand what we need to return to our inner knowing.

The most reliable way to practice returning to mindfulness in our day is by connecting with the body. We can do this by feeling our sensations of breathing, the pulsing of blood in our palms and fingertips, our heartbeat, the warmth or coolness of the touch of air on the skin, or any other object that helps us stabilize our attention so that we can connect with our experience at this moment—without getting lost in judgments and distractions. If for any reason connecting with the body is challenging, we can choose to rest our attention on sounds in the environment or sensations of touch, like the softness of our clothes against our hands.

When we find that our minds are stable and present, we can let go of the object of sensory experience and free our nonjudging awareness to observe our moment-to-moment experience in the real world. We may notice the subtle shifts in our body, feelings, thoughts, and habits of the mind. Or our attention may be drawn to what's happening around us. We might discern, for instance, that the unease in our chest is a contraction associated with a negative judgment we're passing about what a team or community member is expressing. At this juncture, we simply acknowledge our observations, including the presence of our default habits—in this case, our judgmental mind—without casting judgment on any aspect of it.

In those moments that we're connected with our direct and immediate sensory experience, we let go of our default reactions to our thoughts, expectations, judgments, and emotions. We open to a new way of looking at ourselves—and others—by peeling back the layers of protection, beliefs, shoulds, and identities. That's when we can see things as they are—as if an invisible veil has been removed. With consistent practice, we may find that we don't need to remind ourselves to return; like a sweet fragrance that never leaves the flower, we can feel our spacious awareness with increasing constancy.

LISTEN

Once we're connected with our present-moment experience, we can listen to the wisdom of our body and mind. By listening, we can discern the underlying causes and conditions to understand the situation better from our viewpoint and that of others. We can open our minds to new possibilities and perspectives. Most importantly, we can listen within to what truly matters to us in that situation—our deepest aspirations, values, and intentions.

If need be, we can invite the appropriate mindfulness skills to disrupt our default habits getting in the way of listening within. For instance, if we observed ourselves judging a team member, we might summon compassion at this stage to understand their perspective while also acknowledging our needs in this situation. If our automatic reaction is to be compassionate toward others, we might need the lens of self-compassion to carefully listen to our feelings and frustrations. If we find ourselves stuck in a loop of reactive thoughts, we can introduce curiosity to question our assumptions and beliefs, welcoming fresh insights.

It took me a while to trust my inner knowing, so I want to emphasize: Trust that you will know what you need to know. Be patient and kind to yourself. This isn't an analytical process but more of a heartfelt process. When we find that we're striving or judging, the invitation is to return to the open, nonjudging field that Rumi talks about in "The Great Wagon" and listen:

> The breeze at dawn has secrets to tell you.
> Don't go back to sleep.
> You must ask for what you really want.
> Don't go back to sleep.

Once we return to our field of nonjudging awareness, the invitation is to listen to what lies below the surface of our conscious knowing. When we listen patiently with an open mind, we gain insight into our individual and collective experiences. Rumi urges us to wake up to our inner knowing and discover our deepest aspirations.

In summary, this important step of listening with the eight mindfulness skills first entails disrupting any default habits. This clears the way to gain a deeper understanding of the causes and conditions for the situation to arise, our assumptions and beliefs, other perspectives and possibilities, and our intentions and consequences of the choices we want to make.

BEGIN

In this step, we take the clarity gained from listening into skillful actions in the real world. Before we begin our daily actions and interactions, we realign with the intentions and insight from listening within. It's crucial to understand that profound clarity and insights don't automatically translate into action. Our deep-seated habits may impede our ability to act on our intentions. We may need to harness the eight essential skills once again to provide us with the clarity and fortitude necessary to act in alignment with our values and intentions.

We can make it a practice to realign our minds and body with our intentions throughout the day. We can silently ask ourselves this: *Are my thoughts, speech, and actions aligned with my intentions for how I want to show up in this situation? Are my actions and inactions promoting well-being for me and others, or are they causing harm and divisiveness?* Asking yourself these questions is an important step to returning to mindfulness for real-world change.

The more intentionally we begin our actions in noncritical situations, the more easily we can act mindfully in more difficult situations. We're essentially reprogramming our brains to respond with care and a clearer understanding of our situation and intentions. However, there are instances when we may lack the time or mental bandwidth to thoroughly observe our present moment experience and listen within. During such moments, we can silently pose these questions to ourselves: *What's present? What's important in this situation?* And *What's possible?* With consistent practice, it gets easier and quicker to return and realign with our inner compass.

To illustrate the importance of all three steps and how to practice them in the real world, let's revisit my story. In Chapters 2 and 3, I opened up about my personal experience of feeling anxious before my first political debate. In that moment, I remembered to return to my breath, which provided temporary respite and a glimpse into my anxiety. However, I neglected the crucial next step of listening within, which is essential to understand our circumstances better and take appropriate actions to address the issue at hand.

The next day in meditation, when I did make the time to listen, I discovered that underlying my anxiety were thoughts of self-doubt. As I attended to my thoughts with self-compassion, I noticed that I was comparing myself with the more experienced candidates and trying to be them. There's no way I could've competed with their decades of experience and institutional knowledge. However, I realized I have other skills and experiences they don't. In approaching my self-doubt with compassion and curiosity, I could shift my attention from comparison to my strengths and reconnect with my intentions for a thoughtful approach to helping our town transition to the new form of government.

The third step entailed remembering to return to my present-moment experience, then listening within to my intentions and what is getting in the way of showing up authentically, all before beginning subsequent debates. The eight skills helped me to discern and disrupt any default barriers, thus clearing the path to return to my inner knowing. By shifting my attention from wanting validation to aligning with my skills and intentions, I felt more connected and effective—"One thousand times better," as my campaign manager put it. And that's how much better all our lives can be—one thousand times better—when we return to mindfulness with the eight essential skills.

Practices and Reminders

The remainder of this book is devoted to enhancing your capacity for real-world mindfulness by mastering the eight essential skills. This will empower you to make decisions that deepen personal fulfillment, boost your leadership effectiveness, and amplify your positive contributions to the world at large. To enhance any skill, practice is key. Throughout the book, I also mention play. Why? Because sometimes we think that mindfulness has to be serious and only practiced during difficult times. Instead, I encourage you to find a balance between the diligence and rigor of practice with the wonder and awe that comes with playfulness. Remember to be mindful not only when life is tough but also in fun situations. This book invites you to practice and play in two ways:

1. Dedicated practices
2. Daily reminders or mantras

Both the dedicated practices and the daily reminders in this book have been specially designed to strengthen the eight essential skills that will empower you to live and lead mindfully. They both follow the same three steps—return, listen, and begin. The difference is that the dedicated practices require a time commitment—even if it is only five minutes—to focus on skill-building. However, the reminders are geared toward practicing in the middle of everyday life, throughout your day. They serve as touchstones to help you return to mindfulness throughout your daily activities with that particular skill.

DEDICATED PRACTICES

The purpose of the dedicated practices is to train the mind to regain control over your attention, mental processing of information, and access to insight for effective decision-making. These are the general guidelines for your designated practices.

Return: If you have a meditation practice, you can continue with that to return to your present-moment experience. If you don't have a regular practice, you can settle your attention on any object of your choosing: the breath, body sensations, the vibrations of a chant, other sensory experiences, and movement. If a sitting practice doesn't work for you, I invite you to get creative. You can even use activities like running, swimming, or Zumba™ to train your mind to be present in your experience.

Listen: After the mind has settled, take some time to listen within to gain insight and understanding about your mind and situation. You can employ free-style journaling to tap into your unconscious thoughts and aspirations or mindful walking to uncover patterns and aspirations hidden from your everyday mind.

Begin: The third step in your dedicated practice is to integrate your insight and intentions into your everyday life. Remember to return to your insights and intentions before beginning your actions and interactions. You can also use the daily reminders to align your thoughts, speech, and actions with your insights, values, and intentions.

DAILY REMINDERS

The daily reminders are designed for practicing in the middle of your everyday life. They will empower you to return to your inner knowing so you can adeptly navigate decisions, benefiting not only yourself but also your loved ones, your professional sphere, and your community. There are three ways in which the daily reminders in this book can support you in returning to mindfulness for real-world change:

- Disrupt any default habits getting in the way of being mindful
- Strengthen the particular mindfulness skill
- Provide a mindful lens to restore balance, enabling you to view the situation with clarity and make intentional choices that benefit everyone involved

The dedicated practices and reminders work hand in hand. Think of the dedicated practices as your mindfulness gym, strengthening your mental muscles so you can reliably tap into them when needed throughout the day. The daily reminders, on the other hand, serve as continuous reinforcement of a mindful mindset, integrating the eight essential skills into various aspects of your life and multiple selves so you can make effective decisions in an ever-changing world.

We need different mindfulness skills at different times, but awareness is key to waking up from our autopilot ways of living. Without awareness, we can slip into our default ways of stumbling through life. Let's begin our journey of practicing and playing with the eight essential skills, starting with the fundamental skill of awareness.

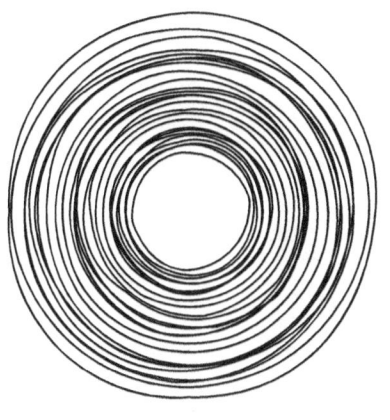

Part II

Mastering the Eight Mindfulness Skills in the Real World

Mindful Awareness: noun

Awareness is our capacity to observe without judgment what's happening in the outer world and the inner self, including our body, feelings, thoughts, habits of the mind, and what we value.

Awareness disrupts our habit of living on autopilot by becoming masterful at observation.

Skill Chapter 1

Awareness

SEE WITH FRESH EYES

I trust the mystery. I trust what comes in silence and what comes in nature where there's no diversion. . . . And the process of deep listening with attention and intention catalyzes and mobilizes exactly what's needed at that time.

—Angeles Arrien

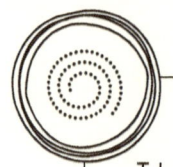

Before You Begin

Take a few breaths to arrive at this moment.

Reconnect with your intention for reading this chapter.

As you read this chapter, the invitation is to be present to the words, listen within to what the words bring up for you, and stay open to any insights or learning that emerges.

The first essential skill for returning to mindfulness is awareness. This is our ability to remain present in our internal experiences and the world around us. But too often, we're on autopilot: zoned out as if hypnotized while rushing through one task after another. It's so easy to miss the magic of being awake in our everyday lives—the lusciousness of decadent dark chocolate, witnessing our children learn and grow, meaningful conversations, and deeper connections within our teams and communities. Such moments can easily pass us by, and we risk wasting as much as 95 percent of our precious time on Earth.[10]

Awareness snaps us out of our trance and gives us a choice: whether we want to continue to auto cruise or reconnect with the aliveness and possibilities in our present moment. Are we heading in the right direction, or do we need to change? Awareness enables us to observe not only what's easily visible but also what is hidden in plain sight. Check out the story of a national nonprofit in the Story Box to see how individual and group awareness transformed a difficult dynamic into an opportunity for growth and transformation.

A national nonprofit was facing a challenging dynamic internally with one of its key team members. As long as the team members' focus was on

---

10 J.A. Bargh and T.L. Chartrand. "The Unbearable Automaticity of Being." *American Psychologist* 54, no. 7 (1999): 462–479. doi:10.1037/0003-066X.54.7.462.

changing his behavior, Johnny resisted, creating awkwardness, and nothing changed. The team leaders invited me to facilitate a retreat to build the team's emotional intelligence. With awareness, the team members were able to see the causes and conditions underlying his behavior, which led to not only Johnny changing his behavior but also how they ran their meetings.

STORY

Awareness: What Lies Beneath Obnoxious Behavior

"He's obnoxious."

Bill, the team leader, cautioned me ahead of time about Johnny, who was going to be at the full-day retreat for the leadership team. The focus for this team retreat was emotional intelligence and communication skills. The nonprofit had grown from a smaller, more cohesive group to a bigger network of people experiencing frequent breakdowns in communication and operationalizing their shared values. One example of this challenge was Johnny's obstinacy and resistance to team rules, including "No cell phones during meetings," which others found disruptive and disrespectful.

He defended his actions: "In an economy where we're competing for donors' money, I have to return texts and emails promptly." And that was that. No one could get Johnny to change. Yet he was good at his job, so they suffered him in silence.

The first half of the retreat time was focused on developing individual skills in awareness and empathy. During the second half, the focus shifted to building group awareness in challenging situations. The "challenging situation" selected for discussion was, no surprise, "Cell phone use during meetings." Team members went around speaking—without judgment or blame—about their need for more focus and a distraction-free environment at meetings. Then it was Johnny's turn.

The silence was palpable. Gazing straight ahead, he started to speak slowly and intentionally, as if trying to give words to what he was just discovering from careful observation of his thoughts and behaviors. For the first time, he vocalized the cause for his frustrations: "The meetings are too long!" He noted that often people weren't prepared, and everything

continued

they could have read ahead of time, which *he* did, had to be explained. He acknowledged that without timely distribution of agendas, which was frequently the case, it was impossible for others to adequately prepare. Now people around him were starting to nod in agreement. They concurred with him that the meetings were lengthy and went on to discuss ways to make them more focused.

By shedding light on the reasons behind Johnny's stubborn conduct, he enabled others to recognize the flaws in their meetings—the absence of agendas, unprepared participants, and excessively lengthy sessions. His behavior was only a symptom of a more profound issue they could now collectively identify and tackle.

What Johnny's story tells us is a common mistake we all make: We focus on what we can see and not the underlying conditions of the situation. The focus all along had been on changing his behavior without understanding the underlying causes and conditions. In fact, even Johnny had not stopped to consider his reasons for stubbornly continuing to text during meetings. When he did bring awareness to his thoughts related to his texting behavior, he discovered that the problem was not him but the long and disorderly meetings. The negative effects of this perceived lack of consideration of others were rippling into all aspects of their work beyond meetings. Had the team not stopped to create a safe space for individual and group awareness, they'd still be stuck in low morale due to adversarial team dynamics and inefficient meetings.

Most likely, we can all recognize ourselves in the story. We've been stuck in a challenging dynamic that's hard to break. Although, of course, we don't have to be in a workplace to find ourselves thrown off guard by someone saying something inappropriate or not respecting our values. It could be that we are the ones triggering others. Maybe it was during a discussion in our classroom, in a virtual meeting with colleagues, or with a friend in the Wild West of social media. One moment, we're getting along, the next, someone says or does something that pushes our reactive buttons, and we have little control over what we say or feel. How do we avoid that blood-pressure-raising cycle of reactivity? Better still, can we transform cycles of reactivity into opportunities for growth and connection?

Enter awareness.

Awareness: Becoming Masterful at Observation

Awareness is our capacity to observe without judgment what's happening in the outer world and inner self; this includes our body, feelings, thoughts, habits of the mind, and what we value. For instance, as you bring awareness to these words you're reading, are you also aware of your breath moving in and out of your body? Is your body posture supporting you in being alert and relaxed? Perhaps you notice a tightness in your body, and your breath is shallow. Now that you're aware of your breath and body, you can soften places that are holding tension and allow your breath to go a little deeper. By returning to your awareness, you can break the autopilot habit and gain more control over how you respond to situations. You're taking back ownership of yourself.

Even though awareness is an innate ability, we forget. We let the momentum of our habits and circumstances take over our lives. David Foster Wallace's commencement speech, "This Is Water," delivered at Kenyon College, depicts our disconnect from awareness with a story of fish swimming in the ocean. An older fish greets two young fish, "Morning, boys! How's the water?" and one of the young fish turns to the other one and asks, "What the hell is water?!" But just like fish fail to see the water they swim in, we, too, are not aware of who and what is before us. We live disconnected from what is, sometimes, most important and from each other as human beings. While it may be easier to live using our default settings to react to life automatically and unconsciously, this approach deprives us of the power to choose how to think and what to pay attention to.

To reliably reconnect with awareness in the middle of life, it's essential to recognize the different pathways that lead back to this innate capacity—inner or outer awareness, sensory or cognitive awareness, and meta-awareness.

INNER VS. OUTER AWARENESS

Inner awareness is our ability to sense and know what's happening within us. The faculty of inner awareness empowers us to recognize our body sensations, thoughts, feelings, judgments, preferences, and values. For instance, when we're triggered, our heart beats faster, our breathing becomes shallow, and our shoulders tense. Internal awareness, like the kind Johnny brought to the thoughts underlying his defiant behavior, helps us understand the causes and conditions of our reactions. Sometimes we don't uncover what's bothering us right away. That's why we will be developing other mindfulness skills to accompany our awareness. A mindful mindset entails different qualities of the mind, and awareness is only the first but necessary skill.

Outer awareness includes not only what's plainly visible but also subtle changes, movements, and patterns of behavior in people around us. It's possible we're so lost in inner awareness that we don't notice the body language and feelings of our children, partners, or colleagues at work. We also need to be able to notice the changes in our environment—such as new technologies, political unrest, climate change, and social movements—so we can adequately adapt, respond, and, when necessary, lead the change. As such, we need to strengthen inner and outer awareness. As we refine our ability to notice more nuanced feelings and sensations within ourselves, the more we can direct our refined awareness toward happenings in the external world. The more masterful we become at observing our inner and outer landscape, the more choices we have to respond in skillful ways, no matter what life throws at us.

SENSORY AWARENESS VS. COGNITIVE AWARENESS

Do you ever feel like your mind is spinning out of control? The constant buzz of thoughts and never-ending to-do lists can spiral into a cycle of stress, but fortunately, there's an easy solution: sensory awareness. Unlike our thinking mind, which plans, remembers, and pursues cognitive tasks, sensory awareness allows us to experience the present moment through sight, smell, touch, or taste in a way that refreshes rather than exhausts. So, in those moments when mental fatigue hits, turn down the thinking volume and indulge in a bite (or two!) of dark chocolate, feel the warmth from your morning cup of joe, and soak up some sunshine. Allow yourself moments like these throughout your day—as they provide tremendous relief for both mind and body and strengthen your ability to return to mindfulness in the middle of life.

Neuroscientists have discovered an important truth: Thinking and sensing are very different activities that can't occur concurrently. So, we can't think and sense at the same time. See for yourself using the guidance in the following simple exercise.

See for Yourself

Begin by immersing yourself in the world of sounds surrounding you. Take a moment to listen to all the sounds, from the rustling of leaves to the distant hum of traffic.

Now, challenge yourself to count backward from one hundred while remaining fully engaged in your auditory experience. It may initially seem plausible, as if you can engage in both activities at once. However, upon closer examination, you'll discover that listening and thinking occur in rapid succession rather than simultaneously.

Take a pause and shift your focus solely to the act of counting backward. Notice how this mental task requires your undivided attention, temporarily setting aside the sensory world around you.

Now it's time to redirect your focus toward simply listening. Tune in to the symphony of sounds, letting go of any thoughts or activity. Observe how the act of listening invites you to surrender any kind of thinking, rushing, or striving, allowing you to fully embrace the present moment.

By tuning into your senses and embracing the present moment, you'll rediscover the ease and tranquility that accompanies pure sensory awareness. The exercise invites you to explore the powerful relationship between sensing and thinking, ultimately highlighting the importance of taking time to rest in sensory awareness.

Why is it important that we understand that we can't think and sense simultaneously? Sensory awareness is a quick way to get out of our heads and return to our awareness of the present moment. It's all too easy to become trapped within our minds—ruminating over past misfortunes or worrying about future anxieties—that we miss out on some of the most beautiful moments this world has to offer: birdsong as it drifts across an open sky, winter days with their soft sunlight, a blanket of white clouds across an azure sky. These are all occasions that offer much-needed respite to our nonstop thinking, rushing, and striving. Intellectually we know all this. Yet, it's hard to disrupt the momentum of habits that we've picked up along the way and seem to have a mind of their own. This is where meta-awareness comes in.

META-AWARENESS

It is the nature of the mind to be distracted, and we also have the capacity to know that we're distracted. This capacity to know the contents of our mind and habits of the mind is meta-awareness. It is what makes it possible for us to know that we're distracted from what's important in the present moment. Like right now, even as you're reading this book, are you aware of all the thoughts in the last few minutes that hijacked your attention—maybe thoughts about an email you need to send, something your partner said earlier today, or the molten chocolate cake in your fridge that will go well with coffee as you read this book? Okay, so the last example wasn't entirely made up. Anyway, the point is that we have developed habits of the mind that leave us distracted and disconnected from what gives us joy and meaning. Meta-awareness is our capacity to recognize these habitual patterns and return our attention to what fulfills our lives in general or at any given moment.

Meta-awareness can also help us regulate the contents of our thinking.[11] When we find ourselves drifting toward thoughts and behaviors that

---

11 Jonathan W. Schooler and Charles A. Schreiber. "Perceptual Decoupling: Accessing Information Without Awareness." *Journal of Experimental Psychology: General* 133, no. 1 (2004): 26–40. doi:10.1037/0096-3445.133.1.26.

aren't aligned with our intentions, this meta-awareness can guide us back on track, prompting actions in alignment with our goals. At the same time, it's important to note that not all mind wandering is bad. In fact, mind wandering has been associated with creativity. When we allow our minds to wander freely, unencumbered by stress, we make unconscious connections that can lead to novel solutions. But we need to know when to allow for mind wandering and when to be present. Meta-awareness empowers us to make that choice!

Do your habits often lead to autopilot living and blur the boundaries between what's in your control and what's not? By developing meta-awareness, you can gain clarity as to when your mind may have strayed from intention—and how to get back on track.

Awareness makes us masterful at observing our inner and outer worlds, sensory and thinking worlds, and how our minds work. Awareness is a foundational skill that empowers us to be mindful in the real world, especially when we want to bring change in ourselves, our families, our organizations, or within communities.

We Can't Change What We Can't See

Have you ever wanted to change for the better but couldn't get yourself motivated? You're not alone. Making any meaningful change can often feel daunting. However, understanding the underlying obstacles to our current situation—whether it concerns physical fitness, organizational change, or broader societal transformation—can help us take more effective action to address the causes and conditions that gave rise to the problems we're seeking to address.

I struggle with change as well. When I was trying to kickstart my running practice, at first I resisted because I felt lazy (or so I thought). It was so hard for me to start running regularly. When I paused to bring awareness to the causes and conditions underlying my discomfort and laziness, I could see what was holding me back. That understanding empowered me to address the cause of my resistance to running. I went from "I'm lazy" thoughts to running regularly . . . and even enjoying it. It all starts with awareness.

STORY

I am not a runner. I am not a gym person, either. Other than Zumba and walking, I pretty much dislike exercise of any kind. My husband, on the other hand, is a marathon runner. I tried running with him a couple of times. Each time after running for a few minutes, I felt my heart was about to explode. I felt so out of breath and uncomfortable that I had to stop. "Clearly, I'm not a runner. This is not for me," I concluded. I silently judged myself as being lazy and unable to stick with running or any other aerobic exercise, for that matter.

One day in meditation, I noticed my resistance to getting up from my comfortable seated position to a standing posture—just standing, no moving involved. But even so, I didn't want to get up. That was immediately followed by my inner judge declaring, "You're so lazy!" That was followed by my mindful self bringing awareness to my resistance to getting up without any judgment. It was then that I clearly saw what was happening. I recognized the causes and conditions for my aversion to movement. I grew up in the Middle East, which was too hot for us as children to go out and play. I spent most of my childhood eating, watching TV, and studying (I still love to study, hence my obsession with research even though I'm not an academic anymore). My entire childhood conditioning was to "not move." That's what my mind knew and was most comfortable with. Of course, I wasn't going to start running suddenly. If I wanted to change my conditioned mind to enjoy moving, I needed to start moving. Period. There are no short-cuts. To rewire my brain for movement, I took small but regular steps to be active.

I used the Pomodoro app to take breaks after every thirty minutes of sedentary work, during which I did jumping jacks or sprinting on the spot. I took up running short distances regularly, judgment-free. Over time, I've learned to shift the causes and conditions to align with my intentions for being active. It's working!

Whether you're looking to change your response to a given situation, a deep-seated habit, or start a new habit, awareness is your ally. Yet, in the middle of life, it is easy to lose awareness, just like the fish in the water. With daily practices and reminders, you can strengthen your ability to return to mindfulness with awareness. But first, do you know where you stand in terms of awareness?

Where Are You on the Awareness Continuum?

Before we dive into ways to deepen our connection with awareness, take a few moments to reflect on your capacity for awareness—inner and outer, sensory and cognitive, and meta-awareness. You can also take the mindfulness assessment on my website (KnowYourMind.training) and use the report as a contemplative tool. The results are not intended to create judgment or get overconfident about your ability to live with awareness. We all have an innate capacity to be aware, and the question is, are you able to bring awareness in situations that matter to you?

Take a look at the Awareness Continuum table on the following page to reflect on the benefits of awareness and your tendencies. See the impact when awareness is mindful, when it's low, and when it's misappropriated by other qualities of the mind that are disguised as awareness and get in the way of being mindful. The last column deserves some explanation. Misappropriated awareness refers to situations when we may think we're very sensitive and aware, but our hyper-vigilance is not coming from a centered place for clear seeing. Rather, we're overly sensitive as a result of past trauma, obsession, or unmet need—all of which obstruct clear seeing.

 ## The Awareness Continuum

LOW AWARENESS	MINDFUL AWARENESS	MISAPPROPRIATED AWARENESS

Tendency to:

- Live on autopilot—unconscious and not intentional about choices and experiences
- Be unaware of your physical needs and bodily sensations
- Disconnect from emotions
- Be unaware of your needs, aspirations, and gifts
- Be unaware of other people's body language, needs, and emotions
- Be unable to enjoy sensory pleasures

Tendency to:

- Be conscious and intentional about choices and experiences
- Be aware of your physical needs and sensations in the body
- Have emotional awareness
- Have social awareness
- Have sensory awareness

Tendency to:

- Be overly sensitive to inner and outer stimuli, which leads to instability and feeling overwhelmed
- Have hyper-awareness of physical sensations and catastrophizing
- Be overly emotional
- Be self-conscious
- Be overly conscious of what others think and say
- Have sensory overload

How to Return with Awareness

Engage with the dedicated "return" practices and the six daily reminders that follow to strengthen your awareness. This will enable you to consistently return to mindfulness throughout your day. To refresh your memory, the practices include three parts—return, listen, and begin—which offer ways for you to return to your present-moment experience, to listen to your inner knowing, and to integrate your intentions and insights before you begin your actions and interactions. The three trainings to return, listen, and begin work together in a cyclical fashion. In the dedicated practice, you may start by returning to the present moment with awareness of your experience. Once you feel connected with yourself in the present moment, take a few moments to listen within—to your inner knowing, insights, and intentions. Integrate your insights and intentions before you begin your next activity or interaction. When you employ the reminders to return to mindfulness in the middle of the day, you can begin by returning to your body or breath, listening to your inner compass, and knowing that it can guide you in showing up intentionally for yourself and others.

Consider selecting one reminder each day, using the central message as a daily mantra to return to your situation with awareness. You can also play with multiple reminders in a day based on your needs. These are suggestions. Trust yourself to know what you need and adapt accordingly so you may see clearly, truly appreciate all of life, and make fulfilling choices that benefit you and the world around you.

DEDICATED PRACTICE

The metaphor of a flagpole may be helpful here. Your awareness is like a flagpole, and your mind is like the flag, fluttering in the wind. No matter how stormy the weather, the flag doesn't fly away because it's anchored to the pole. Similarly, by strengthening your connection to awareness, you'll learn to weather all kinds of storms with stability and grace. You can bring awareness to your breath, body sensations, sounds, other sensory experiences, thoughts, emotions, and your moment-to-moment experience. The practice of open awareness prepares you to meet all of life with fresh eyes.

Maintain a daily dedicated practice, preferably before you begin your day and, if possible, at the end of your day. Most importantly, fix a time for your daily practice that works for you and try to stick with it.

Return. Start by returning to your awareness of the breath as an anchor to the present moment. Once your attention is stabilized, you can open your awareness to body sensations, sounds, thoughts, and eventually to your moment-to-moment experience—allowing all sensations to arise and dissolve in the vast sky-like quality of your open awareness—not resisting or clinging to any experience. Simply be with whatever arises in your experience.

Listen. Take a few moments to listen to any insights about your capacity for awareness. If it's helpful, use the following questions for contemplation or journaling:

- *What did you discover about the quality of your mind and ability to be present in your moment-to-moment experience?*
- *What are the causes and conditions that support your awareness, and what gets in the way of being aware?*

For instance, when I look at the causes and conditions tugging me away from my writing, I may notice that I have an incessant need to check my phone, and when I question that need—is it essential to check my email now?—I may notice that the seeming need to check my phone is just a habit of the mind looking for a quick dopamine rush that comes from getting an email from a client or loved one. But that rush is fleeting, and once it passes, my mind will be looking for the next thing to get that rush. Meanwhile, I've abandoned the more fulfilling exercise of writing. When I see it that way, it's much easier to return to present-moment awareness of whatever I'm doing.

- *What are your intentions for cultivating awareness?*

Reconnecting with my intentions for writing, for instance, also provides a motivation to return to my present moment and write with a revived sense of freshness and purpose.

Begin. Integrate your insights and intentions related to awareness before you begin your next activity. See if you can return to awareness of your thoughts, speech, and all actions and interactions. To remember to return to the present moment with awareness, place the daily mantras or reminders described next in a place you're likely to see them and benefit from them.

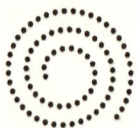

DAILY MANTRAS TO RETURN WITH AWARENESS

Practice and play with the chosen reminders for the day with the following intentions in mind: disrupting your default habit of living and leading on autopilot, strengthening your ability to return to your actions and interactions with awareness, and bringing the lens of awareness to view your experience with fresh eyes, especially when it matters most.

I. Mantra for the Day: Wake Up with the Senses
Cultivating sensory awareness

This mantra is a wonderful way to wake up and start your day. Instead of mindlessly reaching out for your phone, what if you were to take a few moments to look at the morning sky or really enjoy the taste of your morning cup of tea or coffee?

This is also a great practice to do as you move from one location to another at home, school, or place of work—like from one room to another room at home, your house to your car, or walking on your school campus. Instead of looking at your phone or ruminating, use the moments of transition to walk mindfully and strengthen your sensory awareness, which is a direct path to mindfulness. You can also use this practice when you have been engaged in a mental or mundane activity for a while and want to take a refreshing break.

Return. Return to all the senses one by one, or choose one sense that is calling your attention the most. Spend about one to five minutes with each sense. The idea is to feel and not think about the sensations experienced through the senses. For a few moments, free yourself from what you know based on your memory or knowledge of the sensory object. Instead, dive into your direct experience using the senses at this moment. Allow yourself to wake up to the present moment with your senses.

For example, feel the sensations of touch—patterns of pressure, sensations in your feet as they make contact with the ground, the coolness or warmth of the floor, and the air touching your skin. Once you have fully explored the sense of touch, you could turn to the sensations of sounds—subtle and big ones—in your environment. Without getting lost in the source and judgments related to the sounds, simply receive the sounds with your entire body. Similarly, take your time with the remaining senses of smell, sight, and taste.

Listen. Take a few moments after returning to your senses to listen within. Make room to gain a direct and intimate understanding of your experience. Reconnect with what's important to you and what you value in this one wild and precious life. If helpful, gently invite these questions to gain an understanding of your sensory awareness—which senses do you tend to use more or less?

- *What are the causes and conditions that leave you disconnected from your senses, and what strengthens awareness of your senses?*
- *What are the consequences—how does it feel when you're disconnected from your senses, and how does it feel when you return to your senses?*
- *Based on your discoveries and insights, set an intention to deepen your sensory awareness. Maybe commit to one activity you will do today, during which you will give your full attention to your senses, like eating, walking, listening to music, or taking a shower.*

Begin. Integrate your intentions and insights before you begin your activities and interactions in the world. Return to your senses in between work or when you need breaks—rest your thinking mind on one sense of your choice.

II. Mantra for the Day: There Is a Body
Awareness of body

If you had to remember one thing in this chapter, this is it. This mantra disrupts habitual thinking by returning you to the body, which always resides in the present moment. By observing sensations in the body—their quality, intensity, and changing nature—you gain insight into your experience. Any change, pleasant or unpleasant, is immediately felt in the body, informing you about the state of your mind. For instance, high levels of stress can become the "new normal" without you realizing it. By paying attention to your body—before stress levels turn overwhelming—you can proactively do something about it and take ownership of your choices.

Return. Returning to your breath moving in and out of your body, silently say, "There is a body." Notice all the sensations within your body. Allow your awareness to go where your body wants it to go. Maybe it's the tingling or circulation of blood in your fingers, maybe you can sense your heart beating, or it's the tightness in your thigh muscles that draw your attention. Be with the sensations without trying to find anything special or fix anything. If you refine your ability to observe and sense, you may notice the pulsing, arising, changing, and dissolving of sensations in the body.

When your mind gets distracted—which it will—again use the phrase, "There is a body," and begin again.

Listen. Once you feel connected with your body, take a few moments to listen to what it has to say. What did you discover about your feelings or needs underlying your body sensations? Use the following questions, if helpful, to deepen your understanding of your experience by attending to the body:

- *What did you learn about your experience with this mantra?*
- *What is your body telling you about your thoughts and emotions?*
- *How might it be useful for you to return to your body during the day?*

Begin. Integrate your intentions and discoveries before you begin an activity or interaction. Check in with your body and posture before you begin an interaction or even in the middle of it to stay connected with your present-moment awareness. You can also check in regularly throughout your day to listen to your body. For instance, I use a Pomodoro app, which keeps me focused for thirty minutes of concentrated work. Then I take a five-minute break during which I check in with my body, "Do I need more hydration, stretching, jumping jacks, or just some unconditional love?"

III. Mantra for the Day: Anchored Awareness
Awareness of thoughts

Our awareness can be hijacked by people and events that we have no control over. However, we do have control over our breath, which can be used to return to mindfulness. The breath is like an anchor to your present-moment experience, especially when you feel distracted or overwhelmed.

Return. Bring attention to the fact that you are breathing, becoming aware of the movement of your breath as it enters and leaves the body, not trying to change it. Once your awareness is steady, open your awareness to thoughts arising and dissolving in the vast, sky-like quality of your mind. Whether there's one thought or many thoughts, witness your thoughts come and go without losing awareness. Allow your awareness of thoughts to be anchored by your breath.

Instead of letting them be a distraction, allow your thoughts to be center stage. Without getting involved in the content, simply see each thought as it comes up as an observable event and let it be, without pushing it away or getting lost in it.

Listen. Once your attention is stabilized, take a few moments to listen within.

- *How does anchored awareness help you see clearly and act intentionally?*
- *What are the causes and conditions that are taking you away from your anchored awareness, and what can support you in returning to it?*
- *What shifts when you observe your thoughts without following them?*

Choose regular activities you do in your day, such as checking your phone, sending an email, or eating, as cues to return to your anchored awareness. Set an intention to return to your awareness of thoughts for the selected activities in your day and when you feel overwhelmed.

Begin. Return to anchored awareness before you begin the next activity. Anytime you find that your awareness is being hijacked by others or events beyond your control, remind yourself to return to anchored awareness with your breath.

IV. Mantra for the Day: Invite Your Feelings
Emotional awareness

Rumi, the Persian poet, reminds us in his poem, "The Guest House," "Meet them [your feelings] at the door laughing, and invite them in . . . each has been sent as a guide from beyond." Use this practice as an invitation to welcome all feelings, even the difficult ones. Our emotions and feelings are there for a reason, to protect us and help us meet our unmet needs, but our default tendency is to avoid, suppress, or push away difficult feelings. We will explore what our emotions are telling us with other essential skills like curiosity and inner calm. But first, we have to learn to recognize and make room for all our feelings, and that's what this practice will achieve. This is a great reminder when you feel triggered at home, at work, or in your community, and also to nurture your emotional awareness.

Return. Using the breath, return to yourself. Just for a few moments, allow yourself to feel whatever is there with no need to fix anything or feel anything special. Allow each breath to create space in your mind and body, and with each exhale, let go of any tension you may be holding in your body. Once you feel ready, turn toward your emotions with kindness. Without any judgment, simply note your emotions, such as calm or confused, anxious or amused, excited or bored.

If you're feeling pleasant emotions that are calming, like contentment, relief, or appreciation, acknowledge them without getting attached to how they feel—make space for the calming emotions to be experienced in your whole body.

If you're feeling unpleasant emotions like anxiety or fear, see if you can make space for them to be there, without suppressing or trying to fix them. Breathe into places in your body where you're holding the emotions. If you still feel anxious, make a note of whom you can reach out to for help.

If you're feeling a high-intensity emotion like excitement, turn toward that as well. See if you can receive the gifts in this situation—a sense of joy and enthusiasm without needing to rush or react. Make space for it all.

Listen. Take a few moments to listen within. What did you discover about your emotions? Use these questions to gain emotional awareness:

- *What are your emotions telling you about your situation?*

- *What are your default habits related to emotions, and how might you befriend your emotions?*
- *What is one small shift you noticed by making space for your emotions and not pushing them away?*

Begin. Before you begin your next activity, take a moment to "meet and invite your feelings." Return to the mantra "invite your feelings" throughout your day, like while trying a new challenging exercise routine, having a conversation with a loved one, or doing challenging tasks at work. Explore how recognizing your feelings allows you to see the situation more clearly and act intentionally. Feeling your emotions fully will also make your life so much richer and more rewarding.

V. Mantra for the Day: See with Fresh Eyes
Interpersonal awareness

We get into habitual ways of interacting with people, even those we love and especially those with whom we disagree. This stops us from seeing the whole person with fresh eyes and how they, too, are changing over time. We see more clearly when we soften the grip of judgments and expectations with respect to others. In this practice, you'll be building the habit of seeing people with fresh eyes. You can practice and play with this mantra with respect to people who you find are friendly and neutral, and eventually with those you are having difficulty with.

Return. When you're in the company of someone—it could be your partner, child, team member, neighbor, or teacher—take a breath to return to your nonjudging awareness of this person. Soften your gaze and soften the labels or judgments that you hold for this person. See the person as if you're seeing them for the first time. Allow yourself to notice things you might miss when you're interacting with them on autopilot, such as the shine and depth in their eyes, their body language, and the tone of their voice. See if you can bring awareness to what is being said and also what is not verbalized.

Listen. Take a few moments to listen within. If helpful, use the following questions for reflection:

- *What did you discover about your awareness of interpersonal relationships? For instance, where did your awareness linger most naturally—on the words, body language, tone, or something else?*
- *What are the causes and conditions that leave you disconnected from this person?*
- *Does seeing this person with fresh eyes shift your interactions with them?*

Take a few moments to set your intention of seeing everyone you interact with today with fresh eyes.

Begin. Before you interact with anyone today, return to your intentions to see with fresh eyes.

VI. Mantra for the Day: Amplify Awareness
Amplifying awareness

The more you return to awareness in ordinary moments, the more easily you'll be able to access it in critical situations. When you're present, you may discover that even everyday experiences like eating a raisin or taking a walk can be extraordinary. How miraculous is it for so many different parts of your body to instantly coordinate to recognize a raisin, see it, pick it up, chew, and taste it while you're still breathing? With this mantra, you can use your breath to return to mindfulness whenever you find yourself mindlessly rushing through life.

Return. Return to your present-moment experience by bringing attention to your breath. No need to change your breathing—if it's shallow, let it be shallow. If it wants to go deep, let your breathing be deep. Keep it simple.

Your sensing of the breath moving in your body is effortless. Return to this effortless knowing again and again.

Make a gentle note of whether your experience is pleasant, unpleasant, or neutral. With this practice, you're becoming masterful at observing your experience without grasping what is pleasant or resisting what feels unpleasant.

Listen. Take a few moments to listen to what is emerging within when you return to the present moment with your breath. Gently invite these suggested questions to listen within:

- *What did you discover about your inner and outer experiences?*
- *Did seeing the experience as pleasant, unpleasant, or neutral shift your experience in any way?*
- *What is your intention for this situation?*

Begin. Before you begin the next activity, like checking your phone or eating, bring awareness to your present moment. This includes any thoughts, needs, and emotions. Check in with your intentions for the activity and begin with awareness.

Take a Moment to Celebrate!

You made it through the first essential skill! Congratulations!

Just your intention to read this book is something to celebrate. When you try even one of the suggested ways to stop and see the world with fresh eyes, you return to mindfulness, the place we know as home. Every time you disrupt your automatic ways of being and moving in the world, you're strengthening your ability to be more awake, more aware of this precious life and the opportunities it presents to grow, share your gifts, and find fulfillment. Onward to the next mindfulness skill—compassion. This is not only essential for your personal growth but also instrumental in building trust within your organization and community.

Compassion: noun

Our innate ability to feel, understand, and be motivated to alleviate suffering in ourselves and others when we understand our interbeing.

Compassion disrupts our tendency to act on our automatic judgments about ourselves and others by seeking to understand.

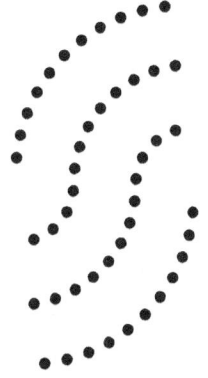

Skill Chapter 2

Compassion

SEEK TO UNDERSTAND AND INTERBE

If you are a poet, you will see clearly that there is a cloud floating in this sheet of paper. Without a cloud, there will be no rain; without rain, the trees cannot grow; and without trees, we cannot make paper. The cloud is essential for the paper to exist. If the cloud is not here, the sheet of paper cannot be here either.

—Thich Nhat Hanh, *Peace Is Every Step*

Before You Begin

Take a few breaths to arrive at this moment.

If it's helpful, place a hand on your chest to rest your mind on the breath moving in and out of your chest. Connect with your intention for cultivating compassion—for yourself and others.

As you read this chapter, the invitation is to be present to any judgments—about yourself or what you're reading—and see if you can soften the grip of judgments with kindness and seek a deeper understanding of what underlies your judgments.

Welcome to the second mindfulness skill: compassion.

Compassion has received somewhat of a bad rap for being "soft" or "too nice." Yet, compassion gives us the courage to lean into our discomfort and try to seek understanding when our natural inclination might be to judge and avoid the situation. When we're looking to change something within us—including our default habits of judging and avoidance—we're bound to experience some resistance. Awareness may be the first step in recognizing that we need change—and our resistance to it—but compassion paves the way to sustainable progress. Our biggest roadblock to change? Judging rather than understanding. Compassion is the practice of transforming our habit of judging into seeking understanding.

Sometimes our harshest convictions are directed toward ourselves. Self-compassion enables us to replace limiting beliefs that keep us from reaching our goals with understanding and actionable steps. Danielle's story is a powerful reminder for us to be more compassionate with ourselves in order to reach our goals. Danielle, a successful middle-aged client, spent prolonged hours hunched over her computer, which led to pain in her back and joints. With self-compassion, she was able to face her inner critic and discover what was paralyzing her from starting a fitness regimen

STORY

Why Bother?!

Meet Danielle, a successful middle-aged woman who seemed to have it all—a flourishing career and a content life with her beloved cat. However, there was one thing that kept eluding her—fitness. Stiff joints and an aching back became unwelcome guests in her life. It was then that her doctor prescribed a strength- and fitness-training program that would rejuvenate her weary body.

Despite her desire to start exercising, life always seemed to throw obstacles in her path. Whether it was work emergencies, the needs of her feline companion, or simply a lack of time, Danielle felt powerless to break free from her sedentary routine.

But little did she know, it wasn't her busy schedule or lack of energy that held her back. It was her own inner critic, whispering doubts in her ear, telling her she would never keep up with an exercise routine. That voice, filled with negativity, had paralyzed her from taking that first step toward fitness.

That all changed when Danielle attended a mindfulness class that introduced her to the power of self-compassion. Through exercises that encouraged her to embrace her struggles with kindness, she realized that she wasn't alone in her pursuit of change. Every human being faced challenges and felt stuck at times.

With this newfound understanding, Danielle mustered the courage to confront her inner critic and challenge its limiting beliefs. She made a commitment to join a gym and embark on a strength- and fitness-training program. Each class she attended, she felt herself growing stronger, both physically and mentally.

As the weeks passed, Danielle's limiting beliefs transformed into self-confidence, propelling her forward on her fitness journey. She no longer saw exercise as a burden but rather as a source of empowerment and liberation from her sedentary lifestyle. And with each achievement, she proved to herself that she was capable of far more than she had ever imagined.

Danielle's story is a testament to the transformative power of self-compassion to understand and overcome our own inner barriers.

recommended by her doctor. Once she uncovered her unconscious beliefs, she knew what to do to change them.

Are you friends with your inner critic? We all have one, regardless of how successful we are. This is the voice within us—sometimes a faint whisper, and at other times that's all we can hear—that we're not enough. We could be, should be better. When we look at ourselves and others through this invisible veil of judgments, it's hard to see the unique gifts we bring and our shared humanity. This is what takes us away from our human nature—to feel, understand, and take steps to alleviate suffering in ourselves and others.

Regardless of your intentions and goals—be it running a marathon, becoming a better actor, or reaching your sales quota—compassion can make all the difference. You just need to understand what it means so you can recognize it within yourself and learn to return to this innate capacity, even when you're feeling compelled to confine yourself or others to a little box.

Compassion: Transforming Judgments into Understanding

Compassion originates from the Latin word *compati*, which means "to suffer together." Joseph Goldstein, my favorite mindfulness teacher and co-founder of Insight Meditation Society in Barre, Massachusetts, describes compassion as "the strong wish of the mind and heart to alleviate all suffering."[12] We all have a sense of what it means to "suffer together" when people we love or care about are going through a difficult time. When your child or partner trips and falls, you immediately reach out to help. You don't first think, *I should help*. You help because it's the most natural thing for you to do.

However, how can we acknowledge and alleviate suffering in strangers or people with different beliefs from our own? This is an important capacity in the interconnected world we live in: We work closely with people we may disagree with; we live in communities divided by politics and social values;

---

12 Joseph Goldstein. *Mindfulness: A Practical Guide to Awakening* (Sounds True, 2013).

we're part of an ecosystem that is hugely impacted by our mindless consumption habits; we're all human, and we have to learn to live together if we want to create conditions for all to thrive. From an evolutionary perspective, Charles Darwin informs us that communities with the greatest number of people who care for one another flourish best.[13] I know all this. Yet, I have failed to be compassionate in my role as a town councilor more times than I would have liked.

MY FAILURE TO BE COMPASSIONATE IN TOWN COUNCIL

Although I thought my regular mindfulness practice had made me a mindful leader, it became obvious that wasn't always the case when sitting on the town council. Instead of offering understanding and empathy to my colleagues, too often, I succumbed to judgments about those who focused on their version of reality and didn't make space for all perspectives to be heard. I understand that we all—and that includes me—have our biases and beliefs that shape how we think and vote. It's in our nature to take a position without grasping all aspects of the issue, but it is paramount for us as leaders—and people—to listen with open minds before reaching any conclusions. I discovered that when people didn't respond according to my expectations, I felt powerless over my reactions. My judgments seemed to control both how I processed information and acted upon it . . . almost no matter how hard I tried to check myself.

Ahh, the irony! Here I was, judging my fellow town councilors for making snap judgments. But I, too, was behaving in a similar manner, judging them without trying to understand the reasons behind their actions. Instead of curiosity about their perspectives and asking more questions, I became judgmental in the heat of a moment.

However, deepening my understanding and practice of compassion has helped me better manage these overwhelming moments so that I can be more effective at solving problems in collaboration with my colleagues. I

13 Clara Strauss, Billie Lever Taylor, Jenny Gu, Willem Kuyken, Ruth Baer, Fergal W. Jones, and Kate Cavanagh. "What Is Compassion and How Can We Measure It? A Review of Definitions and Measures." *Clinical Psychology Review* 47 (May 2016). doi: 10.1016/j.cpr.2016.05.004, CC BY-NC-ND 4.0.

don't always succeed in achieving full understanding—due to the fast pace of government meetings—but I know how to disrupt my righteous judgments and seek to understand instead.

As human beings, we desire to be empathetic and understanding toward the people we work and live with, but it can be so hard when we enter into heated conversations, especially if things reach an impasse. In such moments, when we feel disconnected from our natural capacity for compassion, it can be beneficial to remember what the different components of compassion are so that we can return to it.

EMPATHY, SYMPATHY, AND THE FIVE COMPONENTS OF COMPASSION

It's easy to mix compassion with empathy or sympathy. While empathy involves feeling others' pain and understanding their perspective, compassion goes one step further toward doing something about it. Sympathy involves caring about the suffering but from a distance, which often sounds something like, "Poor you," with the subtext, "Thank God it's not me." Any motivation to help because of pity is not guided by our shared humanity but by fear and separation. When we experience sympathy, we're also experiencing discomfort, which creates a desire to fix the problem, rather than truly being there for the person.

When it comes to being mindful in the real world, understanding the difference between sympathy, empathy, and compassion is a must. Sympathy involves observing others' suffering with detachment and is often accompanied by judgment, while empathy enables us to step into someone else's shoes and feel their pain. However, compassion surpasses empathy by generating a genuine desire to help.

In an increasingly divided world, sympathy, though well-intentioned, has the potential to widen the chasm between individuals. It can inadvertently reinforce differences between those who offer help and those who need help. However, compassion invites us to recognize and embrace our interconnectedness through the lens of our shared humanity. The helpers and those being helped are seen as equally important members of an interdependent ecosystem, each one contributing in unique ways at different points in time. Compassion holds the power to bridge gaps, foster under-standing, and promote peace and collective well-being.

Empathy without compassion can be detrimental to how we experience suffering, resulting in empathic distress, also known as empathy fatigue, which can lead to despair and hopelessness. When we're exposed to the injustices in our world, racial discrimination, climate change, or the extreme poverty in which so many young children live, it's easy to start feeling over-whelmed. However, as soon as we return to compassion—and shifting attention to what actions we can take to help, however small they may be—we can feel motivated and hopeful.

GEEK OUT!

Compassion Overcomes Empathic Distress

Scientists[14] looked into the brains of people who were trained in empathy and, subsequently, in compassion. In subjects trained only in empathy, videos of human suffering activated parts of the brain associated with pain and negative affect. After training in compassion, exposure to human suf-fering triggered parts of the brain associated with positive affect and resil-ience. A short-term training (six hours) in compassion reversed feelings of distress, generated positive feelings of warmth, and increased activations in brain networks related to reward and affiliation.

Compassion is more comprehensive and effective than empathy. It encompasses the following five components that give it the power to trans-form suffering:

1. Recognizing the struggle
2. Understanding the universality of human suffering

---

14 Olga M. Klimecki, Susanne Leiberg, Matthieu Ricard, and Tania Singer. "Differential Pattern of Functional Brain Plasticity After Compassion and Empathy Training." *Social Cognitive and Affective Neuroscience* 9, no. 6 (June 2014): 873–879. doi: 10.1093/scan/nst060.

3. Feeling empathy for the people involved
4. Tolerating the discomfort that arises in response to the suffering person (e.g., distress, shame, anger, fear)
5. Being motivated to alleviate suffering

To summarize, compassion is our ability to feel, understand, and be motivated to alleviate suffering in ourselves and others based on an understanding of shared human experiences.

Compassion in Action

Going back to my town council experience: When I don't naturally feel compassionate, remembering the different aspects of compassion helps me return to a kinder place within. The first step when I am triggered is to stop and recognize that I am struggling. Once I do, I place my hand on my heart, which helps me move away from a reactive mental space to a calmer heart-centered space.

Just this stopping and returning to a more compassionate space reminds me that struggling is a shared human experience, and I am not alone in feeling this way. This normalizes my discomfort; it becomes easier to be with it. Then I can turn toward my colleagues, actively seeking to understand their perspectives. What might they know that I don't? What are their intentions? What are my intentions in this situation? What are the commonalities in our perspectives? By asking questions instead of rushing to judge and declare my perspective, I make room for more information to shape my understanding and make more informed decisions.

It's still a messy process. I'm not always sure that I made the right decision. But my commitment to compassion—seeking to understand the perspectives of all involved and to take actions that benefit all involved—gives me the courage to show up with an open mind and heart, even when I want to shut down or walk away.

Compassion cuts through our judgments and reveals our shared humanity. Yet, the pull of a judging mind is so strong that it can be hard to disrupt the momentum of judgments. Can you think of situations in which your judging mind overtakes your desire for empathy and under-standing? Why is it easy to naturally want to understand and help in some situations—such as for your loved ones—and so hard in other situations, such as town council meetings?

Othering: Us vs. Them Thinking

We can process others' pain in our minds as if we're experiencing it ourselves. This scientific fact demonstrates our innate capacity for empathy. However, we also know from other studies—and perhaps our own experience—that this empathic capacity is reserved for people whom we consider to be part of our in-group. Dr. Eagleman, a leading neuroscientist, found that our brain cares less about members of the out-group.

GEEK OUT!

Whose Pain Do You Feel?

Dr. Eagleman's lab[15] looked into the brains of their participants while they watched a video of a hand being stabbed by a needle. They dis-covered that empathic response was larger when participants viewed pain inflicted on hands labeled with their religion (in-group) than on hands labeled with a different religion (out-group). Counterintuitively, those who considered themselves to be more empathic showed a larger in-group bias.

Consciously or unconsciously, we label people as belonging to our in-group or out-group based on different attributes such as age, race, gen-der, political views, values, religion, gender, and socioeconomic status. The

15 D.A. Vaughn, R.R. Savjani, M.S. Cohen, and D.M. Eagleman. "Empathic Neural Responses Predict Group Allegiance." *Frontiers in Human Neuroscience* 12 (2018). https://doi.org/10.3389/fnhum.2018.00302.

process of creating walls around us based on our differences is called "othering." When we view people's differences as a threat to our way of life, we see them as *the other*, not to be trusted. It's hard to see the positive attributes in those who are in the out-group or understand their perspectives and needs.

Othering creates an "us versus them" way of thinking, which prevents us from feeling empathy and having genuine dialogue. Taken to an extreme, it creates an illusion that the only way to win is to defeat others at any cost. The Holocaust, slavery, and acts of terrorism are extreme examples of denying people in the out-group basic rights to live a free life or live at all.

In our everyday life, we all engage in othering. This happens in big and small ways: when we automatically make assumptions about the motivations of people in the out-group, exaggerate their mistakes, and believe that the only right way is our way of thinking. Othering can take place within families, social circles, at work, in our communities, and within politics. Not caring for our environment as we care for the inside of our home could be considered another way of othering. It's ubiquitous and can exist without our conscious awareness. And as we know, we can't change what we can't see. Awareness that we're engaging in othering is the first step to showing up mindfully, but we also need compassion to understand the nature of our human mind.

The reasons for othering can be complicated. A basic cause of othering is a lack of knowledge and understanding about others and their way of life. Our education, culture, personal experiences, and exposure to popular media shape our beliefs about ourselves and others, who is in the in-group and who's in the out-group. However, there's an even more fundamental factor underlying othering—when we forget our interbeing.

Interbeing: Seeing Our Interconnectedness

Thich Nhat Hanh coined the word *interbeing*—interconnectedness and interdependence. His invitation to see the "cloud floating in this sheet of paper" is not only poetic but also reveals this fundamental aspect of reality. Two seemingly unrelated things—cloud and paper—remind us that all things in the universe are interconnected through a chain of relationships. Even something basic like water involves a web of interconnections between people, systems, and nature.

These interconnections seem obvious, but they can elude us when we're in the middle of a difficult conversation or a challenging situation that divides people into "us versus them." In those moments, we're focusing on a slice of reality that's distinct from the whole. And yet, as Martin Luther King Jr. also reminded us in his famous letter from Birmingham jail, "We are caught in an inescapable network of mutuality, tied in a single garment of destiny. Whatever affects one directly affects all indirectly."[16] When we view situations through the lens of interbeing, we see that our needs are not competing with those of others; they're interdependent. This is similar to the concept of Ubuntu in the Xhosa culture, which has been translated to mean, "I am because we are."

STORY
Ubuntu[17]

An anthropologist proposed a game to the kids in an African tribe. He put a basket full of fruit near a tree and told the kids that whoever got there first won the sweet fruits. When he told them to run, they all took each other's hands and ran together, then sat together, enjoying their treats. When he asked them why they had run like that, as one could have had all the fruits for himself, they said, "Ubuntu." ("How can one of us be happy if all the other ones are sad?")

A Thich Nhat Hanh poem that I have returned to again and again for guidance in the middle of conflict is called "Call Me by My True Names." Here are a few lines that cut through my tendency for othering and remind me of our interbeing. Thay, as he was lovingly called, wrote this poem after meditating on a tragic incident involving the rape of a twelve-year-old refugee by a Thai pirate.

16 Martin Luther King. *Why We Can't Wait* (New York: Signet Classics, 2000).

17 Julia Travers. "Children, Ubuntu, and Interbeing." *Mindfulness Bell,* accessed 2023. https://www
    .parallax.org/mindfulnessbell/article/children-ubuntu-and-interbeing/.

I am the twelve-year-old girl,
refugee on a small boat,
who throws herself into the ocean
after being raped by a sea pirate.
And I am the pirate,
my heart not yet capable
of seeing and loving . . .
Please call me by my true names,
so I can wake up,
and so the door of my heart
can be left open,
the door of compassion.

Thay's invitation is to view all situations from at least three perspectives: that of the victim, the perpetrator, and the observers. Even though our instinct is to empathize with the victim, Thay invites us to put ourselves in the shoes of the perpetrator as well; had we grown up under the same conditions as the pirate, we'd have also most likely grown up to be a pirate. As observers, politicians, world leaders, teachers, and social workers, we are all responsible if we don't do anything to help change the conditions for the people in that village, leading to them growing up to become pirates. Of course, this doesn't mean that the pirates aren't accountable for their actions. It invites us, nevertheless, to expand our view to see the causes and conditions that create pirates and what we all can do to change the conditions—like providing education and jobs in the villages.

Imagine if we dissolve our judgments with the understanding of the causes and conditions that make people think and act the way they do. Then we can direct our resources toward changing systems, processes, and behaviors that are harmful rather than punishing the individuals who are merely a product of those systems. When we learn to clasp each other's hands and run together like the children in the Xhosa culture, we, too, can share the fruits of our shared victory. We, too, can learn to be truly happy by reminding ourselves and each other, "We are interconnected."

Where Are You on the Compassion Continuum?

Based on the results of your mindfulness assessment or a reflection of your self-talk, you may have a sense of your default compassion with respect to yourself and others. You can use the Compassionate Continuum table to see the ways in which compassion shows up in your life: when it's present, when it's low, and when it's misappropriated by other habits of the mind that come disguised as compassion.

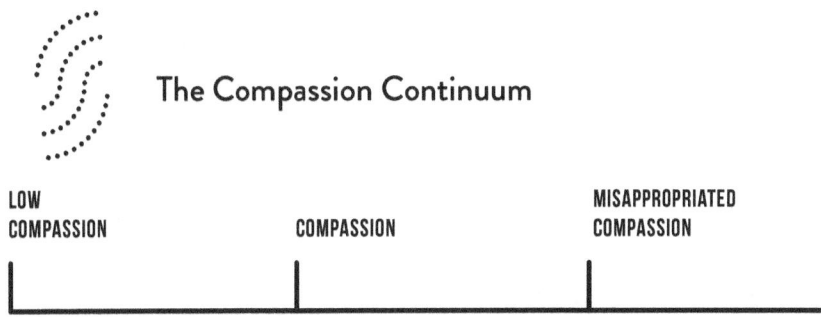

The Compassion Continuum

LOW COMPASSION	COMPASSION	MISAPPROPRIATED COMPASSION
Tendencies to:	**Tendencies to:**	**Tendencies to:**
• Be uncaring about people in the out-group	• Build trust and psychological safety in groups, which is essential for high-performing teams	• Care about others out of guilt or other hidden agendas, like wanting to belong
• Be critical of or uncaring toward the body	• Unconditionally accept the body and tend to its needs	• Indulge, such as overeating, or avoiding discomfort, such as exercising, in the name of compassion
• Be self-critical or lack confidence, which impedes progress	• Understand and accept your strengths and limitations, which help reach your goals	• Be overconfident, which gets in the way of learning and growth
• Engage in othering, which leads to divisiveness	• Bridge divisiveness by seeing interbeing	• Be unable to say no because of low self-esteem or delusion
• Focus on selfish interests	• Think about the benefit of all involved	• Become a martyr

High Self-Compassion: If you got a high self-compassion rating in the assessment or feel like you listen and attend to yourself with kindness, yay! You are in the minority. More than 500 people who took this assessment for a study, and most of my clients, have reported low self-compassion. Being high on self-compassion means you're aware of your needs and know how to take care of yourself. A high level of self-compassion may be overconfidence in disguise. If you find that your thoughts and feelings preclude others, especially when making decisions that impact others, developing compassion for others using the following "return" practices will broaden your lens and offer possible solutions that are more inclusive and kinder.

Low Self-Compassion: In the absence of awareness, a low self-compassion level can manifest as a negative self-image, insecurity, feelings of isolation, disconnection from self, lack of confidence, and ignoring your personal needs to take care of others, among additional detrimental outcomes. All of these negative self-perceptions and self-talk have consequences that can be detrimental to your career, relationships, and health in general.

High Compassion for Others: If you find that your natural disposition is to understand people and their unique history and situation, and you feel motivated to help others in need, you have high compassion for others. This will probably result in making you likable and even loved in your family, place of work, and community. When out of balance, high compassion for others can come at the cost of ignoring your personal needs. I have often heard my clients observe through the "return" practices that they were compassionate and kind toward others but unkind to themselves. If this is the case, a deeper inquiry into your motivation for being compassionate toward others may reveal that you are being nice because of expectations of some kind of gain. Gestures of compassion premised on expectations of some kind of return may lead to disappointment because others may not be seeing your expectations. It's important to be honest with yourself about why you're doing something. There's nothing wrong in doing something to get something in return, but it's important to be clear about your motives and expectations, both in regard to yourself and others.

Low Compassion for Others: If you got low compassion for others in your assessment, you might notice that you tend to judge strongly, are impatient in your dealings with others, and lack the motivation to help others without immediate benefit for yourself. Low compassion for others can interfere with enjoying genuine and strong relationships. Try the suggestions in the "return" practice to foster compassion for others.

Returning to compassion in ourselves involves disrupting our default habits such as rushing to judge, defending our ways of thinking, and avoiding suffering. The more we practice and play with compassion practices and reminders shared later, the stronger we become at facing our differences with an open mind and heart.

How to Return with Compassion

The practices and reminders are here to support you in disrupting your default habit of automatically judging and reconnecting with compassion for yourself and others. Compassion will give you the courage to be with the discomfort of staying open in the midst of differences and doubt and seeking to understand by returning to your experience, listening to yourself and others, and beginning all actions with compassion.

Look out for thoughts that involve a certain idea of how you should or need to be in order to be compassionate: "I should help this person," "I can't say no to this person," or "I must be nice, no matter what." Such thoughts are signs that you're trying to be compassionate and that you're not in full alignment with your intentions for yourself and others. Compassion isn't something we do, but rather who we are when we're naturally feeling connected, and we want to do what we can to help.

Given that there will be many situations—involving people we don't care about or consider challenging—in which we won't naturally feel compassionate, we can strengthen our capacity for compassion. We do this by cultivating a deeper understanding of our interconnectedness with each other, the causes and conditions for how things are, and the consequences of our choices. Deepening our understanding of our suffering with kindness and care will help us in directing compassion toward others.

No worries if you don't see your interbeing with others right away. Baby steps. Just reading this is a step forward. As long as you keep returning to your intention for living and leading with a desire to seek understanding—even if you don't know at that moment what it means to be compassionate—you will, over time, strengthen that capacity to recognize the interconnected nature of all beings.

DEDICATED PRACTICE

Depending upon where you fall on the compassion continuum for yourself and others, choose from the following dedicated practices to strengthen compassion for yourself and for others. At 30,000 feet in the air, we're reminded to secure our own oxygen masks before helping those around us. The same is true with compassion—if we hope to extend understanding and care toward others, then self-compassion must come first.

Self-Compassion Practice

We're so busy doing stuff that we don't make time to meet ourselves. By meeting ourselves, I mean paying attention to ourselves: our bodies, feelings, thoughts, needs, and aspirations. It's harder to turn our attention inward when we're experiencing difficult thoughts (self-judgments), emotions (anxiety, shame, grief), and body sensations (pain, fatigue, illness). When we turn away from ourselves because it's hard or painful, we also turn away from our gifts and passions.

Take out time today and every day to meet yourself. The practice guidelines are only suggestions. Trust yourself to know what needs your full care and attention: body, thoughts, emotions, intentions, unmet needs, or anything else that's surfacing for you. Trust yourself to care for yourself.

Return. Find your favorite space in your home or out in nature—like under the open sky, by a river, or in a field. Lower or close your eyes to return your attention to yourself, sitting and breathing. With each inhale, feel the space created in your body, and with each exhale, feel your mind and body softening.

1. Now return to sensations in your body—pleasant, unpleasant, and neutral—with kindness. See if you need to adjust your posture to find more comfort in this moment. Give your full care and attention to your body.

2. Next, turn your attention to feelings and emotions—pleasant, unpleasant, or neutral—with kindness. Like a good friend, attend to how you are really feeling right now—no need to fix or justify. Just be willing to meet your emotions with honesty and care. Stay here as long as you need to. Even if your mind drifts away, that's okay. Come back to awareness of your emotional landscape.

3. Now turn your attention to the thoughts underlying your emotions. Notice all the shoulds and coulds without any judgment: "should've done that," "shouldn't have said that," "how could I." Make space for it all.

See yourself fully—body, emotions, thoughts, and anything else. Just make space to meet yourself as you are. If there's a cacophony of thoughts, emotions, and body sensations, see if you can approach that with kindness and understanding. If there's absolute quiet, welcome that with kindness.

Stay here as long as you need. If possible, give at least five minutes to yourself for this practice and a few more minutes for listening within.

Listen. Take a few moments to stay in this space of connection with yourself and listen within. Here are a few suggested questions if you're feeling stuck and unable to meet yourself:

- *What is asking for your attention today?*
- *Are there unmet needs that you need to pay attention to?*
- *What intentions and gifts do you want to share with others?*

Begin. Based on your reflection, what is one action you can take toward meeting your unmet needs or sharing your gifts with the world? Begin your activities—especially challenging ones—with this understanding of self-compassion.

Compassion for Others Practice

It may be difficult to feel compassion when we're rushed or dealing with people whom we consider to be in the out-group. If we can learn to see our shared humanity, we can see that we're all more similar than different, ultimately allowing empathy to arise for all beings naturally.

I first learned this meditation—*Just like me*—from Mirabai Bush, who is one of the first teachers to bring mindfulness into corporations, education, and nonprofits in the United States. Her mantra, which I find so inspiring, is "Love all, serve all."

You can do this practice with a partner or on your own. If you're doing this on your own, think of another person or gradually expand your circle of concern as you do in other compassion practices. The first part of this practice is recognizing our shared humanity. After that, you will be sending out loving-kindness wishes to the person or people you're thinking about.

Return. Start by lowering or closing your eyes and returning to the breath moving in and out of your heart region.

1. When you feel connected with yourself in the present moment, you can look into the eyes of the person sitting in front of you or keep your eyes closed as you consider the following similarities:
   ◦ This person is also a fellow human being, just like me.
   ◦ This person has a body and mind, just like me.
   ◦ This person in front of me has feelings, emotions, and thoughts, just like me.
   ◦ This person in front of me has, at some point in life, been sad, disappointed, angry, hurt, or confused—just like me.
   ◦ This person in front of me has experienced physical and emotional pain and suffering, just like me.
   ◦ This person in front of me wishes to be free from pain and suffering, just like me.
   ◦ This person in front of me has experienced many joys and times of happiness, just like me.
   ◦ This person wants to be happy and healthy, just like me.

2. Now, let's allow some wishes to arise:
   - I wish for this person to have the awareness to be free from suffering.
   - I wish for this person to be happy.
   - Wish for any other wishes that are spontaneously arising in you for this person.

3. Before ending, take a moment to look at your partner again. Thank your partner in whatever way feels natural to you.

Listen. Take a few moments to observe your experience. Ask the following questions, if they're helpful, to intimately note your experience and patterns of your mind:

- *Were you able to give and receive loving-kindness wishes if you were doing this with a partner?*
- *If not, what is stopping you from seeing this person as a fellow human being just like you?*
- *What are your intentions for yourself and others?*

Observe your emotions without suppressing or letting them take over.

Begin. Based on your insights and intention, commit to one interaction where you will bring compassion. If you feel resentment or challenged by someone during your day, begin the meeting with compassion and with three breaths.

1. With the first breath, calm the mind and body.
2. With the second breath, see a similarity with this person.
3. With the third breath, send loving-kindness wishes that would be helpful to this person.

DAILY MANTRAS TO RETURN WITH COMPASSION

Practice and play with the chosen reminders for the day with the following intentions in mind: disrupting your default habit of judging yourself and others, strengthening your ability to see your interdependence and interconnection with others, and bringing the lens of compassion to seek a deeper understanding of others and yourself, especially when it matters most.

I. Mantra for the Day: Interbeing
Seeing interdependence

This practice is an invitation to see our interbeing and strengthen our capacity to see this in the middle of it all. Before you begin, bring to mind someone you are or will be interacting with at home, work, or in your community with whom you want to explore your interbeing. This could be someone you want to connect with more deeply or someone you're having a conflict with.

Return. Direct your attention to the breath moving in the region of your chest. If your mind is active, place one hand on your chest and one hand on your belly as you feel the rising and falling of your body under the gentle touch of your hands.

Listen. Once your mind is stabilized, quietly ask yourself this:

- *What are my needs in this interaction?*

Stay here with kindness, without forcing an answer. Listen to your response within. Don't go with the first response. Wait. Listen. Notice any kind of rushing, judgments, or fears about what you may discover. Make space for that and let it be there while you continue to listen internally to your needs in this situation.

Once you feel connected with your needs, quietly ask yourself the following:

- *What are the other person's needs?*

Again, no need to search for answers. Just wait and listen within. You may have self-doubt: *How can I possibly know what they need?* Trust yourself to know what you need to know. All you're doing is making inner space to shift how you see things, preferably from their perspective; you will see a little more than you would otherwise. Keep returning to your breath moving in your chest as an anchor to your natural place of connection, with your body, yourself, and others.

Take a few moments after the practice to make a note of your observations during and after the practice. Even the subtlest of shifts in your perspective can have a big impact on how you show up, which will impact how the other person responds. Based on your reflection, how might you show up for yourself and that person today? Create an intention to show up with understanding and kindness.

Begin. Before you begin your interaction with that person, return to your contemplation of interbeing and your intentions for meeting your needs and theirs.

II. Mantra for the Day: Be Kind to the Body
Body scan with compassion

It's easy to ignore the body, especially when we are busy. By attending to the body with full care and attention, we learn to access vital information about how we are feeling, and we can let go of the harsh voice of judgments aimed at the body. Instead, we can attend to the body with loving-kindness. Feel free to practice and play with this reminder as you navigate through your daily activities, such as work, exercise, mealtimes, and periodic check-ins.

Return. Return to your body sitting here. Notice your body posture with kindness. The way we sit in the practice is how we learn to show up in our lives. Make sure you are sitting in a posture that is dignified and easeful. Eyes can be lowered or closed.

Move your attention at your own pace from the top of your head all the way down to your feet—notice any sensations there. Bring a gentle awareness accompanied by nonjudging acceptance of your body. Take this opportunity to relax your muscles as much as you can. End with noting sensations in your legs and feet, feeling the support of the ground below your feet.

You are perfect at this moment as you are. Take a few moments now to listen to your body.

Listen. Listen to what your body needs—more nutrition, hydration, movement, rest, or just your unconditional love. Here are suggested questions to listen to your body:

- *What did you observe by attending to your body with care?*
- *What is the quality of your inner dialogue as it pertains to your body?*
- *What are your intentions for your body?*

Begin. Based on your reflection and intentions, how can you better care for your body? What's one thing you can do today to better care for your body? Before you begin eating or exercising, connect with your intentions and the wisdom of your body.

III. Mantra for the Day: I See Me
Meeting yourself with kindness

Throughout the day, particularly when facing demanding tasks or transitioning between activities, remind yourself, "I see me." This may also be a good reminder in the middle of a difficult or demanding situation.

Often, the world makes us believe that we are never quite good enough, leading to self-doubt and causing us to present ourselves as diminished versions of who we truly are—sometimes even becoming invisible to those around us. Instead of attempting to fix yourself, allocate moments to genuinely connect with your inner self without any expectations. Maybe what we need isn't external validation, but rather us recognizing our own worth.

Return. Take a conscious, nourishing breath. Place a hand on your chest or belly. Like a good friend, ask yourself, "How are you really feeling?" Pay attention to your breath, body sensations, thoughts, and emotions. Remember, this is a judgment-free zone. If you feel confused or need additional direction to see yourself, you can do this practice by seeing yourself at different life stages—as a child, teenager, in college, and so on. When you see yourself, what qualities or experiences stand out?

Listen. Listen gently without trying to change anything. Reflect on the following questions for additional guidance to meet yourself:

- *What parts of you need nurturing?*
- *What gifts do you want to share with the world?*
- *What are your intentions for yourself?*

Begin. Honor and nurture your needs and gifts. Before you begin any activity, remind yourself, "I see me." Proceed with self-compassion.

IV. Mantra for the Day: I See You
Compassion for others

When we can see our similarities, we can better move through our differences. This is a good reminder when your judgments about others are preventing you from connecting with them. This may occur during a difficult conversation with a family member, leading an essential change at work that people are resisting, or participating in a divisive issue in your community. Before you begin the practice, consider a person with whom you want to cultivate a better understanding.

Return. Settle your attention on the breath moving in and out of your chest region. Relax your body and mind for three breaths. Consider similarities that you share with this person. In case you can't think of anything in common with them, return to the *Just like me* practice. Consider the following statements:

1. This person is a fellow human being, *just like me.*
2. They have experienced suffering, *just like me.*
3. They want to be happy, *just like me.*

Listen. Notice what's shifting and moving within you without resisting or judging. Consider the following questions to deepen your experience of compassion:

- *What are you noticing about your capacity for compassion for this person?*
- *What's getting in the way of your natural capacity for compassion?*
- *What are your intentions for yourself and others in this situation?*

Begin. Can you let go of your judgments and begin your interactions with compassion? What might be one step you can take to understand this person better?

V. Mantra for the Day: Causes and Conditions
Foster understanding

Often, we react to situations based on what's most easily seen or visible. We judge and automatically jump to correcting the problematic behavior without understanding the causes and conditions that gave rise to such behaviors. However, when we understand how something came to be—maybe because of someone's upbringing, culture, education, or traumatic experiences—it's easier to feel empathy and work toward better outcomes.

Identify a difficult situation that you're dealing with—like starting a new habit, disagreements with team members at work, or community members you've been judging harshly about something. For a few moments, set it aside to stabilize your mind.

Return. Feel the rising and falling of your chest with each inhale and exhale. Every time your mind wanders to the difficult situation you identified before starting this practice, return with kindness to your breath. Once you feel your mind is stabilized, move to the next step of listening within.

Listen. Once your attention is stabilized, open your mind to the causes and conditions of the situation. Listen within. Inquire within with the help of the following suggested questions:

- *What factors might be causing your resistance or judgments?*
- *If someone else is involved, what might be contributing to their attitude or behavior?* Sometimes it's hard to know what the causes and conditions are; in which case, seek to get more information about the person and get to know what's going on with them.
- *What are your intentions for yourself and others involved in the situation?*

Begin. Based on your reflection and intentions, how might you foster understanding rather than judgment or assumptions?

VI. Mantra for the Day: Offer Goodwill to All
Compassion for all

All beings deserve happiness and well-being—yourself included. This practice inclines the mind toward loving-kindness for yourself and others. You can do this as a formal practice or while waiting in line or working in a public space. The more you practice compassion, the more it becomes a habit. You can dedicate this compassion practice to someone going through a hard time, to someone you see randomly, or systematically cultivate compassion for all beings.

Return. Let the warmth of your hand on your heart center return you to the present moment. Feel the rising and falling of your chest with each in-breath and out-breath.

1. Start the compassion practice by thinking about the person you are

with or someone who naturally evokes warmth and kindness in you, like a child or pet. Gradually you can add a benefactor, someone neutral, someone with whom you have a challenging relationship, and then all beings. Neutral would be a person whom you don't think about much, even though you see them regularly, like a neighbor, colleague, or someone working at a café you usually visit. The idea is to start with people you care about and gradually expand your circle of compassion to all sentient beings. If you don't have time, then focus on the people involved in the interaction.

2. You can silently repeat the suggested phrases or whatever comes naturally to you:

May you be happy.

May you have the awareness to be free from suffering.

May you be healthy—in your mind, body, and heart.

May you be safe.

May you live with ease.

Don't get lost in trying to find the appropriate phrases. Simply offer the previous phrases or those that emerge spontaneously. The repetition of the previous phrases is also training the mind to settle on the suggested words.

3. Repeat these phrases a couple of times for each person they're directed toward or until you experience a shift or connection.

Listen. Notice your thoughts, emotions, and body sensations. Make a note of how it feels to be kind to others proactively. If you had difficulty offering loving-kindness to yourself or others, don't beat yourself up. It's common for people doing this practice for the first time to feel as though it's fake or doesn't resonate. With kindness, explore your experience. Here are a few questions for a deeper exploration to listen within:

- *Does your level or quality of kindness change across people?* Observe that. With kindness, of course.

- *What's stopping you from being authentically kind to others involved in the interaction?* What stops you from extending loving-kindness to certain people—maybe the neutral people or the people you have difficulty with?

- *What are your intentions with respect to compassion for others?*

Begin. You can create habits of kindness by repeating actions that are kind to others. For example, before leaving home for work or before a presentation, I do a version of this practice: I send loving-kindness wishes to the people I'm going to meet and align with my intention of being of service for everyone's benefit. Return to this practice before you begin a meeting, a new project, or a difficult interaction.

Take a Moment to Celebrate!

Congratulations on finishing the chapter on compassion! Pause to acknowledge your readiness to face discomfort within yourself and others.

Hopefully, you made a new friend in this chapter—your inner critic. Even if you're not friends yet, just stopping to listen within—to your thoughts, emotions, and underlying needs—with kindness is a big step forward in living mindfully. We can't truly be kind and curious toward others when we're unable to do that for ourselves. Every time you don't automatically act on your critical thoughts, you're changing your default habit of judging to self-compassion.

Along with compassion for self comes the wisdom of interbeing—we're all interconnected in the universe. Even if you don't know what it means in some situations, just opening your mind to that idea of interbeing is inclining your mind toward understanding the fundamental reality of our co-existence on this planet we all call home.

Mindful Curiosity: noun
Our ability to be genuinely interested and care with the purpose
of understanding the situation, even when it's challenging.

Curiosity disrupts our confirmation bias
by staying open and patient in the face
of uncertainty and new information.

Skill Chapter 3

Curiosity

ASK WHAT, NOT WHY

Have patience with everything unresolved in your heart
and try to love the questions themselves, as if they were locked
rooms or books written in a very foreign language.
—**Rainer Maria Rilke,** *Letters to a Young Poet*

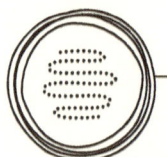

Before You Begin

Just a friendly reminder to return to your body, mind, and intentions before you begin. Take a few deep breaths.

Give your full care and attention to the breath moving in and out of your chest. Connect with your intention for cultivating curiosity.

As you delve into this chapter, the invitation is to explore new ways of being open to information, even if it challenges your current beliefs. Be receptive to any insights or learning that emerges.

Life is full of surprises, and that can sometimes be overwhelming. We've all been there—unexpected events throwing us way off balance with our emotions running high while searching for an appropriate response. That's when one attribute can be super helpful: curiosity.

In a survey asking thousands of CEOs worldwide what key leadership qualities are required for success during turbulent times, many pointed to curiosity as being vital.[18] Indeed, curiosity is the surest way to return to a balanced and open mind, which enables us to see clearly and act intentionally. This is especially true in situations where we want to default to our impulses— it takes strength, but it's worthwhile to stop, step back, and get curious.

As a town councilor, I return to the mindfulness skill of curiosity most frequently. It disrupts my automatic reactions in triggering situations. This makes space for new perspectives and renewed energy to engage in meaningful ways. In a controversial vote involving large-scale solar on private land with trees, curiosity became my superpower. Three fellow councilors backed by a majority of vocal residents wanted a temporary moratorium until we had a bylaw for large-scale solar projects. A routine aspect of my decision-making process is seeking input from multiple viewpoints. This time, however, topic experts and

---

18 Warren Berger. "Why Curious People Are Destined for the C-Suite." *Harvard Business Review*, September 11, 2015. https://hbr.org/2015/09/why-curious-people-are-destined-for-the-c-suite.

committee members whom I reached out to refused to be involved. Voting against a large-scale solar moratorium was "political death," they said.

There were other factors that contributed to the complexity of this decision. I felt conflicted. My mind was spinning with the same thoughts playing over and over again. I had to continually stop and get clear about my intentions—to do what is best for the environment. Next, I opened my mind to possible actions that I could take and the consequences of my actions (and inactions) on the environment. Once I was in touch with my inner knowing, it was clear that I had to keep investigating the issue until I had enough information to decide how I would vote.

I searched for scientists and solar professionals using my personal and social networks. Talking with many people with an open mind, willing to be proven wrong, led to a third way of dealing with the large-scale solar venture. Instead of the either-or situation—yes or no to a moratorium—I learned about ways to thoughtfully deal with each large-scale solar project till the solar bylaw was written.

STORY
A Third Way

Advocates of the temporary large-scale solar moratorium provided compelling information about the harm of cutting down trees for solar panels. The lens they used to approach the issue primarily focused on the negative impacts of large-scale solar projects in forests. However, I found myself grappling with an unanswered question: "What were the negative implications of an eighteen-month moratorium on the environment?" Further, did we have any mechanisms in place to ensure that large-scale solar developments could be handled carefully until a solar bylaw was written to guide future projects more thoughtfully? Before deciding how I'd vote— yes or no—I stayed open to new information and patiently reached out to all potential leads to experts in climate change.

Complicating matters further was the fact that the moratorium could potentially impact a friend who'd also been a past mindfulness client and regularly sent her employees to my trainings. Many residents advocating for the moratorium demanded my recusal because of my

continued

personal and professional relationship with this person. I consulted with the ethics commission officer, who was clear that I didn't have a conflict of interest, but the residents remained unconvinced.

I felt torn. Even though a vocal group of residents wanted me to recuse myself from voting, the way our local law is structured, my recusal would've ended up helping my friend. Recusal seemed to be the easier path. However, I questioned whether it was the best choice for the environment. My strength on the town council lay in my ability to research issues from all angles. A recusal would have prevented me from sharing my insights with the council.

Before proceeding, I stopped to get curious about my intentions, possible actions, and the consequences of my actions (and inactions) on the environment and other stakeholders. Returning to my inner knowing with curiosity, I could see clearly that I had to stay involved to gather information that others might not pursue.

Keeping an open mind, I patiently reached out to different people in my network, who eventually led me to a group of experts. These scientists provided compelling evidence that an eighteen-month pause on large-scale solar developments (that were carefully planned) would do more harm than good. They emphasized the need to protect forests and their potential to sequester and store carbon, while also accelerating decarbonization via rooftop and utility-scale solar. In lieu of a moratorium, they suggested permitting processes to guide responsible decisions around solar development. Additionally, I learned from speaking with professionals in the solar industry that the state had created specific mechanisms that could guide towns in ensuring the integrity of the sites for large-scale solar panels and ensure their safe implementation.

Consulting with a diverse range of individuals beyond my immediate circle provided me and the rest of the town council valuable perspectives to make a more informed decision. Ultimately, moratorium didn't pass, and the town had a way to proceed thoughtfully until a solar bylaw could be crafted to guide future projects.

Despite facing opposition, my commitment to the environment and curiosity enabled me to navigate a complex decision with diligence. While some residents were still dissatisfied with the outcome, I firmly believe that gathering information from diverse sources is crucial in making well-informed decisions. Actively seeking diverse perspectives helped our community move forward with caution and care, considering the best interests of both the environment and concerned constituents.

How Do You Respond to Crises or Difficult Situations?

Consider something as basic as losing your keys. Do you immediately jump into action—launching a frantic search for them, growing increasingly agitated? Or do you pause, take a deep breath, and approach the situation with curiosity? John, a successful middle-aged businessman, would go into a panic whenever he felt out of control, even for simple things like misplaced keys. His automatic reaction—which involved a series of loud, angry swears in his deep, intimidating voice—wasn't helpful to anyone. With practice, he was able to disrupt his default reactivity with mindful curiosity. He learned to take a few breaths to calm down and ask questions, "When did I last use them? What was I wearing?" Then he'd trace his steps backward in his mind. Curiosity returned him to a calm and clear mind, with infinitely better outcomes, which reinforced his new habit.

This new skill also helped him at work when he got impatient during long-winded meetings. His immediate way to deal with frustration was to suppress it, which wasn't helpful. It came across as passive-aggressive or straight-up aggressive. By strengthening his curiosity, he learned to turn toward everyone with an open mind. He asked questions to understand their perspectives and struggles better. Once he knew more about where people were coming from, he could engage more productively.

Mindful curiosity is like an untapped superpower we all possess. Unlocking its full potential can be tricky—but it doesn't have to be!

Curiosity: Genuine Care and Wonder

We have an innate capacity to be curious—to have genuine interest and a sense of wonder about our experiences and other people. Consider this scenario: You want to bake a carrot cake for your partner's milestone birthday. Without curiosity, you would likely default to a familiar recipe, perhaps one passed down from your mother or a tested-and-tried favorite. You would recall how much your partner enjoyed carrot cake the last time he had it at your friends' anniversary and get to baking.

However, if you're curious, you'll challenge the tendency to rely on information that confirms your existing beliefs. When you approach the situation with an open mind, you may realize that it's you who loves carrot cake—your partner prefers chocolate cake! To find the perfect recipe, you turn to the website IAmBaker.net. There, you're greeted by a stunning array of forty-eight types of chocolate cake—including delectable options like molten lava chocolate cake and chocolate cake with red-wine-soaked cherries. As you peruse the website, your mind absorbs the visual cues about taste, texture, moisture, toppings, fillings, and maybe calories, all while considering your partner's preferences. You engage with the website with interest because you care. That's curiosity.

Mindful curiosity is our ability to bring genuine interest and careful attention to enable a better understanding, even in challenging situations. *Merriam-Webster* defines curiosity as a "disposition to inquire, investigate, or seek after knowledge—a desire to gratify the mind with new information or objects of interest; inquisitiveness" (see the online version of C. & G. Merriam Co. from 1913).

Our everyday use of the word *curiosity* connotes an intellectual or cognitive activity. However, the late-fourteenth-century origin of curiosity—careful attention to detail—is closer to the meaning we ascribe to curiosity in mindfulness. Curiosity as a mindfulness skill is our ability to be genuinely interested and care, which returns us to our capacity for a broader and deeper understanding. It's an intimate and honest look at our embodied experience to discern what's true in any situation. However, it can be tricky to detach from what we believe to be true because of our confirmation bias.

We See What We Want to See

The mind clings to what it believes to be true. Consequently, we see what we want to see. Our tendency to seek information that confirms what we believe is known as confirmation bias. This bias creates a lens through which we're likely to only see, recall, and interpret information in ways that are consistent with our beliefs. This bias, like others, is often unconscious and hard to detect, but it hampers our ability to see clearly.

One way that confirmation bias gets in the way of being mindful in the real world is by creating an echo chamber effect. We naturally gravitate toward partners and friends who share our beliefs and values. In this echo chamber, our perspectives are never challenged, and we are only surrounded by like-minded people.

Confirmation bias can also impact our ability to make mindful decisions. When we've committed to a particular conclusion, it's hard for us to see or accept information contrary to that because it's ridiculously hard to admit we're wrong. Our sense of self is based on the beliefs we've shared with others. The stronger the beliefs, the bigger the threat to self when we're proven wrong. Sometimes, we'd rather make a decision that's bad for us and for others than be proven wrong.

So often, we get stuck in a rut of believing things that might not be true simply because it's easier than having to admit being wrong. Unfortunately, this can have serious consequences. If we're put into leadership positions and refuse to accept the truth about ourselves or our decisions, then everyone around us is going to suffer for it too. But instead of facing up to reality, many times, we'd rather keep deluding ourselves with information that only confirms what we already want (or choose) to believe.

Mindful curiosity cuts through our delusion and confirmation bias. It prepares us not only to be open to new information and experiences, but also to gain insights by paying attention to our emotions and physical sensations. The body never lies. If we're feeling agitated, frustrated, or reactive, we'll recognize it in our body. With curiosity, we can uncover the thoughts and beliefs that are holding us captive and disallowing new information to enter our awareness. Once we're aware of our biases, we can let down our guard and get curious about opposing views without an agenda.

Listen Without an Agenda

When we listen, especially in difficult conversations, we generally have an agenda—to prove that we're right and convince others to adopt our point of view. Incidentally, the other person is also coming to the conversation with a similar agenda. We're not really listening to each other when we're attached to our points of view and busy preparing what we will say next that will change the other person's mind.

It's hard to listen with an open mind and suspend all agendas, but it is possible. All it takes is awareness and intention. As soon as we become aware that the body is tensing up, we can examine our thoughts to see if we're clutching too tightly to our perspectives. Then we can return to our intention to listen with an open mind, letting go of our agendas.

There's real power in listening with mindful curiosity and without an agenda. When people meet, not bound by their beliefs about each other and a need to change each other, true transformation is possible—transformation in which both people are changed for the better by the exchange. In the Geek Out Box, I cite two research projects involving people with strong prejudices and political views. In both cases, the process of deep canvassing was used to engage with the people with curiosity—it was free from a desire to convince or change people's minds.

GEEK OUT!

The Power of Listening Without an Agenda

A Stanford study[19] showed that a single, approximately ten-minute conversation encouraging perspective-taking and deep listening markedly reduced intergroup prejudice in people with transphobia for at least three months. The same approach used by People's Action,[20] a multi-racial movement to build a government and economy that puts people and the planet first, yielded results that were 102 times more effective than average persuasion programs to shift the 2020 presidential vote.

19   David Broockman and Joshua Kalla. "Durably Reducing Transphobia: A Field Experiment on Door-to-Door Canvassing." *Science* 352, no. 6282 (April 8, 2016): 220–224. doi:10.1126/science .aad9713.

20   People's Action. "Deep Canvass Experiment," accessed 2023. https://peoplesaction.org/deep -canvass-experiment/.

The reason this approach works is that the canvassers engage the voters with nonjudgment, curiosity, and authentic sharing, which creates an emotional connection and trust. People step into a shared field of nonjudging awareness together. Within a co-created field of trusting awareness, people listen better and feel heard. Often, it's not what people say but the space from which they're speaking that matters. When they're speaking from an inner space that's open with good intentions, it's likely that others will reciprocate. It opens up a possibility for transformation for everyone involved.

Like listening, another sense that's compromised by confirmation bias is seeing.

Looking Is Not the Same as Seeing

We may look at people and everyday objects—spring flowers, the face of a loved one, or information about an emerging technology—without really seeing the essence and complexities. There's sublime information about life's mysteries ready to be unveiled even in seemingly mundane situations if we stop to see with an open mind and heart.

Jennifer L. Roberts, a professor in art history, created an assignment for her class that involves looking at a painting for three hours. Her students, of course, resist the exercise at first. But once they overcome their initial hesitation, they're astonished by the depth of information this slowing down reveals. The prevailing belief is that vision is immediate, seemingly straight-forward, instant, and complete. This is perhaps why it has become the dominant sense that we rely upon for information delivery in our modern technological era. However, this assignment provides students with a deep understanding that any piece of art contains intricate details, sequences, and relationships that require time to appreciate fully.

The importance of this kind of training in critical attention and strategic patience extends beyond art history. In the training that I run, diverse groups of people—CEOs, students, educators, and parents—go through a similar exercise of looking at a picture and commenting on what they notice before and after a mindful pause. The pause of just a few minutes shifts their experience. Rather than merely looking at objects in the picture and labeling them, participants typically move to a deeper place of connection with the image. They're able to see with more depth, feel the aliveness of the objects, and connect with the contents for a more meaningful experience. Looking is not the same as seeing.

See for Yourself

Pick an object in your environment and quickly list the first five things that come to mind.

Now take a few moments to close your eyes and rest your awareness on the breath moving in and out of your body. Allow yourself to feel the breath moving in your body—the temperature, sensations, and tingling of the breath and a rising and falling in the body.

Once your mind feels more settled, open your eyes to look at that object again. What do you see when your mind is more relaxed and not rushing?

Did what you see and your experience of observation change by taking a mindful pause? Common responses from participants in my workshop are that they see things they had missed earlier and feel a deeper connection with the object than they had before the mindful pause.

How can infusing your curiosity with a mindful pause shift your experience in conversations, problem-solving, and your everyday activities? See for yourself.

If we can slow down to notice—without any kind of striving to look for something special—we may end up seeing more and having more fulfilling experiences than when we gloss over posts on social media and in life without really seeing any of it.

One practice that can help us move from living in our heads to seeing more and being open to new information and insights is asking more "what" than "why" questions.

Ask *What*, Not *Why*

"What" questions disrupt our confirmation bias by inviting us to notice elements in our experience and surroundings that we may have missed earlier. "Why" questions tend to invite responses based on what we already know. Asking yourself, "Why am I doing this?" as a way to return to your intrinsic motivations or purpose is helpful. But when you want to gain insight into or access new information, asking *what* is better than asking *why*.[21]

For example, Sheila, a participant in one of my mindfulness classes, was struggling with curiosity in her mindfulness practice. She complained that curiosity "didn't work" for her. She shared a situation in which she was angry with her partner, Tom. When she decided to stop and "be curious" about her emotions of anger toward Tom, she ended up feeling even more angry. The question she was using to get curious, which many of us might ask in a similar situation, was, "Why am I angry with Tom?" Her "why" question led to many more reasons for her anger. Before she knew it, Sheila was lost in a spiral of angry thoughts, which cemented her narrative about Tom. She felt justified in getting angry.

When we become attached to a particular point of view, it's hard for us to detach and look for other perspectives. Asking "what" questions can expand the lens we're bringing to the situation and return us to our inner field of infinite possibilities. Instead of "why," had Sheila asked "what" questions, she could've returned to mindfulness, seeing the situation from different points of view. Questions such as these: *What am I observing in my body? What are the thoughts underlying my anger? What are my unmet needs and intentions for this situation? What was going on for Tom when he did what he did? What else is possible?*

The purpose of looking at her experience with patience and kindness is to return her to a spacious mind that can gain more information and insight into the causes of her anger. Once she knows the causes, she can do something about it. For instance, had Sheila asked "what" questions at the time, she may have discovered her unmet needs, her history with this person, or a pattern that's emerging. She could then choose to ask for what she

---

21 Tasha Eurich. "What Self-Awareness Really Is (and How to Cultivate It)." *Harvard Business Review*, January 4, 2018. https://hbr.org/2018/01/what-self-awareness-really-is-and-how-to -cultivate-it.

needs—with curiosity for herself and the other person—without her default emotions, judgment, and blame.

Our emotions are there for a reason: to give us information hidden from the conscious mind about a threat to our well-being or our unmet needs (see table later in the chapter, "Purpose of Emotions and Questions to Uncover Unmet Needs").

Can you think back to a time you became emotional and needed to pause to figure out what was underneath your reaction? Or maybe in the moment, you were caught off guard by the avalanche of emotions and were able to pause only later? Retrospectively, what might mindful curiosity have looked like for you in that situation?

Where Are You on the Mindful Curiosity Continuum?

A healthy level of mindful curiosity means that you're genuinely interested in your own and others' experiences and perspectives, even in the midst of difficulty.

When someone is out of balance, an overexpression of curiosity can contribute to distractibility and an inability to focus.[22] In a series of experiments, psychologists discovered that curiosity could also drive people to engage in risky behaviors.[23] You may know from your experience how a quest for answers can take you down the internet rabbit hole with nothing much to show for it two hours later.

Instead, mindful curiosity invites you to be curious in a gentle and embodied way. This happens when you return to your immediate and direct experience in your body rather than just focusing on thinking and analyzing. Balance excessive mental curiosity with awareness of your body (body scan)

---

22 Celeste Kidd and Benjamin Y. Hayden. "The Psychology and Neuroscience of Curiosity." *Neuron* 88, no. 3 (2015): 449–460. doi:10.1016/j.neuron.2015.09.010.

23 Christopher K. Hsee and Bowen Ruan. "The Pandora Effect: The Power and Peril of Curiosity." *Psychological Science* 27, no. 5 (2016): 659–666. https://doi.org/10.1177/0956797616631733.

or practices in inner calm (Skill Chapter 6), focus (Skill Chapter 7), and equanimity (Skill Chapter 8).

If your curiosity level was low on the assessment, you may find it challenging to remain open to ideas and perspectives that differ from your own. A lack of curiosity can dull our minds and enthusiasm for learning. As a result, you may experience disinterest, depression, boredom, and closed-mindedness. If you identify with any of these characteristics, pay special attention to the "return" daily practices and mantras to strengthen curiosity. In addition, strengthening the mindfulness skills of energy (Skill Chapter 4) and appreciative joy (Skill Chapter 5) can also support a curiosity-based mindset.

You can use the table to reflect on the benefits of curiosity and your tendencies. See the impact when curiosity is mindful, when it's low, and when it's appropriated by other habits of the mind (or in excess).

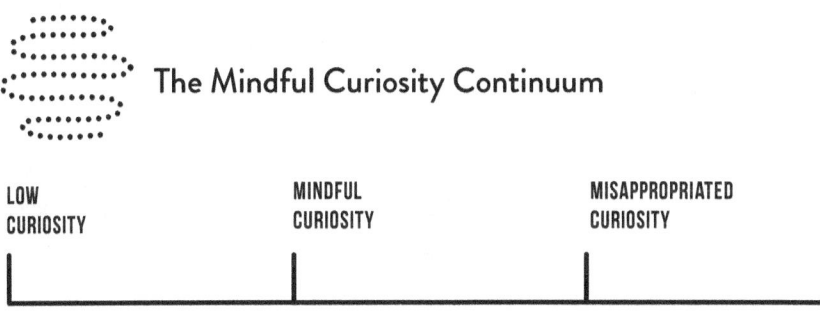

The Mindful Curiosity Continuum

LOW CURIOSITY	MINDFUL CURIOSITY	MISAPPROPRIATED CURIOSITY
Tendency to:	Tendency to:	Tendency to:
• Not be open to information that is inconsistent with beliefs and points of view	• Be open to learning and new information	• Overexpress curiosity, which can lead to inability to focus
• Be fixed-minded	• Overcome bad habits and addictions	• Engage in risky behaviors
• Be depressed and disinterested	• Have meaningful interests and desires	• Obsess
• Create an echo chamber	• Innovate	• Be restless and disruptive

Return with Curiosity

Mindful curiosity is an important skill to disrupt our confirmation bias—returning us to an open mind that helps us to understand what's true for us and others. When we see the truth underlying any situation, we're freed from the grasp of our attachments and aversions. Mindful curiosity is like a sword that cuts through our delusion. For example, curiosity about sensations arising and dissolving in the body can help us recognize impermanence in an embodied way, which weakens our attachments because we can see that there's no sense in holding on to things that aren't going to last. When our attachments to our views are weakened, we're more willing to receive information that contradicts our views. This, as we know, is important for creative problem-solving.

DEDICATED PRACTICE

You can develop curiosity by creating the right conditions in your mind to give your full care and attention to your daily experiences with a sense of awe and wonder. I often hear participants say that it's hard to maintain curiosity in situations that involve boredom or difficulty. This is why practicing mindfulness by bringing curiosity to the breath, a most mundane bodily process, can help you develop and direct curiosity to other aspects of life, however challenging they may be. More specifically, you can cultivate curiosity by attending to any or all of the four aspects of your experience—body, emotions, thoughts, and mental habits. The following is an example of mindful curiosity of the body.

Return. Give your full care and attention to the sensations in your body sitting or lying in a comfortable posture. Notice your direct experience in the body without clinging (what's pleasant) or resisting (what's uncomfortable). Bring curiosity to the subtlest sensations. Here are a few suggestions to pique your curiosity:

1. Notice your posture. Is it open or closed, rigid or relaxed, leaning forward or backward?
2. Find one place in your body where you can feel the sensations most clearly—like your hands, feet, chest, or anywhere else in the body.

What do you notice? Patterns of pressure, temperature, tingling, and blood pulsing?

3. Let go of the labels—hands, feet, chest—and be with your direct experience of sensations in the body. Can you feel how the sensations are changing in quality, intensity, and location?

Listen. Take a few moments after your attention is stabilized to listen to your body. Suggested questions for reflection:

- *What is your body telling you about the quality of your mind?*

- *What does your body need—better nourishment, more hydration, movement, rest, or just your unconditional love?*

- *What supports you in staying connected with your body, and what gets in the way?*

Begin. Carry forward the insights from this practice into your day. Before you begin any activity today, bring mindful curiosity to your body—check in with your posture and body sensations to prepare your mind before any action or interaction.

DAILY MANTRAS TO RETURN WITH CURIOSITY

Practice and play with the chosen reminders for the day with the following intentions in mind: disrupting your default habit of seeking information that confirms your beliefs, strengthening your ability to love the unsolved questions in your heart, and bringing the lens of curiosity to gain a deeper understanding of your reality. By doing so you can empower yourself to enhance personal fulfillment, be effective as a leader, and have a positive impact on a global scale.

I. Mantra for the Day: Love the Unsolved Questions
Patience and openness in mundane activities

> Have patience with everything unresolved in your heart and try to love
> the questions themselves, as if they were locked rooms or books written in a
> very foreign language. Don't search for the answers, which could not be
> given to you now, because you would not be able to live them. And
> the point is to live everything. Live the questions now. Perhaps then, you
> will gradually, without even noticing it, live your way into the answer.
> —Rainer Maria Rilke[24]

Rilke captures the essence of mindful curiosity in his *Letters to a Young Poet*.
His advice to the young poet seeking answers to life's big questions is to tend
to the unanswered questions with love and patience. That's the approach
that mindful curiosity also invites with regards to our direct experiences.
This intimate observation of our sensations, without rushing or reacting,
opens the way to a clearer seeing. Please note that this is NOT a license to
procrastinate. Rather it's a very intentional act of making space to hold the
question with patience and care.

Simply remember the mantra throughout your day and especially
when embarking on a project that is creative or requires a novel solution.
This reminder can disrupt your tendency to rush to a resolution and seek
answers that conform with what you want to believe. You can also return
to this mantra to cultivate curiosity using something mundane and ordinary, like breath.

Return. Return to your breath moving naturally in and out of your body.
Here are a few questions to pique your curiosity:

1. Can you feel the breath the moment it enters your body?

---

24 Rainer Maria Rilke, translated by Stephen Mitchell. *Letters to a Young Poet* (New York: Random
House, 1987).

2. Is it a distinct moment or a subtle unfolding?

3. When you breathe in, where do you most feel an expansion—in your nostrils, chest, or belly?

4. Notice when the breath ends and changes to an out-breath. Can you catch that moment? See the moment the out-breath ends. Does a new breath enter right away, or is there a gap?

Look at the number of things you observed about your breath by being curious.

Listen. Take a few moments to listen within.

- *What did you learn about your ability to stay open and patiently observe your breath?*

- *What gets in the way of your innate capacity to be curious?*

- *What are your intentions for curiosity?*

Begin. Begin your activity by returning to your mantra, "Love the unsolved questions." This will remind you to keep an open mind to your experiences without rushing to fix or find a solution.

Look out for opportunities in your day to observe, sense, feel, and ask questions, and through that exploration, feel your way into the optimal solutions. Good luck!

II. Mantra for the Day: Arising and Dissolving
Mindful curiosity of the body

This one practice, done wholeheartedly, is enough to liberate us from default habits of pushing (away what's unpleasant) and pulling (in what's pleasant). Bringing curiosity to our sensations in the body allows us to see the impermanence of all phenomena in an embodied way, not just intellectually. Over time, feeling the sensations in our body shifting and changing weakens our attachments because we realize that there's no sense in holding on to things that aren't going to last.

Practice and play with this mantra at regular intervals in your day. Once you cultivate mindful curiosity about your body, you can direct curiosity toward other actions and interactions in your day.

Return. Direct your attention to the sensations in your body sitting or standing. Notice the beginning and end of each breath in the body.

Shift your attention to the sensations in your feet. Notice the sensations of touch, temperature, tingling, or pulsing of the blood circulating in your feet. At first, you may not feel the arising and dissolving sensations. As you refine your ability to stabilize your attention and notice, you will start to feel that all sensations in the body (even the uncomfortable ones) are changing.

If you have the time, continue to scan the rest of your body for sensations—arising and dissolving.

Listen. Take a few moments to listen to the wisdom of impermanence in your body. Every breath and every sensation in the body has a beginning and an end. Nothing lasts forever. Stay open to your experience or invite the following questions to deepen your understanding:

- *Were you able to notice any sensations in your body?*
- *Did you see your breath and body sensations arising and dissolving?*
- *Did you notice how sensations are different in intensity and quality in different parts of your body?*

Begin. Incorporate the mantra "arising and dissolving" in your daily routine to return to your experience with curiosity. Before beginning any action or interaction, pause to inhale deeply, consciously feeling the beginning and end of one entire breath cycle in your body. What emotions or thoughts surface when you witness the beginning and end of your breath? Utilize the curiosity of your body to see what you may be holding on to at this moment.

III. Mantra for the Day: Ask What, Not Why
Expanding your understanding and clarity

Asking why-based questions when we're feeling stuck or triggered typically leads to answers that draw from what we already know. Many of our thoughts, feelings, and motivations are operating at an unconscious level, and we can't access them by asking why—asking why, especially in undesirable situations, invites unproductive negative thoughts and rumination that are not helpful.

Return to this mantra to expand your understanding of a situation and see clearly. When feeling stuck, asking "what" is better than "why." Employ what-based questions to carefully observe your thoughts, feelings, body sensations, and what's occurring in your environment. Asking what-based questions widens your container of knowing by inviting new information and insights that you might typically miss when rushing and reacting.

Before you begin this practice, clearly articulate in your mind or write down what the situation is for which you'd like to expand your understanding. Then set it aside for a few minutes while you stabilize the mind with mindful walking or bringing attention to your feet touching the floor.

Return. Invite your mind to return to your body standing, sitting upright, or walking. Allow the breath to move easefully without trying to change anything. Just for these few minutes, let go of any thoughts about the situation and give your full attention to your feet making contact with the floor.

Now direct your attention to the situation you wish to understand better. You may silently repeat what you articulated before. For example, "I want to deepen my understanding of my uncomfortable experience with . . ."

Start by noticing the sensations in your body even as you think about this situation. You may ask yourself the following:

1. What am I feeling in my body?
2. What emotions are becoming known, or what am I feeling?
3. What are my thoughts underlying my feelings?

Listen. Take a few moments to reflect or journal your discoveries for deeper insights and understanding.

- *What are the assumptions I am making here?*
- *What other explanation is possible?*
- *What might be going on for others involved in this situation?*
- *What are my intentions for this situation?*

Based on your expanded understanding of the situation and your intentions, what actions can you take?

Begin. Pause throughout your day to ask "what" questions, especially when you need clarity.

The more you build the habit of posing "what" questions in noncritical situations, the more proficient you become at opening your mind to new information in critical situations.

IV. Mantra for the Day: Emotions Are My Friends
Mindful curiosity of emotions

This being human is a guest house.
Every morning a new arrival.
A joy, a depression, a meanness,
some momentary awareness comes
as an unexpected visitor.
Welcome and entertain them all!
—Rumi[25]

25 Jalal Al-Din Rumi, translated by Coleman Barks. "The Guest House." In *The Illuminated Rumi* (New York: Harmony/Rodale, 1997).

Upon reading Rumi's poem "The Guest House," maybe your immediate thought is, *There's no way I can or want to welcome depression and meanness.* And that's a natural reaction. Remember, we're wired to resist unpleasant feelings. Yet, all our emotions—including depression and meanness—are here for a reason. And that's to help us safely navigate changes in our inner and outer environment.

Return to this mantra, especially when you experience difficult emotions. This is a reminder to disrupt your default inclination to push away or suppress difficult emotions. Mindful curiosity is your ability to notice first the knocking on the door—like the breath is constricted, the heartbeat is up, or the mind is restless. Next, mindful curiosity opens the door to welcome every emotion that's been knocking. And most likely, it will keep knocking if you don't acknowledge the potential threat. So, you don't really have a better option than to open the door.

The other aspect of mindful curiosity you are also cultivating is to be patient because you may not understand the language of the emotion right away. When you are feeling stuck and can't translate what emotions are trying to tell you, refer to the following table based on Karla McLaren's book, *The Language of Emotions: What Your Feelings Are Trying to Tell You.* Remember Karla's words of wisdom, "There is no such thing as a negative emotion. All of your emotions are essential to your well-being."

Return. Find a posture that's most supportive to you. It could be sitting, standing, lying down, or walking. Use a basic mindfulness practice like your breath, body scan, mindful walking, or a loving-kindness practice to settle the mind.

Once your mind and body feel settled, direct your attention to how you are feeling. Simply notice and acknowledge without judging or trying to fix anything. Emotions are like guests—welcome them all. You may notice that some emotions feel pleasant, some unpleasant, and some are neutral.

Listen. Listen to your thoughts or emotions experienced in your body. If you feel that your mind is spinning, try journaling or take a break and go for a walk. Keep your mind's door open without expectations, and patiently wait till you receive new information. You could also use this table as a tool for contemplation. After you've identified the emotion you're feeling, look at the purpose it serves in the table and how it may be relevant in your situation. Contemplate the related question to gain insight into your unmet needs.

Purpose of Emotions and Questions to Uncover Unmet Needs

EMOTION	PURPOSE	QUESTION
Anger	Defend violations of your boundaries or others' boundaries	What must be protected or restored?
Boredom	Protect you from uncomfortable situations	What's being avoided and what must be made conscious?
Guilt and shame	Ensure that your behavior is honorable and good	Who has been hurt and what must be made right?
Hatred	Bring awareness to what you're denying seeing in yourself	What am I not seeing about myself and what needs to be reintegrated? What repressed aspect or talent does this person represent?
Fear	Give you energy and focus to deal with novel situations and change	What is feeling threatened? What action should I take?
Panic and terror	Help confront trauma and reintegrate yourself to heal	What's been frozen in time and what healing action must be taken?
Jealousy and envy	To protect you from deceit in intimate relationships and unfair distribution of resources and recognition	What's been betrayed and what must be healed and restored?
Grief	To feel the deepest and most true connection with all of life	What must be mourned and transformed?

Begin. Based on your insights, what action can you take to attend to your unmet needs? Can you commit to one small step to better care for your emotions? This is a good mantra to return to before responding in situations where emotions are running high. In the absence of understanding your emotions, you may miss an opportunity to realign your actions to meet your needs. Further, the better you understand your needs, the more easily you can discern the emotional needs of others and respond skillfully.

V. Mantra for the Day: Friendly and Patient
Friendly and patient in interactions

In today's interactions, replace reactivity and rushing with friendliness and patience. I've found this mantra particularly helpful in the middle of town council meetings when I am frustrated or impatient that the people are not open to my point of view or taking too long on an issue that I don't think is important for our town. The "friendly and patient" reminder invites me to return to mindful curiosity about whatever is unfolding and keep an open, friendly mind. This doesn't mean I have to agree with what's being said, but I can listen with a willingness to receive new information that may conflict with my beliefs and values.

With this reminder, you will be strengthening your ability to be friendly and patient in your interactions, which allows you to listen and connect with an open mind. When you cultivate these qualities in noncritical situations, you can rely on them in critical situations.

Return. Steady your mind on the breath moving in and out of the heart region. With each in-breath, feel the spaciousness in your mind and body. And with each exhale, soften any desire to rush or react. Invite the mantra "friendly and patient" as a reminder to be present in your interaction with an open mind that's willing to be surprised.

Notice the quality of your mind and body as you invite a friendly mind-set into your interaction. Notice any judgments toward this interaction. Invite a sense of awe and wonder for this fellow human being with their unique journey on this planet Earth.

Listen. Take a few moments to notice your experience and insights about your capacity to be friendly and patient. Here are suggested questions for listening within:

- *What supports you in being friendly and patient?*
- *What's getting in the way of you being friendly and patient?*
- *Can inviting a friendly and patient mindset shift your interactions with others, especially in difficult conversations?*

Begin. Before you begin an interaction, invite the mantra "friendly and patient." What might be possible if you approached a frustrating situation by slowing down? Play with the mantra, especially when you notice impatience or rushing in your interactions today.

VI. Mantra for the Day: Not Difficult, Just Different
Wonder and care in difficult situations

We're wired to resist change. Change can be perceived as a threat to our survival, and we view it as discomfort, something to be avoided. If we notice our direct experience with curiosity, we may discover that it's not difficult, just different.

Return to this mindful curiosity reminder to look at your difficult experiences—such as a new exercise routine, a challenging project, or big changes in your community—with wonder and care.

Return. When presented with something new or challenging, return to the sensations in your body. Observe what arises without pushing or pulling. Notice the labels your mind gives to sensations that are unfamiliar such as "hard" or "too difficult." Return to your direct experience in the body, free from labels.

Listen. Can you see that what the brain views as difficult is just unfamiliar sensations? What if this were an opportunity to grow, have fun, or learn something new? Listen within.

Begin. If feeling overwhelmed, break things down into manageable chunks. Before beginning new or difficult activities today, remind yourself, "Not difficult, just different!"

Take a Moment to Celebrate!

Curiosity is your capacity to question and wonder. Take a moment to return to this innate ability. Acknowledge the ways that showing up with patience, friendliness, and an open mind serves you in the real world. However, I get it that curiosity can wane when we find ourselves physically and mentally drained. That's where the next mindfulness skill comes in—mindful energy.

Mindful Energy: noun
The vigor and vitality essential for activity and accomplishment

---

Energy disrupts the tendency to avoid the discomfort of any kind of change, also known as status quo bias, by realigning with intentions that are beneficial to all involved.

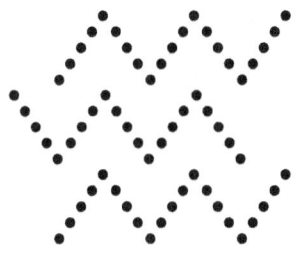

Skill Chapter 4

Energy

CHOP WOOD, CARRY WATER

With passion pray.
With passion make love.
With passion eat and drink and dance and play.
Why look like a dead fish
in this ocean of the divine?

—Rumi

Before You Begin

Take a moment to pause for three energizing breaths. Allow each inhale to refresh your mind and body. With each exhale, soften any tension you're holding in your mind and body.

Connect with your intention for cultivating energy. As you read the chapter, explore what it feels like to engage with the contents with effortless effort.

We've all experienced days where we're so low on energy that it feels almost impossible to do anything. It can be hard enough to get out of bed, let alone tackle a project, go to the gym, or attend a community event. But have you ever stopped to consider what would happen if you stepped outside your comfort zone and took on the activity, despite feeling low on energy? How would that feel?

When our energy is flagging, it can be tempting to take the easy route and take a break. After all, who doesn't want the compassionate solution of taking time out for self-care? But should we always listen to that voice when it tells us to rest? Let me share a personal experience: I had only two days left to complete one of my least favorite tasks as a business owner— accounting for taxes! As soon as I started working on it, I felt a heaviness in my body and a sense of sluggishness creeping in. Every part of me screamed, *Take a short nap!* While that might have been the easier choice, doing so could have caused me to miss the deadline. So, what's the best course of action here—rest or push through despite the fatigue?

It's tempting to give in to what our mind is telling us. At the other end of the continuum, we may ignore our fatigue and forge ahead with the task at hand. Instead of these extreme choices, it's important to pause and inquire within with compassionate curiosity. So, I asked myself, "Are my mind and body really feeling tired? Did I get enough sleep last night? What activities have I engaged in that would cause me to feel tired?" My inquiry revealed that my inclination to sleep was actually a way of avoiding a tedious task, like dealing with tax returns. When I let go of my resistance, I was able to tap into my inner reserves of energy and got the job done. I realized that when I didn't give in to the temptation to rest (even though it sounded enjoyable) and finished my taxes instead, the relief afterward was incredibly freeing. I felt energized after completing the task!

The pandemic felt like an ongoing frenzy, leaving many of us overwhelmed and unable to get our tasks done. Greg is no exception; a senior executive at a large market research company, he had seen his team members being furloughed and was struggling with the politics in his leadership group. Despite these obstacles—and low energy thanks to recent stressors—Greg challenged himself one weekend by tackling all of the little things that had been a source of procrastination: paying bills and cleaning out a cluttered office space. And you know what? After completing this to-do list, however mundane it may seem, he experienced both clarity AND vitality . . . all because he tackled tasks that needed his attention.

Max, who works at a nonprofit, used to cope with his tiredness by turning to food or other distractions after work. Despite graduating from Cornell University with two degrees to pursue the life he wanted, he felt held back by the sudden onset of chronic fatigue.

However, after starting the "Return" program, Max shifted his approach to tiredness. The concept of mindful energy helped him recognize how taxing it had been to constantly complain and worry about feeling exhausted. "It made decisions so difficult because I couldn't predict my energy levels, and I felt so much pressure to make the 'perfect' choice that would please and impress my colleagues and friends, without them knowing how tired I really was," he told me. He rewrote this narrative as he learned about mindful energy. The Four Rooms meditation (described later in this chapter) helped him discern the best next step to balancing his energies, which wouldn't have happened had he turned toward eating or other distractions. Because he was sitting in front of the computer most of the day, he found that exercise was often balancing, even when he felt tired. He also started taking intentional breaks to rest his body and mind throughout the day. His newfound realizations empowered him to make more fulfilling choices: "I recognized how much energy it took to worry about my fatigue. It locked me into a scarcity mindset and I doubted my capacity to complete my assignments on time. When I notice myself worrying, these practices taught me to check in with my intentions and take an imperfect step toward them, without wasting more energy overthinking and striving to make the 'perfect' decision."

In today's fast-paced world, finding ways to optimize our energy for making fulfilling choices can be a challenge. An understanding of mindful energy helped Greg and Max overcome their resistance and accomplish their work with renewed vigor. Let's take a closer look at how mindful energy empowers us to achieve what truly matters to us.

Chop Wood, Carry Water

It's clear that reaching our goals requires commitment, hard work, and dedication; however, it is not enough to simply rely on willpower and self-control to get there. Research shows that our brain can only handle so much before we run out of energy completely. This phenomenon, known as "ego depletion" in the field of social psychology, explains why we're less likely to work out or meditate at the end of a full day. Our daily decisions and activities deplete our brain resources. This leaves us with little energy at the end of the day to engage in activities we don't consider fun and thus require effort.

This is where returning to mindfulness with mindful energy comes in. You may have heard the Zen saying, "Before enlightenment, chop wood, carry water. After enlightenment, chop wood, carry water." What's different before and after enlightenment is the quality of mind of the person implementing the ordinary tasks. What we're aspiring for with practice is to shift the mindset with which we approach what needs to be done. Letting go of our resistance to any task empowers us to draw from our field of inner knowing and energy. In fact, the more we *chop wood, carry water* without resistance, the more energy we will have for other purposeful tasks. However, at first, when we're still building a habit of returning to mindfulness, we will need mindful energy to disrupt our resistance to discomfort of any kind.

Mindful Energy: Transforming Resistance into Right Effort

Rumi's thought-provoking question, "Why look like a dead fish in this ocean of the divine?," urges us to reflect on how we're living our lives. This metaphor invites us to consider whether we are truly embracing the richness and vitality of life. That spark of spirit we experience when feeling alive? Psychologists call it "energy."[26] As a mindfulness skill, energy overlaps with its psychological connotations of vigor and vitality. On the flip side, when we don't have enough energy, we feel depleted or drained.

The most straightforward meaning of energy is the capacity for activity and accomplishment. But how can we muster enough energy to tackle our endless to-do lists while taking Rumi's advice to live with passion? The answer lies in *right effort*.

THE SECRET TO ENERGY: RIGHT EFFORT

In the context of mindfulness, right effort refers to taking actions that enhance the welfare of all involved. The term *right* specifically denotes alignment with intentions of promoting the well-being of all involved. At a minimum, if it doesn't benefit anyone, it shouldn't harm anyone involved. For instance, we may resort to snacking or watching Sunday football when low on energy—instead of exercising or prioritizing essential tasks. But science has proven that a brisk ten-minute walk is better than eating a candy bar to get the necessary boost of energy and overcome fatigue.[27]

The secret to energy is that when we put effort into what's wholesome, we end up feeling more energized than if we wait for more energy to do what's wholesome. Joseph Goldstein and Jack Kornfield, my favorite mindfulness teachers and the authors of *Seeking the Heart of Wisdom*, explain it this way:

---

26   Richard M. Ryan and Christina Frederick. "On Energy, Personality, and Health: Subjective Vitality as a Dynamic Reflection of Well-Being." *Journal of Personality* 65, no. 3 (1997): 529–565. doi:10.1111/j.1467-6494.1997.tb00326.x.

27   Robert E. Thayer. "Energy, Tiredness, and Tension Effects of a Sugar Snack versus Moderate Exercise." *Journal of Personality and Social Psychology* 52, no. 1 (1987): 119–125. doi:10.1037//0022-3514.52.1.119.

We tend to be stingy with our effort. We think, "Well, I only have so much energy, and if I practice hard today, then tomorrow I'll run out of energy. So maybe I should take it easy today." The way energy works is just the opposite of what we fear. We are not like a battery that runs down.[28]

Giving our wholehearted effort to our mindfulness practice, and beyond the practice to wholesome actions and interactions, gives us energy rather than robs us of it.

RIGHT EFFORT: NOT TOO MUCH OR TOO LITTLE

Right effort entails not only doing what's essential in the present moment but also doing it with the right amount of energy. Doing something with a striving mind that exerts too much energy is cumbersome and not sustainable—on the other hand, doing something with little or no energy results in dullness of the mind and listlessness in the body.

For example, when you experience relief upon hearing the bells denoting the end of a meditation, it's a sign that you've been exerting too much effort. However, if the bells wake you up at the end of the meditation, it's clearly a sign of a lack of energy. The key is to find the sweet spot where we can maintain an optimal level of energy that allows us to be both alert and relaxed. When we strike this balance, practicing mindfulness becomes effortless.

Similarly, in life, we need energy to respond to situations with mindfulness. When we experience a challenge or conflict, it's easy to react based on our past conditioning. It takes energy to stay open and curious in a difficult situation. To not give in to the flood of thoughts and emotions that feel legitimate and push us to react in habitual ways. Even just stopping and not reacting immediately takes energy.

Of course, the more we practice mindfulness, the more efficient we become with our use of energy. I now navigate situations I used to find

---

28 Joseph Goldstein and Jack Kornfield. *Seeking the Heart of Wisdom: The Path of Insight Meditation* (Boston: Shambhala Publications, 1987).

challenging when I first started to practice (such as big networking events) with far greater ease. That's because mindfulness has trained me—trains us—to approach everything in life with more love and less resistance. And this takes practice and perseverance.

STORY

Perseverance

At a ten-day silent retreat, I was stretched out of my comfort zone in many ways. Every day was the same. Our day would begin with meditation at 4:30 a.m.—a challenging start for someone who isn't an early riser—lasting for a couple of hours, followed by a break for breakfast. Then we'd meditate for another couple of hours, eat lunch, go for a silent walk, and meditate again until a dinner of tea and fruit. We'd conclude the day around 9:30 p.m. with more meditation and discourse.

Every morning, I'd make it to the meditation hall only to doze off on my meditation cushion. Daily, I struggled between sitting upright and falling asleep in an upright position, with a recurring thought: *This is futile. I'm not cut out for morning meditations.* I felt tempted to quit. It took energy to show up despite failing every day.

On the seventh day, I finally conquered my morning drowsiness and stayed alert throughout the entire meditation. The feeling afterward was freeing. Indeed, I was liberated from my default habits of not rising so early, as well as the nagging fear that I wouldn't be able to do it. Energy manifesting as perseverance empowered me to face the challenge and keep going until I was able to overcome my deep-seated habits. And that, too, in just seven days.

MINDFUL ENERGY AS PERSEVERANCE

Mindful energy, in the form of perseverance, refers to the sustained effort we need to overcome deep-seated tendencies of the mind that prevent us from pursuing a fulfilling life. When working with habit patterns, persistence and perseverance are key to avoiding giving in to our default habits, especially the fear of failure.

The mindfulness skills of awareness with compassionate curiosity can aid in recognizing our resistance to challenging endeavors, supporting our ability to persevere. By developing mindful energy, we strengthen the mindset needed to show up for activities that align with our values and intentions, even when they make us uncomfortable. Whether it's simple tasks like washing dishes or more complex projects, we can approach them with love and care. Like the enlightened monk, we can learn to reset our minds, enabling us to perform our daily activities—chop wood and carry water—effortlessly.

EFFORTLESS EFFORT

Many of us can relate to the feeling of resistance when it comes to tasks we're less than excited about yet need our attention. Filing taxes, going to the gym, making a difficult decision . . . it can be so easy to put these off! Rather than tackling them head-on and getting through them, we procrastinate and postpone until finally, there's no choice but to deal with them. Yet when we approach tasks with resistance, our bodies feel heavy and constricted while doing whatever task needs completing. It takes a lot more energy to resist than to just do what is necessary.

Here comes the good part: Although dealing with what needs to be done involves effort at first, once that challenge has been conquered, a sense of lightness will surely follow that's accompanied by more energy. Remember, our inner field of nonjudging awareness is unencumbered. When we soften our resistance to return to mindfulness, we can channel our energy more efficiently than when we use force or willpower. When we're free of repression and conflict, we have more vitality and creativity. This is why mindful energy is more effective than using self-regulation or self-control to get the job done.

Grasping also depletes energy. Note the amount of effort you're using to hold the book or device you're reading from. Normally, you'd put in just the amount of effort needed so the book doesn't fall from your hands. If you were to hold the book tighter, grasping it, you'd expend more energy than required and get tired quickly.

Holding a book without grasping it is simple. However, in other areas of our lives that we care about—relationships, professional goals, and our commitment to bigger issues such as climate action goals—it may be challenging to not cling to and become overly attached to what's important to us. We use up precious energy in holding on to our attachments, refusing to let go. Yet, if we manage to let go, we might find ourselves pleasantly surprised by the lightness and newfound energy to pursue the life we want.

Mindful energy is the ability to channel our inner resources into meaningful relationships, activities, and goals with the least amount of resistance and force. Consequently, when we engage in meaningful activities, we fuel our energy.

Autonomy and Purpose Fuel Energy

Our sense of vitality is impacted by the level of autonomy we feel. When our actions are self-motivated and purposeful, that's when we feel truly alive. Perspective can play a huge role in determining how invigorating an activity or task will be; the same burden could prove exhausting for one person yet energize another if approached with enthusiasm fueled by meaningful purpose. Even mundane tasks become so much more stimulating when they're aligned with our purpose and values. One way to be mindful in our day is to reconnect with our intrinsic motivations for the choices we're making.

As our responsibilities continue to grow, especially in leadership positions, it's important to learn ways to renew our mental energy. In the top ranks of any organization, decisions involve risks with higher degrees of uncertainty and more at stake. According to Merete Wedell-Wedellsborg, author of *Battle Mind*, women at the top struggle with risk-taking more than men.[29] To overcome the anxiety of high-stake risk-taking, she advises focusing on our values and doing what's right, regardless of what others think. Setting clear intentions to guide us through challenging times and doing the right thing greatly reduces the amount of energy wasted on complaining, resisting, and wishing circumstances were different.

Where Are You on the Mindful Energy Continuum?

There is an Indian proverb or axiom that says that everyone is a house with four rooms: physical, mental, emotional, and spiritual. Most of us tend to live in one room most of the time but unless we go into every room every day, even if only to keep it aired, we are not a complete person.
—Rumer Godden[30]

If you found you had a low level of energy when you took the free mindfulness assessment, you may have an imbalance in terms of the time and energy you spend in the four domains of your life—physical (related to your body's needs), emotional (related to social and emotional needs), mental (related to activities involving the mind), and spiritual (what gives you meaning and makes you feel alive).

Practice and play with the exercises to return with mindful energy at the end of this chapter. You can also increase your energy by cultivating curiosity (Skill Chapter 3) and appreciative joy (Skill Chapter 5). Moreover, bringing attention to our purpose and limited time in this world can motivate us to use our time and energy more wisely.

---

29 Merete Wedell-Wedellsborg. "How Women at the Top Can Renew Their Mental Energy." *Harvard Business Review*, April 26, 2018. https://hbr.org/2018/04/how-women-at-the -top-can-renew-their-mental-energy.
30 Rumer Godden. *A House with Four Rooms* (New York: William Morrow, 1989).

If you found you had a high level of energy on the assessment, you have vitality and look forward to your day with enthusiasm. You feel alert and engaged in your daily activities and interactions.

When out of balance, a high level of energy can entail restlessness in the body and anxiety. This might also involve unskillful efforts that embody continuous striving and attachment to unrealistic expectations. Counter your restless energy with calming practices such as the body scan and pay special attention to the stabilizing mindfulness skills like inner calm (Skill Chapter 6), focus (Skill Chapter 7), and equanimity (Skill Chapter 8).

You can use the table to reflect on the benefits of energy, such as when it's mindful, when it's low, and when it's appropriated by other habits of the mind or in excess. Where are you on the continuum for mindful energy?

The Mindful Energy Continuum

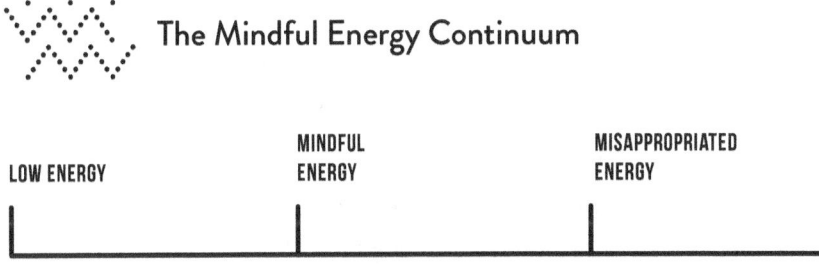

LOW ENERGY	MINDFUL ENERGY	MISAPPROPRIATED ENERGY
Tendency to:	Tendency to:	Tendency to:
• Feel dull and depleted	• Feel enthusiastic about life	• Feel restless and anxious energy
• Procrastinate and be unable to take steps to reach your goals	• Pursue goals with ease	• Strive and put in effort to reach goals, which can be depleting
• Be out of balance in the four domains of life—physical, mental, emotional, and spiritual	• Be balanced in the four domains of life—physical, mental, emotional, and spiritual	• Overcommit in the four domains of life, which is not sustainable
• Give in to status quo bias and avoid change	• Disrupt status quo bias and be open to beneficial change	• Have an overly regulated life that depletes energy[*]

* Roy E. Baumeister, Ellen Bratslavsky, Mark Muraven, and Dianne M. Tice. "Ego Depletion: Is the Active Self a Limited Resource?" *Journal of Personality and Social Psychology* 74, no. 5 (1998): 1252–1265.

How to Return with Mindful Energy

Just do it. Nike coined this slogan in the 1980s. Four decades later, it's still popular. And for a good reason—we all face difficult challenges that require us to push through and keep going. However, catchy slogans alone can't fuel our actions. This hit home for me when I realized how overworked and fatigued so many of us have become lately—myself included. The idea of working longer or faster isn't sustainable if we want to take care of our health, relationships, and communities—something has to give. So, ask yourself this: Are you operating at full capacity without giving your body and mind adequate rest and nourishment required along the way? Are you unable to disrupt your default habits that are leaving you depleted and unfulfilled in life? If you answered yes to either of these questions, then maybe now's a good time to add the daily mantras to your practice, to cultivate the habit of mindful energy throughout your day. Replenish energy in four domains—physical, emotional, mental, and spiritual—and remind yourself to live life with passion and effortless effort.

GEEK OUT!
High-Intensity Emotions Are Draining

Have you ever wondered why we feel exhausted at the end of a workday? Even if we don't do physically demanding jobs, we still get tired. Yes, physical factors can deplete our energy, like when we hold tension in the body and lack of sleep, exercise, or good nutrition. But there's another big reason for feeling drained—our *high-intensity emotions*—and not just the seemingly negative ones like anxiety and fear, but also positive ones like excitement and elation. High-intensity emotions are physiologically taxing because they activate our stress response—the fight-or-flight system—just like fear or anxiety does. This is not to say that we shouldn't feel any high-intensity emotions. Rather, the invitation is to turn toward our emotions and channel them in ways to support our goals without burning out.

DEDICATED PRACTICE

Return. As you've been doing with other practices, the first step is to return to your present-moment experience, such as breath moving in and out of your body. Check in with yourself to see whether you have too much energy or too little. Also, make a note of the quality of energy—such as stable, excited, dull, depleted, or restless.

You will likely notice one of two things. There may be excess energy, in which case you may experience restlessness or irritability. Engaging in mindfulness practices that increase concentration can help calm down restless energy. Stabilizing your attention on any object, such as the breath or body, can relax the mind and body.

On the other hand, if you're experiencing too little energy, you may experience fatigue or dullness in the mind and body. In this case, focusing on the breath, especially the inhale, can help energize the body. It may also be helpful to incorporate mindful walking or mindful yoga into your schedule. That way, you can move the stagnant energy in the body. Intentionally slowing down your pace while walking can generate more energy. This may sound counterintuitive, but slowing down requires more effort and can generate more energy than walking fast.

Listen. Once you've stabilized and energized your mind with an appropriate mindfulness practice, listen within to the causes and conditions for your energy levels and quality of energy. Check in to see what domain you haven't visited lately. Your overall level and quality of energy depend upon a healthy balance of experiences in the different rooms. Use the Energy Matrix, if helpful, to identify what nurtures and depletes your energy in the four rooms.

Begin. Based on your discoveries from listening within and discerning which room (or rooms) need attention, begin to enliven that room. We've established that *right effort* creates energy. Sometimes when I'm writing, I get this feeling of being so tired that all I want to do is take a nap or eat some chocolate. Sometimes, it's true—a nap or chocolate helps! But often, if I take the time to investigate what's going on, what I really need is to rest my thinking mind and just move. So, I go for a quick walk or run, and this gives me the boost

The Energy Matrix

ROOMS	NURTURING ACTIVITIES	DEPLETING ACTIVITIES	CHALLENGES TO VISITING EACH ROOM	COMMITMENT TO VISIT EACH ROOM: WHAT/WHEN
PHYSICAL (BODY)	• e.g., Right nutrition and hydration • Movement and rest • Unconditional love and acceptance	• e.g., Excessive sugar and alcohol • Not enough movement or rest • Self-criticism and comparison	• e.g., Lack of resources • Too busy to exercise and get enough rest • A sedentary childhood	• e.g., Creating a plan for the kind of movement activities that are enjoyable and sustainable on a regular basis
EMOTIONAL (EMOTIONS)	• e.g., Channel high-intensity emotions to prevent burnout • Supportive friends • Wise restraint of where to spend energy	• e.g., Extremely high or low energy • Relationships that are draining • Not enough social interactions	• e.g., Being a workaholic • Codependent relationships • Having low self-esteem	• e.g., Making time to nurture relationships that are uplifting and meaningful • Creating healthy boundaries
MENTAL (MIND)	• e.g., Trying new things • Meditation • Being in nature • Return to your senses can rest the thinking mind • Cooking nutritious food	• e.g., Spending too much time in this room • Lack of exercise • Unable to unhook from thinking • Excessive time on social media	• e.g., Being a workaholic • Addiction to social media	• e.g., Intentional use of social media • Trying activities that engage the mind in new ways like cooking, painting, learning an instrument, or writing poetry

The Energy Matrix

SPIRITUAL (PURPOSE AND MEANING)	• e.g., Define purpose and what you value • Make time to meet yourself with no agenda and judgment • Spending quiet time in nature • Meditation • Dance and singing	• e.g., Doing work that is not aligned with values • Spending excessive time listening to news or scrolling on social media	• e.g., Growing up in a culture that focuses on external goals but not introspection • Not knowing how to be with oneself without an agenda • Driven only by material wealth	• e.g., Make time and space in the house or in nature that is dedicated to being with yourself in silence • Spend time at regular intervals to connect with your gifts and ways to express them • Make time to meditate, walk in nature, do Tai Chi, or swim in fresh water

of energy I need to churn out another 2,000 words. Try it for yourself. When you're feeling tired, go for a walk, exercise, or put on music and dance. Begin to take action, however small, to strengthen mindful energy.

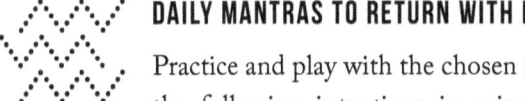 ### DAILY MANTRAS TO RETURN WITH ENERGY

Practice and play with the chosen reminders for the day with the following intentions in mind: disrupting your default habit of living and leading with status quo bias, nurturing your energy in the four domains of life, and bringing the lens of energy to view your experience and make choices in alignment with your purpose and values for personal fulfillment, effective leadership, and global impact.

I. Mantra for the Day: Visit the Four Rooms

Balance the four domains—physical, mental, emotional, and spiritual energy

We are like a house with four rooms—physical, mental, emotional, and spiritual. If we don't make time to care for them, they can become dusty with neglect. During transitions in your day, as you move from one activity to another, take a few moments to discern which room or rooms need your attention. You can also practice and play with this reminder when you are feeling drained or if you've been devoting an excessive amount of time in a particular room, like training for a marathon or working tirelessly to meet a publisher's deadline for your book project.

Return. Return to your breath. Breathe in deeply, and as you exhale, let out a sighing sound. Repeat as many times as you need.

Listen. Check in with your body, mind, emotions, and spirit (purpose). Which room needs your loving attention? If it's helpful, use this list with suggestions:

- *Physical energy: Is my body energized or fatigued? Do I need better nutrition, more hydration, more rest, or more movement?*

- *Emotional energy: What is the quality of my emotional energy? How can I support my emotional needs, such as belonging, love, and emotional support?*

- *Mental energy: Is my mind awake or dull? What do I need to nurture my mind?*

- *Spiritual energy: Do I have a sense of meaning and purpose? Am I giving time to what makes me come alive?*

Begin. Commit to one action of self-care in the room that needs it most and begin. Even if it's a simple action—like stretching or drinking water, calling a loved one, resting the mind, or reconnecting with your purpose—just do it. Begin your next activity with mindful energy.

II. Mantra for the Day: Chop Wood, Carry Water
Mindful energy in mundane activities

Before enlightenment, chop wood, carry water.
After enlightenment, chop wood, carry water.
—Zen proverb

Daily tasks can often feel monotonous and unremarkable. However, what if we consciously introduced a sense of purpose into these seemingly mundane moments? By tapping into what's important and fulfilling about the task, we can discover joy even in ordinary activities. Each action we take can be an opportunity to let go of our resistance and move in the world with more ease. As the Zen proverb says, "Before enlightenment, chop wood, carry water. After enlightenment, chop wood, carry water." Who knows? Maybe your next household chore could be an enlightening experience!

Return. When cleaning the house, cooking, working, or doing other mundane tasks, return to your body for three deep breaths. Soften any resistance to the task.

Listen. Reconnect with your intention for the task—how might it serve you, your loved ones, team members, or the community? Listen within. Feel the energy that arises when you connect with what's meaningful at this moment.

Begin. Before you begin any mundane activity today, remind yourself, "Chop wood, carry water." Proceed with purpose and ease.

Return to this mantra when you feel resistance to undertake tedious tasks and enjoy a boost of energy when you drop your resistance and connect with what matters at that moment.

III. Mantra for the Day: Live with Passion
Living with energy and enthusiasm

With passion, work. With passion, love. With passion, play....
Why look like a dead fish in the ocean of the divine?
—Rumi

The daily grind of everyday life can dull our enthusiasm and sense of wonder. When you find yourself feeling low in energy, remind yourself of Rumi's invitation to live with passion. Playfully, ask yourself, "Why look like a dead fish in the ocean of the divine?" Every time I ask myself this question, I can't help but smile—perhaps it'll do the same for you!

Return. Return to a body posture that is empowering, energizing, and grounded.

Listen. Listen within to what excites you about the activity or interaction before you.

Begin. What would it feel like to bring passion to that activity or interaction? Begin your activity or interaction with genuine passion.

IV. Mantra for the Day: Abort! Return to Love
Mindful energy in actions and interactions

Here's a lighthearted reminder to hit the "Abort!" button when you find yourself feeling trapped or provoked. Rather than succumbing to a vortex of emotional reactions, let this cue steer your attention toward the essence of the situation, allowing your love for the people and things that matter to illuminate the path forward.

Return. When you notice that you're triggered, immediately abort any action, and return to your breath moving in and out of your chest. If it's helpful, place your hand on your chest and feel the warmth of your hand.

Listen. Once you're breathing normally or feel more settled, listen within to what or who you care about in this situation. How does your energy shift when you hold love at the center?

Begin. Begin your action or interaction with love.

You can practice and play with this reminder on your own or with others in your family or team. Love is a powerful source of courage; the intention is to take you out of the realm of "shoulds" and into inspired and intentional action based on what you care about.

V. Mantra for the Day: Time to Replenish
Energizing a tired mind

Meditation replenishes our tired minds and reveals what we need to return to balance. Mindfulness practices stabilize attention so you can see your resistance. This frees up energy to do what's needed with more ease. So, even when—maybe especially when—you're busy, make time for meditation. As the Zen proverb suggests, "You should sit in meditation for twenty minutes every day—unless you're too busy. Then you should sit for an hour." Make time to replenish your energy in between activities in your day.

Return. Return to your body. Allow yourself to relax your eyes. For at least three cycles, receive the gift of each new breath. With each exhale, let go of the tension in your body. Repeat for at least three cycles, resting on the breath.

Listen. Listen within—what do you need to do or let go of to restore balance?

Begin. Begin your next activity or interaction with an energized mind.

VI. Mantra for the Day: Values Fuel Energy
Boost energy with values and intentions

Energy is sustained by integrity: Align your actions with your values and intentions. You could seek inspiration from people who have displayed (or currently display) courageous energy in pursuit of that which they value. What do you value in your life that's worth cultivating this kind of powerful resolve?

Return to this reminder when you experience dullness of mind or lack of motivation to do what you need to do. See for yourself: Even small actions that are aligned with your values and intentions will boost your energy.

Return. Notice the experience of vitality in your body—your heart beating, blood pulsing in your palms, or breath moving in your body. Is your energy dull, restless, or balanced?

Listen. Consider what thoughts, speech, or actions will bring you into greater alignment with your values and intentions.

Begin. Before you begin activities that may evoke resistance, reflect on your core values. Trust in your inner knowing and align with your values.

Take a Moment to Celebrate!

Appreciating yourself for the big and small steps you're taking to live with purpose and enthusiasm is energizing—more on that in the next chapter on appreciative joy. But for now, find your way to feeling good about yourself for taking the time to visit one or more of your rooms—physical, emotional, mental, and spiritual. Nurturing your energy across these four dimensions will enhance your inner resources to do what it takes to live and lead a fulfilling life. And if you haven't made time to visit all four rooms, no worries—you can begin now with one small step.

Appreciative Joy: noun

Our innate capacity to delight in what's good in the present moment.

Appreciative joy disrupts our negativity bias—which is the tendency to see more wrong than right in our lives— by savoring what is going well for us.

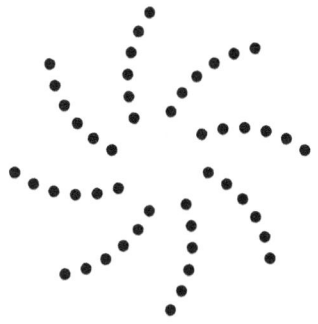

Skill Chapter 5

Appreciative Joy

MEET LIFE WITH LOVE AND GRATITUDE

If I pull from places of faith, joy, and gratitude, then I have the wind of
creativity behind me. And, my work in the world is much more effective.

—Elizabeth Lesser

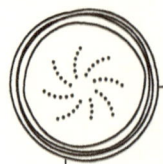

Before You Begin

If possible, take a few deep breaths to invite your mind and body to be present at this moment. Once you're here, take a moment to delight in this time you've carved out for yourself. Then connect with your intention for cultivating appreciative joy.

As you read this chapter, the invitation is to be present to the words, listen within to what the words bring up for you, and stay open to any insights or learning that free you to feel the limitless joy in you.

The fifth habit of the mind that empowers us to be mindful in the real world is appreciative joy. Now, of course, there are different flavors of joy—like excitement, exhilaration, appreciation, contentment, and fulfillment—and not all of them support us in seeing clearly and acting intentionally, especially in the middle of challenges. For instance, the adrenaline-pumping joy from activities like white-water rafting, a live concert featuring your favorite rock star, or watching your sports team win the final game can make you come alive. It's energizing, but the joy is short-lived and doesn't automatically translate into making fulfilling decisions for ourselves, our projects, or our community.

On the other hand, we have access to a special kind of joy that's available to us at all times, regardless of our circumstances. It arises when we're present to our experience with an understanding that life's okay at this moment. This innate capacity to delight in what's good in the present moment is called "appreciative joy." You may recognize this kind of joy as a serene experience when you look at the purple skies at sunset, a more intense feeling of rapture playing music, or a kind of release when you have an aha moment that resolves a complex situation. But what does all this have to do with seeing clearly in the middle of discomfort or reaching our goals? A lot, actually.

Joy in the Middle of Discomfort

I had a real breakthrough in my understanding of appreciative joy because of a difficult conversation with Ashok, one of the most important people in my life. He propped up an unethical leader, which left me feeling confused and frustrated. My logical arguments about the consequences fell on deaf ears—no matter what I said, it felt as though he was totally shutting down; that's until I interrupted my reactive thinking to return to mindfulness.

In that moment, two words appeared in my mind: *appreciative joy*.

It dawned on me that Ashok's comments had me so worked up that I could only focus on the one issue about which we disagreed. His single opinion overshadowed the fifty years of kindness and generosity he had shown me up until that point. My desperate efforts to sway his thinking only resulted in tension and unease on both sides—not an ideal environment for having a meaningful conversation or a shift in perspective.

Once I realized what had transpired, I made a deliberate choice to invite a lens of appreciative joy. Instead of fixating on what we disagreed about, I reoriented myself toward gratitude for all he had done over his fifty-year journey with me. This intentional shift disrupted my negative focus so I could return to my inner spaciousness. As a result, our conversations became more productive, with both of us experiencing a newfound openness. Whether the changes in our respective positions are lasting remains uncertain; either way, this shift brought us closer together emotionally.

Since then, I've come to notice that not only in difficult situations but also when doing work we love, we can get hyper-focused and lose touch with appreciative joy and all the benefits it brings. For instance, have you noticed that your brain gets hooked by negative words and experiences more than positive ones? If you answered yes, you're certainly not alone. There's an explanation for why bad stuff sticks and good stuff slides.

Why the Bad Stuff Sticks

Negative events and experiences register faster, linger longer, and have a greater impact than positive ones.[31] This positive-negative asymmetry, known as the negativity bias, was present in my conversation with Ashok. Even though his good qualities far outweighed his one undesirable perspective, my brain hooked on to what it perceived as negative.

This type of bias causes us to dwell on the bad stuff, even though there are good elements in equal or greater proportion in every situation. For instance, if you receive ten positive comments from your clients, and one client gives you negative feedback, it's very likely that you will obsess over the latter. At the end of the day, do you rejoice over everything you got done? Or do you focus on what you couldn't get done? Very few of us truly say to ourselves, *Bravo! Look at all I've accomplished today!* Again, the purpose of appreciative joy is not to avoid the bad stuff but to approach it from a balanced perspective.

Like many other human biases, this one can also be attributed to our outdated wiring for survival, where we're always on edge, always vigilant.[32] This helped our ancestors stay alive by noting the slightest rustling in the bushes to warn them of a hungry tiger and to kick in the fight-flight-freeze (FFF) response. Our ancestors survived if they missed an apple on the tree, but if they missed the rustling in the bushes, chances are they'd end up as dinner for the tiger. We have the genes of those who were vigilant, which means we've inherited the tendency to be on edge, always looking for lurking danger. However, in the modern world, when we encounter challenges like the difficult conversation I had with Ashok, we don't need to activate the FFF response. You know from previous chapters what happens when we go into FFF mode—we're unable to see clearly and act intentionally.

Appreciative joy enables us to disrupt our negativity bias and return

---

31 R.F. Baumeister, E. Bratslavsky, C. Finkenauer, and K.D. Vohs. "Bad Is Stronger than Good." *Review of General Psychology* 5, no. 4 (2001): 323–370. https://doi.org/10.1037/1089-2680.5.4.323.

32 A. Vaish, T. Grossmann, and A. Woodward. "Not All Emotions Are Created Equal: The Negativity Bias in Social-Emotional Development." *Psychological Bulletin* 134, no. 3 (2008): 383–403. https://doi.org/10.1037/0033-2909.134.3.383.

to the strengths, allies, and resources available to us, even amid adversity.[33] Imagine a situation where you're giving a presentation and see someone yawning or looking bored. It's natural for situational cues—such as a bored look—to kick in the negativity bias that triggers the FFF response, which then leads to thoughts of self-doubt (*I should have prepared better* or *I'm not a good presenter*) or criticism of others in the situation (*The audience sucks!*). These self-deprecating thoughts, or those directed at others, can derail you, and you may end up doing or saying things that you regret later. By returning to the appreciative joy of what's true for you in that situation—such as your hard work leading up to this point or your love for what you're doing—you're more likely to feel balanced and empowered to proceed with confidence. That's because you're broadening your focus that's fixated on only the negative cues to also consider what's positive in that situation. This more inclusive focus may not happen automatically at first, but the good news is that you can retrain your brain for appreciative joy with practice.

Adrenaline or Bliss Junkie

Even though the brain tends to pick up on the bad more than the good, when something good happens, our brains can also get hooked on the pleasant experience. There's nothing wrong with seeking pleasure and enjoying it fully. However, when we overdo it or don't want the pleasure to end, we create suffering for ourselves and others.

Before we go into more detail, take a few moments to remember and jot down three to five recent experiences that made you happy recently. For example, my list includes the following activities:

- My first white-water kayaking trip
- Meditation in the sun after a cold spring
- Cooking with my son, who was visiting home

---

33 Michael Bergeisen. "The Neuroscience of Happiness." *Greater Good Magazine*, September 22, 2010. https://greatergood.berkeley.edu/article/item/the_neuroscience_of_happiness.

- Eating a decadent triple-layer chocolate cake
- Supporting the folks in my senior center to get more resources from our town

All these activities brought me joy, but the nature and intensity of happiness varied across the different experiences. Some activities, like kayaking, were exciting yet exhausting after a while. Others, like meditation, supporting seniors, and cooking, evoked a more serene kind of joy and a deeper connection with myself and others. The triple-layer chocolate cake was a religious experience! In the past, I'd have devoured it quickly and suffered from a sugar overload afterward. Eating it mindfully allowed me to really enjoy it until I felt full, then packed the rest for the next day, prolonging my joy.

Did you see any patterns in the kinds of experiences that are enjoyable to you? For example, did your list primarily comprise thrilling activities like rock climbing and riding roller coasters? Or more serene activities like hanging out with a loved one, meditation, or a mix of both? There's no judgment here, just discernment. Ask yourself whether each experience left you feeling nourished or craving more excitement and pleasure.

Serene and excited forms of joy impact us differently.[34] Serene joy restores the body to equilibrium and activates the parasympathetic system (the rest-and-digest functions). You may experience serene joy as feeling harmonious and connected with yourself and the world. On the other hand, excited joy can be intense and high energy, which activates the sympathetic nervous system (fight-flight-freeze).[35]

The adrenaline rush from high stress and exciting activities can be addictive and lead to burnout.[36] We see this burnout in professional athletes. Take, for example, the legendary basketball player Michael Jordan, who won his third NBA title at age thirty. However, upon announcing his

34 Matthew Kuan Johnson. "Joy: A Review of the Literature and Suggestions for Future Directions." *The Journal of Positive Psychology* 15, no. 1 (2020): 5–24. DOI: 10.1080/17439760.2019.1685581.

35 Craig Lambert. "The Science of Happiness." *Harvard Magazine*, January–February 2007. https://www.harvardmagazine.com/2007/01/the-science-of-happiness.html.

36 Ron Friedman. "Staying Motivated After a Major Achievement." *Harvard Business Review*, February 3, 2015. https://hbr.org/2015/02/staying-motivated-after-a-major-achievement.

retirement (the first of three) that same year, he said, "I didn't feel all the same appreciation that I had felt before, and it was tiresome."

Similarly, in 2021, tennis superstar Naomi Osaka made headlines when she announced that she would be taking a break. "When I win," she said, "I don't feel happy, I feel more like a relief. And when I lose, I feel sad. And I don't think that's normal."[37]

Perhaps what these two successful athletes were experiencing was this: The combination of excited joy and pressure that accompany success is not sustainable. These events trigger the FFF response, which gives us a burst of energy to deal with the situation, after which we're expected to return to equilibrium. But when we're continuously "on" because we have to regularly perform in high-stress situations or because we care deeply about our work, which we'll discuss later in this chapter, we risk experiencing burnout and becoming overwhelmed.

Serene joy is a more sustainable source of pleasure than excited joy. However, this is not to say that we mustn't pursue activities that bring us excited joy or try to contain our excitement when we hear good news or celebrate success. Enjoying moments of excited joy keeps us motivated and stimulated, which are wholesome qualities. However, since excited joy creates an imbalance in the body, we need to be careful that we don't become adrenaline junkies. This is a tendency that can be found not just in adventure seekers and risk-takers but also in workaholics who get addicted to the thrill of meeting tight deadlines and pursuing ambitious goals.

Serene joy is less known for becoming addictive, but it, too, can create attachments that get in the way of being mindful. I remember early on in my mindfulness practice when I had just discovered the joy of being present. The feeling of inner calm was so blissful. I didn't want it to end. I spent many hours and many dollars on books, retreats, and, of course, the right apparel and accessories to re-create that joy and try to make it last. To a lesser or greater degree, I've noticed this in my clients as well. When they first realize that it's possible to let go of their stress, they get addicted to that feeling of

37 Steve Tignor. "Naomi Osaka Isn't Enjoying Herself Even When She Wins—So You Can Understand Her Need for a Break from the Game." Tennis.com, September 4, 2021. https ://www.tennis.com/news/articles/naomi-osaka-isn-t-enjoying-herself-even-when-she-wins -so-you-can-understand-her-.

ease, which can get in the way of them being present in their relationships and work. In mindfulness circles, people who get addicted to the feelings of joy that meditative activities bring and incessantly chase that happy state are known as "bliss junkies."

However, it is possible to experience the full joy of excitement and serenity without falling into the trap of becoming an adrenaline or bliss junkie. Enter appreciative joy.

Appreciative Joy: Delight + Gratitude

The essence of appreciative joy, captured in poet Mary Oliver's "Sometimes," lies in giving our full attention, marveling at the wonders in our world, and sharing our experiences. In other words, when we're present, we will notice the beauty and awesomeness in and around us. Appreciative joy is our ability to notice and delight in all that's good in the present moment.

This may sound simple, but it's not. The kind of joy we tend to chase after usually depends upon circumstances that we may or may not have any control over—such as the joy of winning, finding the ideal partner, or securing the dream job. Still, other types of joy can lead to burnout, as we saw in the case of Michael Jordan and Naomi Osaka. Even serene joy can be addictive and leave us unfulfilled. However, by building our capacity for appreciative joy, we can learn to savor the different experiences of joy available to us without any attachments. Instead of becoming ensnared by the allure of pleasurable feelings, we can cultivate the skill to discover goodness even amid adversity.

An important distinction between appreciative joy and other types of joy is that with appreciative joy, we don't hold on to our attachment to pleasant feelings. We allow ourselves to be nourished by enjoyment and let go of the pleasurable feeling when it's time to move on. Can you see what kinds of attachment to comfort and pleasure get in the way of being mindful in your day? The invitation of appreciative joy is to allow the bliss from our enjoyable experiences to fill our cup so that we can take that into all our actions and interactions.

The second aspect of appreciative joy that makes it different from other types of joy is that it's available to us at all times, regardless of the circumstances: pleasant, unpleasant, or neutral. The purpose of returning to appreciative joy, especially in the middle of a challenge, is not to simply feel good and avoid meeting the discomfort. Rather, it's to return to a place of balance, where we can see the big picture by acknowledging the good along with the bad.

The third aspect of appreciative joy that increases opportunities for happiness is appreciating the good qualities and fortune of others. Our innate capacity for empathy allows us to feel not only others' suffering but also their happiness. This lesser-known aspect of joy is also known as empathic joy, which allows us to rejoice in the success of people we care about. We can also train our minds to feel empathic joy even for people we don't care about.[38]

When we uncover our layers of conditioning—including our tendency to push (away what's unpleasant), pull (in what's pleasant), and run in circles (lost in distractions and doubt)—what remains is a state of appreciative joy. You might be wondering, "Even if I could let go of my pushing, pulling, and running in circles, would I really feel joy? Or will it be emptiness or sadness or something else?"

You don't have to believe what I have to say. See for yourself! If you have a few moments, follow the guidance in the See for Yourself Box. If you're currently short on time, simply think back to a pleasant experience, like the touch of a cool summer breeze on your skin, an art project you were immersed in, or an enjoyable conversation with a loved one. The experience felt pleasant because, in those brief moments, you were absorbed in what was there and not wanting something different from that. When we train ourselves to feel appreciative joy, we realize that it doesn't take much to uncover endless possibilities in this very moment—to live with a sense of awe and wonder for all that's available to us and find fulfillment.

Appreciative joy disrupts our tendency to hold on to the bad stuff and allows us to return to feelings of harmony, equilibrium, and freedom from afflictions, thereby offering a stable foundation for success.

---

38 Amy L. Eva. "How to Nurture Empathic Joy in Your Classroom." *Greater Good Magazine*, February 2, 2017. https://greatergood.berkeley.edu/article/item/how_to_nurture_empathic _joy_in_your_classroom.

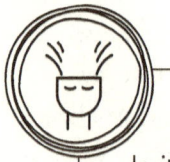

See for Yourself

Invite your mind to be with your body. Make yourself comfortable wherever you are. Take a deep breath, and as you exhale slowly, let your shoulders drop and your body soften. Simply feel your breath fully as it enters your body and as it leaves your body. Be with the sensation of your breath flowing effortlessly into your body and then leaving gently. Soften the urge to find anything special or to do better. Allow yourself to receive the gift of this breath in this moment.

Repeat these steps for a couple of rounds.

Pause and reflect on how you felt during those moments. When you were fully present to and accepting of your breath, just the way it is, without trying to change it in any way, did you experience a sense of ease? This ease is the wellspring of joy that resides within you, that you can always return to whenever and wherever you are. If you don't feel the joy now, that's perfectly all right.

Sometimes, when we're not actively seeking it, joy can surprise us in the most unexpected places: a long-forgotten favorite song playing on the radio, the sight of a radiant rainbow, or the act of helping a neighbor.

For now, remain open to the possibility of experiencing joy, knowing that it is always within reach.

Joy Leads to Success

It turns out that we're bad predictors of what will make us happy. We assume achieving our goals will lead to joy when in reality, our chances of reaching those goals increase when we're already content. That's what researchers Sonja Lyubomirsky, Laura King, and Ed Diener discovered.[39] It's counterintuitive. But what they propose is that if we have a happy disposition, we're more likely to be successful across multiple life domains, including work, relationships, and health. In other words, joy leads to success.

---

39 Sonja Lyubomirsky, Laura King, and Ed Diener. "The Benefits of Frequent Positive Affect: Does Happiness Lead to Success?" *Psychological Bulletin* 131, no. 6 (2005): 803–855. Copyright 2005 by the American Psychological Association.

Interestingly, the Buddha, too, discovered that appreciative joy was an essential quality of the mind in order to sit in stillness and overcome the mental hindrances obstructing his ability to see clearly. His remarkable discoveries that continue to enlighten us 2,600 years later emanated from a mind that was steeped in joy.

STORY

Buddha's Discovery About Joy

Before the Buddha came to be known as the Buddha (which is a name given to someone who has gained freedom from suffering), his name was Siddhartha. He was the only son of a king who was raising him to be a king. Siddhartha enjoyed all the worldly pleasures: the best foods, fine clothing, exotic gardens, and a wise and beautiful wife. However, at a young age, he realized that none of these sensory pleasures could free him from the inevitable suffering brought about by sickness, old age, and death.

Driven by an insatiable thirst for liberation, Siddhartha made a drastic decision. He renounced his luxurious life as a prince and adopted an ascetic lifestyle so he could fully focus on his search for a way out of suffering. With unwavering determination, he mastered various concentration techniques and willingly let go of all comforts, ensuring that nothing would distract him from his ultimate goal.

One fateful day, exhausted and on the brink of starvation, Siddhartha found himself saved by the kindness of a village girl. Her act of generosity, providing him with nourishment in the form of rice and milk, was a lifeline that revived him from unconsciousness to continue his quest. Upon recovering, he realized that extreme renunciation created suffering just as extreme indulgence did. Neither was the path to liberation. He resumed his search for answers but now following a moderate path.

Upon regaining his strength, Siddhartha came to a profound realization. Reflecting on his past, he recalled a childhood memory of sitting beneath a rose apple tree, observing his father perform a ceremony in the fields. In that innocent moment, he had experienced a natural state of absorption, a stillness and calmness of the mind that had eluded him despite all his interactions with learned teachers and extreme acts of renunciation.

continued

This recollection sparked a compelling question within him—could the joy arising from being fully present, free from striving and resistance, be the gateway to the wisdom he sought? And indeed, he went on to discover that appreciative joy was essential to sustaining his meditation practices. This revelation unraveled profound truths about the inner workings of the mind and ultimately led him to the cessation of suffering. His journey serves as a testament to the power of joy in helping us return to our potential for liberation from the hindrances to a fulfilling life.

Fast-forward to the present, research confirms that happiness is a foundation for success. What this means for us is that when we return to a mind that is at ease and see the goodness in life, we're more likely to think, feel, and act in ways that build our resources, skills, energy, and friendships, which help us pursue our passions and purpose, without burning out.

Passion and Purpose Can Burn You Out

Appreciative joy plays a valuable role not only in challenging situations but also in situations where we love what we do. There's a common belief that if we love what we do, we won't work a day. It may be true that people who love their work can work long and hard, but when out of balance, that passion can lead to exhaustion and becoming overwhelmed. Michael Jordan and Naomi Osaka are examples from the sports world of professionals who loved their work. They were incredibly good at their chosen sport when they declared their retirement because they were burned out. They're not alone in this predicament.

Professionals—such as nurses, ER docs, chefs, teachers, cops, and firefighters—who are passionate about their work or do purpose-driven work are at an increased risk of burnout.[40] For one, they can't stop working. I know this from personal experience. As a mindfulness practitioner and teacher, I love what I do. I can keep going, especially when working incessantly on

---

40 Jennifer Moss. "When Passion Leads to Burnout." *Harvard Business Review*, July 1, 2019. https://hbr.org/2019/07/when-passion-leads-to-burnout.

a project like writing or creating a new mindfulness program. Ironically, I've experienced burnout in my work helping others avoid burnout, when I forgot about joy.

It's easy to get wrapped up in the work that matters so much to us, but it's essential—especially if we're engaged in a field of caregiving or teaching—to prioritize actions and interactions that bring joy. Empathy is an invaluable tool for professionals, yet we can often forget about cultivating appreciative joy, which, in turn, helps counteract any negative effects from empathic distress (excessive negative feelings experienced when the self-other distinction becomes blurred and the suffering of others becomes overwhelming).[41] Life is busy, and it's easy to forget about joy, which is why some organizations are prioritizing appreciative joy.

Prioritizing Appreciative Joy

Making appreciative joy a priority in your family, school, work, and community may take some effort. But it's worth it! If you're not intentional about ways you're going to appreciate yourself and others, chances are you'll get hijacked by all the other priorities and deadlines in your life and forget to celebrate your loved ones and colleagues.

Within organizations, when appreciative joy is a priority, employees feel more valued, motivated, and cohesive. In the *Harvard Business Review*, the author Alex Liu makes a case for joy as an intrinsic motivator and powerful connector among people at work.[42] His team surveyed employees around the world and consistently found that employees who feel more joy at work also have more experiences of harmony, shared impact, and acknowledgment at work.

In her book *Braiding Sweetgrass: Indigenous Wisdom, Scientific Knowledge, and the Teachings of Plants*, Dr. Robin Wall Kimmerer talks about the Onondaga Nation school, where the students are taught the value of appreciative joy

41 Kelly Carter and Anne Hawkins. "Joy at Work: Creating a Culture of Resilience." *Nursing Management (Springhouse)* 50, no. 12 (December 2019): 34–42. doi: 10.1097/01.NUMA.0000605156.88187.77.

42 Alex Liu. "Making Joy a Priority at Work." *Harvard Business Review*, July 17, 2019. https://hbr.org/2019/07/making-joy-a-priority-at-work.

at an early age. They don't recite the Pledge of Allegiance, but they do recite the Thanksgiving Address. This is a scientific inventory of the natural world and an appreciation of the interdependence and functions of each element in the ecosystem. Can you imagine a culture in which children grow up prioritizing appreciative joy for one another, their teachers, the environment, and all living things? The children begin the Thanksgiving Address with these words:

> Today we have gathered, and when we look upon the faces around us, we see that the cycles of life continue. We have been given the duty to live in balance and harmony with each other and all living things. So now let us bring our minds together as one as we give greetings and thanks to each other as People. Now our minds are one.

The address comes from the Haudenosaunee, also known as the Iroquois or Six Nations—Mohawk, Oneida, Cayuga, Onondaga, Seneca, and Tuscarora. Each speaker of the Thanksgiving Address varies the words slightly. The verses I've included here from *Braiding Sweetgrass* are from the 1993 version by John Stokes and Ohén:ton Karihwatéhkwen.[43]

Part of the reason this example is so powerful is that these children are taught to be genuinely grateful for one another and the abundance in their lives; it's not another routine they go through without a deeper appreciation. Similarly, for the appreciative joy practices and processes to have the desired outcomes in families and a work setting, all family members, employees, and leaders need to understand the "why" behind it, and share how they can create a culture of appreciative joy in ways that are meaningful to them.

One group I worked with during the pandemic was professionals experiencing burnout. Before offering solutions, I first needed to understand the causes of the burnout. One of the problems identified was a lack of focus in meetings and a breakdown in communications. A solution to promote shared understanding and appreciative joy, in this case, was to start each video meeting with a few minutes for participants to read the agenda and share their intentions in the chat box. They ended each meeting by stating

---

43 John Stokes and Ohén:ton Karihwatéhkwen. *Thanksgiving Address: Greetings to the Natural World* (Six Nations Indian Museum, 1993).

one thing about their team they were grateful for (which left the members with a feeling of pride in the work they were doing together).

In another example, a friend shared that her family had a gratitude tree for Thanksgiving. Family members hung little notes cut out like flowers to share what they were thankful for in their family. Especially during challenging times, it's important to remember to find ways to appreciate each other.

Celebrate the Small Wins

When change makers and leaders set ambitious goals that are hard to reach, it's important to celebrate the small steps and successes along the way. As a town councilor, I often practice appreciative joy to find balance in an environment fraught with divisiveness and obstacles to reaching our goals related to complex issues such as racial equity, climate change, and homelessness. I've seen the magic of appreciative joy in uplifting even a divisive group of people undergoing a very difficult time. At the last district meeting one year, I took a risk and ended the meeting with an appreciative joy practice. See the Story Box for what happened.

We often forget or can't see the good in our situation or in ourselves. We all need to be reminded about the difference we're making. A recognition of the efforts we're making on what feels like a futile journey may be just what we need to hear to keep going. The more we feel good about ourselves, the more we can share that joy with others and multiply our happiness.

STORY

Appreciative Joy Is Contagious!

Pandemic-related stress and burnout in our community had exacerbated the existing political divisiveness. We had a few minutes to spare at the end of our last district meeting for the year. I invited the residents attending the meeting over Zoom to acknowledge someone in the community, like a friend, neighbor, or town employee, who in some way had brought them comfort or joy.

continued

My impromptu suggestion was met with an awkward silence. Sharing good stuff wasn't typical at political meetings. But I dug deep within myself to find something that I genuinely appreciated in my co-councilor and sincerely acknowledged her environmental focus that had greatly influenced our town council decisions. My colleague followed suit.

Then, one person raised their hand to say, "The Merry Maple," a community tradition to launch the Christmas season in the town commons with the lighting of the maple tree accompanied by children's carols, warm apple cider, and donuts from our local store. People nodded in agreement. Soon, others started mentioning different experiences of joy and gratitude. There was the outdoor symphony organized by the senior director, the local artists who painted the dividers for outdoor seating, and the efforts of the Amherst Chamber of Commerce and the Business Improvement District (BID) in supporting small businesses and local families.

As people started to share their stories of appreciative joy, somewhat awkwardly at first, things started to shift. With each joyful experience that was shared, I saw more people's faces over Zoom light up, nodding, smiling, and raising their hands to share their experience, which would then send out another ripple of shared smiles and laughter. Appreciative joy is contagious! I saw it happen before my eyes.

After the meeting ended, I texted the executive director of the BID to let her know that at the meeting, she was appreciated for her hard work in supporting our businesses in a time of a pandemic. She replied, "Wow! Thank you Shalini. This is coming right when we're hanging our heads and wondering if it [their hard work] makes a difference."

In that moment, I realized the power of acknowledging and celebrating the positive contributions of others. It not only brings joy and gratitude to those being recognized but also has the ability to uplift an entire community, even in the midst of challenging times.

Multiply Happiness

Appreciative joy allows us to see that happiness is not a limited resource. We don't need to compete with others for happiness. In fact, we can derive happiness from others' joy by appreciating their success and well-being. There's evidence that feeling empathic joy—feeling others' happiness—has positive outcomes for everyone involved. For example, the study "Empathetic Joy in Positive Intergroup Relations" discovered that when teachers had empathic joy for their students, the teachers performed better, and their students had better test scores.[44] Empathic joy not only improved teachers' interactions with their students but also the academic performance of their students. How can empathic joy benefit you and your loved ones?

It may be easier to celebrate the success of our loved ones than that of our competitors or people we don't care about. In those situations, it may not be easy to step away from comparing and competing—as if joy were a limited resource. For instance, what might be your first reaction when hearing someone you know just hit the jackpot, got a six-figure job, found an attractive partner, bought a bigger house, or moved to an idyllic location in Hawaii? Even if your immediate reaction is that you're thrilled for them, there may be a teeny-tiny voice within that's wondering, *Why them and not me?* Hey, I've been there and go there all the time. Every time I see a Facebook acquaintance who has published a book about mindfulness, my stomach contracts, and I wonder when my book will be done. It's almost as if there's a limited supply of success and happiness out there; if someone gets it before I do, there'll be none left for me.

I'm not suggesting these reactions are the case for everyone all the time, but if every now and then you experience envy, I invite you to return to appreciative joy. Not in a fake way to bypass your experience, like when you say something like this but don't mean it: "I'm absolutely *thrilled* for you" or "No one in the galaxy deserves it more!" Instead, take a moment to appreciate the efforts of the person who's sharing their happy news and acknowledge what you might genuinely appreciate about their success: *I know how hard it is to write a book. Congratulations for completing this milestone!* or *I'm envious, I admit. But getting that out of the way, congratulations!*

It's also helpful to check in with your intentions when feeling envious. You may realize that you don't even want what makes others happy. In this case, you can simply rejoice in others' joy. If you do want what others have accomplished, you can be happy for them and see what you can learn from

44 Todd L. Pittinsky and R. Matthew Montoya. "Empathic Joy in Positive Intergroup Relations." *Journal of Social Issues* 72, no. 3 (September 2016): 511–523. https://doi.org/10.1111/josi.12179.

them. Let their success be a motivation for what's available to you as well. That's a good reason to rejoice!

His Holiness, the Dalai Lama, is known to have said that feeling happy when good things happen to others increases his chances to be happy by billions. The good news is that, like the Dalai Lama, we can multiply our happiness by sharing in others' joy. Like any skill, we can get better at accessing appreciative joy with practice. But first, where are you on the joy continuum?

Where Are You on the Joy Continuum?

If you haven't taken the free mindfulness assessment, take a few moments to reflect on your capacity for appreciative joy for yourself and others. The Joy Continuum table illustrates tendencies as they pertain to joy.

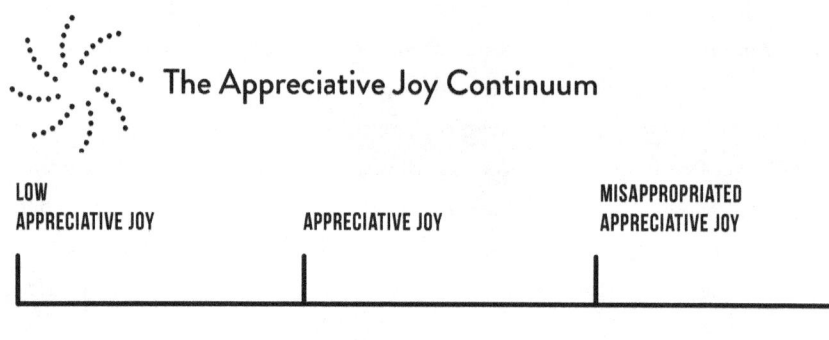

The Appreciative Joy Continuum

LOW APPRECIATIVE JOY	APPRECIATIVE JOY	MISAPPROPRIATED APPRECIATIVE JOY
Tendency to:	Tendency to:	Tendency to:
• Have a scarcity mindset	• Delight in what's good in the present moment	• Be a bliss junkie or an adrenaline junkie
• Be depressed	• Appreciate good qualities and good fortune in yourself	• Be overly optimistic
• Be ungrateful	• Appreciate good qualities and good fortune in others	• Have superficial happiness for others

Too little joy could indicate that you're not taking the time to be grateful for all the good qualities in yourself and others.

High appreciative joy suggests that you tend to see and acknowledge all that is working well in your life. However, it's easy for appreciative joy to be misappropriated by other tendencies that feel like joy but entail attachments or superficial feelings that get in the way of being mindful. For instance, too much joy can lead to attachment to sensory pleasures and enjoyment. Another way that your mind can create a false sense of appreciative joy is when you show excitement for others' joy but don't genuinely feel happy about their happiness.

Practice and play with the daily practice and mantras to find and foster your way of strengthening your capacity for appreciative joy.

Return with Appreciative Joy

Appreciative joy is your innate ability to delight in what's present. Maybe all you need to do is remind yourself to return to it in the middle of your day. However, because of conditioning and negativity bias, you may need to do a little more than remind yourself. Practice and play with the dedicated practices and reminders to return, listen, and begin your daily actions and interactions with appreciative joy.

DEDICATED PRACTICE

Now that you know that your brain may be tilted in favor of seeing threats and missing out on all that is good and working well in your life, you can do something about it. You can retrain your brain to make appreciative joy the default habit that replaces negativity bias. An appreciative mind levels the playing field by returning us to equilibrium. While unhappy people primarily notice the negative stuff, happier people notice the negative *and* positive stuff. What this means is that happy people have a balanced response to both.[45]

---

45 William A. Cunningham and Tabitha Kirkland. "The Joyful, yet Balanced, Amygdala: Moderated Responses to Positive but Not Negative Stimuli in Trait Happiness." *Social Cognitive and Affective Neuroscience* 9, no. 6 (June 2014): 760–766. https://doi.org/10.1093/scan/nst045.

Finding happiness can be as easy as taking three simple steps. Start to practice appreciative joy by noting pleasant experiences in your day. Or you can direct appreciative joy toward yourself, including your body, good qualities, and intentions, or you can show appreciation for those around you, whether they be close friends, acquaintances, or even people who have caused difficulties before. You just might surprise yourself with how much easier it becomes to return to mindfulness when recognizing all sources of good feelings within yourself and your environment.

Return. As you return to your present-moment experience, notice the positive experiences in your day. Here are a few ways to do that.

1. First thing in the morning, as you're waking up, instead of reaching for your phone, take a few moments to appreciate yourself and all that's good in your life. Enjoy your first cup of tea or coffee fully, tasting the warm, yummy cup of deliciousness.
2. Throughout your day, observe the goodness in people working with you and offer sincere appreciation. Return to love for what you do rather than aiming for perfection.
3. End your day with gratitude for even one small step you may have taken to act on your intentions for the day. Notice goodness at least half a dozen times every day, suggests Dr. Rick Hanson, psychologist and author of *Hardwiring Happiness.*[46]

Listen. After acknowledging the positive events, take a few moments to listen to your body and mind. Savor the positive experience and feel the joy in your body for (as Dr. Hanson recommends) twenty to thirty seconds. Allow your mind to catalog the experience and register that there are no threats. Remind yourself, *Life's good at this moment. It's okay to let down my guard and relax.*

Listen within to any insights about your experience. If you're unable to listen within, reflect on the following questions:

46 Rick Hanson. *Hardwiring Happiness: The New Brain Science of Contentment, Calm, and Confidence* (New York: Harmony, 2013).

- *What did you discover about your capacity to appreciate the things going well in your life?*
- *What supports you in returning to appreciative joy, and what gets in the way?*
- *How might appreciative joy help you return to equilibrium in your day?*

Begin. Before you begin your next activity, reconnect with the feeling of goodness and the knowledge that you're okay. It's important to note that you can undo your mind's affinity for the negative by living with a sense of gratitude or appreciation for all that's working well in your life and letting the joy register in both your mind and body.

RETURN TO MINDFULNESS WITH DAILY MANTRAS

Practice and play with the chosen reminders for the day with the following intentions in mind: disrupting your default habit of living and leading with a negativity bias, appreciating the good qualities in you and others, and bringing the lens of appreciative joy to return to your inner equilibrium for making choices that enhance personal fulfillment, effective leadership, and global impact.

I. Mantra for the Day: Appreciate Yourself
I see my goodness

This serves as an important prompt, particularly if you habitually neglect your positive attributes while constantly striving to be better, to do better. Appreciating your wholesome qualities can empower you to show up authentically and purposefully.

If you find it difficult to appreciate yourself, start with someone you feel appreciative joy for naturally. Once you return to that capacity for appreciation, direct that joy toward seeing all that is good within you.

Return. Return to your breath. Notice the way the chest rises with each inhale and falls with the exhale. Stay here for a few cycles of your breath moving in and out of your body at a natural pace. Consider a moment where you felt energized, connected, or inspired. Notice the wholesome qualities you brought to that situation. Directing the appreciative joy phrases toward yourself, repeat the following lines out loud or internally:

1. I appreciate my good qualities. (Name a couple of them.)
2. I am grateful for the good fortune in my life.
3. May my good qualities and fortune continue to grow.

Notice the effects of the different phrases and adapt the phrases according to what feels most natural to you. Allow yourself to acknowledge your good qualities and savor the feeling in your body.

Listen. Listen within to your experience when you appreciate yourself. If helpful, reflect on the questions that speak to you:

- *Can you see the goodness and sincerity in you?*
- *What is getting in the way of you appreciating yourself?*
- *What supports you in appreciating yourself?*

Begin. Prior to diving into any activity or interaction, take a brief pause to remind yourself of this mantra, recognizing the positive qualities you're bringing to the situation. Replenish your inner reservoir and then generously share its contents with the world.

II. Mantra for the Day: Your Body Loves You. Love it Back!
Appreciative joy for the body

It's human nature to notice the body when it's not working as expected or when there's pain. However, taking time to attend to the body with gratitude offers many benefits, including noticing how you can take better care of your body (so it can support you in living and leading successfully).

For example, even during easy hikes, I was starting to get out of breath, and I'd notice that my body wasn't performing the way I expected it to.

Motivated by this observation, I have started to exercise regularly, and when I don't feel like working out, I return to appreciative joy for my body and remember that for my body to help me hike and do the things I want, I need to love it back and take care of it with some exercise.

You can start your day with this practice—return to it at the end of your day before going to sleep or during breaks throughout the morning and afternoon. You can adapt the practice to the purpose and time at hand.

Return. While it may not be perfect, your body is doing its best to support you.

1. Pause when you accomplish something or feel frustrated with your body.
2. Return to your body. Scan through or choose an area of your body that needs loving attention. Place your hands on that part and give your full care and attention.
3. Attend to the sensations with loving attention and offer gratitude to the body part.

If you have time, you can extend gratitude and feel the sensations in your whole body—such as your neck, shoulders, arms, hands, chest, heart, thighs, knees, and feet.

Listen. After you've finished the practice, take a few moments to listen within and trust what you learn about your body and your capacity to appreciate it. How might appreciative joy for your body shift your perspective or choices that impact the body?

Begin. What's one action you can take to care for your body so that it can better care for you?

III. Mantra for the Day: Act with Love
Appreciative joy for your work

Life is messy and imperfect. Focusing on perfection can hold you back from showing up fully. Instead, you can practice reconnecting with your intentions and acting with love.

If you want to do everything perfectly, know that perfection is not the same as doing your best. It's an unrealistic expectation you place on yourself, often because you don't think you're good enough.

You can return to this mantra before you begin an activity at home, school, or work.

Return. Settle your mind on the breath moving in and out of your body. Feel the space created in your chest with each inhale and the relaxation with each exhale. If it's helpful, place your hand on your chest to appreciate the gift of this body and breath.

Once you feel connected with appreciative joy at this moment, bring to mind the activity you will be engaging in. Notice your thoughts related to this activity.

Listen. As you approach this activity, what "shoulds" or "have tos" arise? Consider, instead, what you love or enjoy most about this activity. See if you can gently shift your focus from a need for perfection and compulsion to what you love and enjoy about your work. (It could be that the activity brings you joy, allows you to express yourself, positively impacts people, and so on.)

Realign with your intention on what's important to you.

Begin. Begin the activity with love and intentions for this activity.

Throughout the day, return to love again and again. Love yourself, your mind, your body. Love the gift of this life, the work you do, the opportunities to express yourself, the people in your life, and even those who challenge you. Think, speak, and act from a place of love.

IV. Mantra for the Day: I Am Supported
Appreciating available resources

Now that you know you're more likely to reach your goals when you're happy, you can practice returning to appreciative joy. Repeat the mantra "I am supported," or make up one that reminds you about your inner resources to see clearly and walk intentionally toward your goals. Even though you may not think of yourself as living with abundance, we're using the word to include nonmaterial wealth, such as the gift of rich friendships, a strong heart, and your unique skills.

This is a good practice to start your day or prior to making decisions. You can also return to this mantra when you're experiencing a scarcity mindset or feeling alone while confronting challenging circumstances.

Return. In every situation, we can tap into our inner and outer resources for support. Placing your hand on your chest, bring your attention to the breath moving in and out of your chest till you feel connected with your breath and body.

Bring to mind one way you are supported by a person you love or even by the ground beneath your feet. Feel the support in your body.

Listen. When you feel ready, ask yourself this: What's here to support me— my skills, resources, and connections? Don't go searching for answers or trying too hard to figure out what will support you.

If it's helpful, write down "I am supported," and list all that's here to support you. Listen within to what's emerging when you shift your mindset from scarcity to trust.

Begin. Take a step forward, however small it may be. Trust that you already have what you need to move forward—even if that involves reaching out to a loved one, a mentor, or a colleague who can clarify, guide, or simply listen.

V. Mantra for the Day: Multiply Goodness
Appreciative joy for others

Have you ever noticed that when someone around you succeeds, it can be tough to celebrate with them? Maybe your heart doesn't quite leap for joy even though the other person has worked hard and accomplished something amazing. If this sounds familiar, why not take a look at what could be standing between you and genuine happiness for others' achievements—are there feelings of envy or unfairness somewhere in there? Investing time into understanding these emotions will open up new doorways toward giving (and receiving) heartfelt congratulations. Goodness is infectious. The more you share, the more it grows!

Return. Come to a posture that feels supportive and nurturing.

1. Return to your breath moving in and out of your chest. Stay here for a few cycles of your breath at a natural pace.
2. Consider the positive qualities in those you meet or are about to meet. Feel the presence of this person. Let your attention go to all the good qualities or things going well in the person's life, large and small.
3. If you feel called, let them know, or silently repeat the following-suggested phrases as many times as you like or until your mind feels stable and joyful:
   ◦ I am grateful for your good qualities. (You can name them if they are easily accessible.)
   ◦ I am happy for the good fortune in your life.
   ◦ May your good qualities and good fortune continue to grow.

Listen. How does it feel to share in someone else's joy? Take a few minutes to listen within. If you have time, reflect on the following questions to gain insight into your capacity for joy in others' success:

- *What supports you in feeling appreciative joy for others, and what prevents you from celebrating others' success?*
- *What are your intentions for yourself and the people you invited into this practice?*
- *Can you see the gifts in appreciating others' success—more ideas, motivation, a bigger capacity for joy, or something else?*

Begin. Before your interaction, return to your intention for appreciative joy for people at home, at work, and in your community. When possible, celebrate others' success and let them know they're appreciated.

VI. Mantra for the Day: End with Gratitude
Appreciating what's working well in our lives

By stopping to feel gratitude for all that's working well in our lives, we disrupt our habit of focusing on all that's not working well, is unfinished, or needs improvement. Small and frequent doses of gratitude help rewire the brain for lasting happiness.

You can do this practice alone or with your family, team members, or community. Stopping to feel gratitude could also be a good way to transition between activities or end your day.

Before jumping into your next activity, pause to reflect: What can I feel grateful for about this experience? Notice what comes to mind. Allow the feeling of gratitude to settle into your body.

Return. To settle the mind and body, return to your favorite practice.

Once you feel present, recall one thing you feel grateful for. This could be a project you've completed or the first step you've taken. It could be a family vacation or a meal you cooked together. You get the idea.

1. Allow yourself to notice all that you're grateful for in this situation, including yourself.
2. Take a few moments to experience gratitude in your body. Savor the moment.

Listen. Revel in appreciative joy and listen within. Here are a few reflection questions if you need them. Otherwise, trust yourself. See what you discover about your innate ability to feel gratitude. Reflect on these questions to listen within:

- *What do you naturally feel grateful for, and what took you time to notice?*
- *What supports you in feeling grateful, and what gets in the way?*
- *How does it feel to be grateful, and how does it feel when you're not able to feel grateful?*

Begin. Before you begin a new activity, take a moment to reconnect with gratitude for what you've completed and accomplished. If it's helpful, before bed, journal about three things that occurred that day for which you're grateful.

Play with this practice between activities and share with others!

Take a Moment to Celebrate!

I hope this chapter provided you with many opportunities to appreciate yourself and all that is working well in your life. Throughout your day, return as often as you like to appreciate and share your joy with others. The more you practice returning to joy in ordinary moments, the more easily you will access appreciative joy as a mindfulness skill when you need it to return to your inner equilibrium. Have fun with appreciative joy.

Inner Calm: noun

The ease that flows from letting go of attachments and reactivity when we understand impermanence—the changing nature of our thoughts, emotions, and desires.

Inner calm disrupts our attachments to habitual hurrying, beliefs, and expectations that hinder our inner equilibrium by deepening our understanding of impermanence.

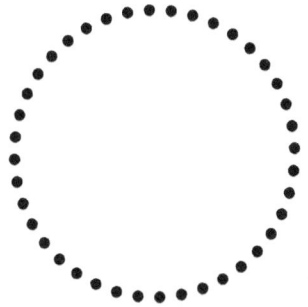

Skill Chapter 6

Inner Calm

EMPTY THE CUP

Rested, we are ready for the world but not held hostage by it;
rested, we care again for the right things and the right people in the right way.
In rest we re-establish the goals that make us more generous, more
courageous, more of an invitation, someone we want to remember,
and someone others would want to remember too.

—David Whyte, "REST" from *Consolations*

Before You Begin

Take a moment to take three deep breaths. With each exhale, soften any tension you're holding in your mind and body and let go of what you don't need to hold on to at this moment.

Connect with your intention for letting go of what doesn't serve you.

Life is full of incredible experiences and unique opportunities to savor, connect, learn, and grow. However, we often limit ourselves and miss out on the joys available if our minds are overly attached to how things *should* be or our habits of hurrying.

Imagine this: You're on your way home from a family vacation when your car suddenly stalls. Undoubtedly, it's a major inconvenience and could potentially be costly. It's only natural to feel frustrated. But here's the question: What is the underlying expectation that is fueling your agitation? Is it the belief that your car should never fail unexpectedly?

Once you accept that it's unrealistic to assume your car will always run smoothly, you can come to terms with the situation. Instead of dwelling on how things should be, you can open up to the possibilities before you. Perhaps this is an opportunity for more quality family time to explore a new city or try something new that you wouldn't have done otherwise.

The same principles of recognizing our attachments and expectations can be applied to our work or community life. By letting go of the hindrances caused by rigid expectations, we clear the space to see the bigger picture and seize the opportunities before us.

Empty the Cup

I'm no stranger to the hustle and bustle of life—balancing being a town councilor, taking on new research projects and clients, *and* writing my first book can be overwhelming. The busier I get, the harder it is to stop and see that I'm not being effective; I get more reactive in meetings, and I am unable to see clearly and act intentionally. Sure, hitting the pause button and allowing myself some time for rest is what I should be doing, but it's not easy when I'm caught up in a web of attachments and racing for several finish lines.

After twenty years of dedicated mindfulness practice coupled with extensive research into how our brains work, I know that breaking free from habits—like rushing and reacting—is possible. The key is learning to empty the cup!

STORY
Empty the Cup: A Zen Parable

An accomplished scholar traveled far and wide to acquire the legendary wisdom of Zen from a wise master but was too caught up in his convictions to truly listen. He went on and on, describing the different theories he knew, leaving no space for the teacher to talk. The Zen master offered him tea with an unexpected lesson in store: He patiently filled the cup until it began pouring over, causing quite a mess on the table. Shocked by this spectacle, the scholar exclaimed, "Stop! The cup is full. Can't you see?" The teacher replied with a smile: "Just like your mind! It must be emptied before any new knowledge can enter."

Can you think of situations when your cup was too full to seize opportunities available to you or to receive new information and perspectives? For instance, in a meeting with different points of view, were you able to make space for all perspectives to be entertained? It's easy to fill our cup with thoughts, expectations, and emotions that limit our understanding and experience of a situation. Sometimes we're not even aware that our cup is full because we're busy or don't know how to look within. We need to learn to regularly empty that cup so we can fill it with stuff we care about.

I had a client who challenged this concept, and perhaps you're wondering the same thing, "What if I love what's in my cup and don't want to empty it?" This is a great question to ask yourself regularly, and only you can answer it. The answer lies in this inquiry: Is the stuff you're accumulating in your cup fulfilling? Or is it full of narratives that occupy your mind space and keep you stuck? In the absence of awareness that's accompanied by an ability to let go, we can hold on to ideas and concepts that are obsolete, redundant, stale, and even toxic. It isn't easy letting go of ideas that have been a big part of our lives for so long, but developing an inner-calm practice can help us clear out old stories and make room for fresh perspectives.

Inner Calm: The Key Is Letting Go

We often hear about inner calm, but it can be so much more than a fleeting moment of peace after yoga or the perfect massage. Inner calm is actually our ability to let go of attachments and reactions to life's events, resulting in ease and clarity. We can't return to our field of nonjudging awareness when our mind is busy judging and reacting. But once we learn to empty our cup, as the Zen teacher suggested, we, too, can make space for peace, healing, and wisdom.

As a mindfulness skill, inner calm is the ability to let go of attachments and reactivity based on an understanding of impermanence—the changing nature of our thoughts, emotions, and desires. When we find ourselves rushing and reacting, we can remind ourselves, *This too shall pass.* The purpose is not to negate what we're feeling but to put brakes on accelerated feelings. Once we return to our inner stillness, we can look at the source of our reactivity, intimately seeing its changing nature: This right here is what frees us.

As a practice, inner calm is the art of stopping, looking, and letting go for purposes of healing and clarity. It involves physical composure and mental tranquility. It can be seen as the ultimate balm for your soul—like a cool breeze on a hot day. Inner calm brings ease to body and mind alike. In the body, composure is experienced in the muscles and as an overall feeling of ease. In the mind, inner calm creates the space to hold everything without attachment and resistance. Conversely, the absence of inner calm may show up as restlessness in the body and agitation or reactivity in the mind.

Seeking inner calm can often leave us wanting more, but it's ironic that true inner calm is achieved when we let go of our desires, even the desire for inner calm itself—a catch-22 if there ever was one. This paradox becomes evident when we consider the case of a client dealing with anxiety who turned to meditation as a way to ease his mind. Surprisingly, he found himself even more anxious post-meditation. He had hoped that meditation would improve his sleep, but he was left frustrated when he observed his restlessness during a body scan meditation, which only seemed to worsen his sleep problems.

The moral here? To find peace, he had to let go first of his expectations around finding peace. In order to let go, he learned to see the three hindrances to his achieving mindfulness: running in circles (a restless mind), pulling (striving to sleep), and pushing (frustrated with his restlessness). With practice, he learned to accept his restless mind, which softened the striving and frustration, and he was able to find ease, even when he couldn't sleep, which ultimately allowed him to sleep.

Letting go of attachments to certain outcomes doesn't, however, mean that we're suppressing or evading challenging situations. Instead, this release occurs organically when we comprehend that emotions arise and dissolve—all within ninety seconds.

The Ninety-Second Rule

Inner calm is not about suppressing, denying, or avoiding our emotions. When we don't give in to the urge to react, we're cultivating the ability to stay with unpleasantness (knowing that emotions are physiological responses in the body that will arise and dissolve). Just as happiness triggered by external events doesn't last, negative emotions also don't last. Have you heard of the ninety-second rule? Neuroscientist Jill Bolte Taylor reveals that all emotions have a beginning, middle, and end—all within ninety seconds from when they first arise.[47]

47 Jill Bolte Taylor. *My Stroke of Insight: A Brain Scientist's Personal Journey* (New York: Viking, 2008).

The reason we continue to experience negative emotions, sometimes for days, weeks, and even years, is that we continue to fuel these feelings with our narratives. Instead, if we stop and let the emotion move through our body, we'll create space in our minds to better understand what they are trying to tell us. Remember the purpose of different emotions in Skill Chapter 3 on curiosity? Rather than suppressing or using positive thinking to bypass our experience, we can form an alliance with our feelings. By doing this, we can uncover how they're trying to protect us, address our unmet needs, or draw our attention to new information in the environment.

The ninety-second rule is a helpful reminder to ride the waves of our emotions, but emotions can sometimes be so powerful that they hijack our rational thought processes. It's helpful in these situations to remember where those emotions come from—deep in the past, when we were hunter-gatherers facing real tigers!

GEEK OUT!
The Dangers of Suppressing Emotions!

A 2013 study showed that people who bottled up emotions increased their chance of premature death by more than 30 percent and being diagnosed with cancer by 70 percent.[48]

48 Benjamin P. Chapman, Kevin Fiscella, Ichiro Kawachi, Paul Duberstein, and Peter Muennig. "Emotion Suppression and Mortality Risk over a 12-Year Follow-Up." *Journal of Psychosomatic Research* 75, no. 4 (October 2013): 381–385. doi: 10.1016/j.jpsychores.2013.07.014.

Remember: There Are No Tigers!

Between stimulus and response, there is a space. In that space is our power to choose our response. In our response lies our growth and our freedom.
—Attributed to Viktor E. Frankl

Inner calm is the space between the stimulus and our response. When we encounter a trigger, this space diminishes. For instance, when someone challenges us publicly, it's no surprise that our instinctive reaction can take over. We may experience physical signs—our body tenses up, maybe our face flushes red, or our chest tightens. Our mind races with unhelpful narratives about the person who is criticizing us, such as, *She is out to get me. I can't believe she's doing this again. She doesn't know what she's saying.*

The momentum of habitual reactivity, like a wild horse, runs amok. We don't have any choice at the moment other than to keep going wherever that energy's taking us. We're likely to get defensive and start justifying our actions instead of being curious about the other person's point of view. As we probably know, it almost never ends well for anyone involved.

This condition, in which our emotions are triggered such that we can't think or see clearly, is called an "amygdala hijack"—a term popularized by emotional intelligence expert Daniel Goleman. The amygdala is the emotional center of the brain. One of its functions is to scan the environment for threats and prepare the body for an emergency response. When it perceives a threat, such as a tiger lurking in the bushes, it sends an immediate signal to release stress hormones—adrenaline and cortisol—that ramp up an emergency response. Blood stops flowing to the organs and instead floods into the limbs to prepare us for fight or flight. Meanwhile, the prefrontal cortex (which is responsible for thinking and executive decision-making) shuts down because there is no time to think and analyze when we're facing what the brain perceives as a life-threatening situation.

So much of our lives are marked by perceived threats to our identity, career, or relationships. Our primal reactions—fight-flight-freeze—may have been beneficial in the face of a tiger. They can be unhelpful when it comes to navigating these everyday psychological and social stressors. What's needed to resolve problems common to the modern world is clarity and creativity, but our reaction is the opposite—to fight, flee, or freeze. This evolutionary response to any threat is automatic and unconscious.

During an amygdala hijack, it is said that our IQ temporarily drops by ten to fifteen points. Maybe this explains that feeling after we've reacted to a verbal trigger: *What was I thinking when I said that?* That's exactly the point. We stop thinking rationally. It also compromises memory, which is why we can't remember a single good thing about a person with whom we have a conflict or why we can't find our keys in the middle of a panic attack. Being in a continuous state of fight or flight from modern threats also compromises the integrity of other systems, like immunity and digestion.

Cultivating inner calm is an important step in avoiding the amygdala hijack so we can think clearly even in highly charged situations. Using practices to promote inner calm—like breath awareness—helps slow our escalating emotions and allows the parasympathetic nervous system to kick back in so we can once again think clearly. Another activity that nudges the prefrontal cortex to start thinking again is "noting" or "labeling." The act of noting or labeling our emotions gets the prefrontal cortex to regain healthy communication with the amygdala and avoids the hijack. Inner calm offers opportunities to learn and improve or for us to provide a deeper understanding of the "what" and the "why" behind our actions. We can replace tension and misunderstanding with harmony and understanding. Inner calm is key for resilience in relationships and life in general.

A Foundation for Resilience

Inner calm is a foundation for resilience. Resilience may conjure up images of toughing it out and going nonstop until we reach our goals. Yet, resilience has more to do with how we stop and recover rather than pushing through despite exhaustion. In their 2016 *Harvard Business Review* article "Resilience Is About How You Recharge, Not How You Endure," best-selling authors Shawn Achor and Michelle Gielan explain that "the key to resilience is trying really hard, then stopping, recovering, and then trying again."

We need to develop habits of self-care on a regular basis so that we can rely on our ability to engage our emotions and respond in a balanced and imaginative manner when we're stressed. It's common among successful executives to have worked nonstop in their earlier years and experience burnout in their middle years.

For instance, Chris, a managing partner in an insurance company, observed that she was getting more easily triggered in meetings than she had when she was younger. She realized that while she took care of her two kids, drove them to their soccer and football practices, planned their meals with her stay-at-home husband, and managed her business in a competitive environment, she didn't take care of herself. A decade of ignoring her needs depleted her inner resources to deal with even the slightest triggers at work. Learning to rest with meditation and gardening helped her replenish her inner resources on a daily basis so she could access inner calm on demand (even in the middle of heated discussions at work). Slowing down to restore our resources is essential to thriving in a modern world.

Slow and Steady Wins the Race

Slow and steady may not be sexy, but it's the way to sustainable growth, especially in a fast-changing world. Many successful executives and professionals, sent to me by their doctors and therapists, are worried that mindfulness will dull their adrenaline-fueled drive and creativity. In fact, that's a major reason for the failure of the world-famous Mindfulness-Based Stress Reduction program at Google.

In a conversation with Mirabai Bush, a mentor of mine and consultant for Google, I learned about some Google engineers' reluctance to let go of stress. They thrived on being stressed, which to them was a source of their creative edge. Interestingly, many of my senior executive clients share a similar sentiment: *I don't want inner calm. I love being stressed. It's what keeps me going.*

However, it's important to understand the effects of stress on our bodies. The stress hormones—adrenaline and cortisol—may provide a burst of energy and focus to deal with a crisis. However, they also elevate heart rate, blood pressure, and sugars in the bloodstream, disrupting the body's natural balance. Once the threat has passed, our hormone levels should return to normal, allowing other bodily functions like digestion and immunity to resume regular activity.

However, a constant state of high stress overexposes us to the stress hormones that disrupt the body's healthy functioning. This puts us at increased risk of many health problems, including anxiety, depression, digestive issues, heart disease, sleep disruption, and weight gain. Adrenaline-driven energy is not sustainable. Sure, stress hormones provide bursts of energy at times— even necessary ones—but you shouldn't rely on them day after day. Give yourself a chance to rest and recharge too.

As leaders, we often overlook the immense value of our inner calm. It is with a calm mind and body that we find the clarity and creativity necessary to effectively tackle both mundane tasks and challenging projects. Contrary to popular belief, embracing inner calm does not mean sacrificing energy or enthusiasm; rather, it enables us to maintain a balanced approach without succumbing to the chaotic rush of adrenaline. Moreover, cultivating inner calm strengthens our capacity for endurance and perseverance, essential qualities for navigating the ever-changing landscape of our world. With a calm and clear mind, we are better equipped to navigate the various challenges we encounter—be it boredom, tedium, resistance, opposition, or any other obstacle hindering our progress toward achieving our individual and collective goals.

Where Are You on the Inner Calm Continuum?

Based on the free online assessment or your reflection, if your inner-calm rating is low, you may get reactive when things don't go as you expected. Continue with self-compassion practices and use the following daily practices and mantras to explore your patterns of reactivity. What are the causes and conditions that promote calm, and what stops you from being calm?

A high score on the inner-calm continuum indicates that you are able to accept life's events without resisting or grasping them. You can be content even when things are not going your way. However, inner calm can be misappropriated by complacency. What may appear as inner calm can be a lack of motivation to bring desirable changes, in which case you'll benefit from cultivating more energizing mindfulness skills such as curiosity (Skill Chapter 3), energy (Skill Chapter 4), and appreciative joy (Skill Chapter 5).

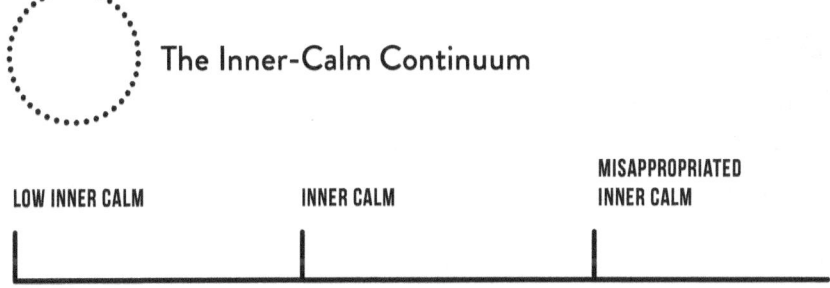

The Inner-Calm Continuum

LOW INNER CALM	INNER CALM	MISAPPROPRIATED INNER CALM
Tendency to:	**Tendency to:**	**Tendency to:**
• Be reactive	• Regulate reactivity	• Be complacent
• Hold on to attachments, which causes reactivity	• Disrupt holding on to attachments, which leads to ease and clarity	• Stay calm on the surface, while holding on to attachments
• Activate sympathetic reaction (fight-flight-freeze), which suppresses immune function	• Activate parasympathetic reaction (rest and digest), which supports immune system	• Suppress emotions, which negatively impacts the immune system
• Have increased cortisol and inflammatory response in the body	• Have lower levels of cortisol and inflammatory response in the body*	• Suppress emotions, which increases the chance of premature death and cancer**

*   Melissa A. Rosenkranz, Antoine Lutz, David M. Perlman, David R.W. Bachhuber, Brianna S. Schuyler, Donal G. MacCoon, and Richard J. Davidson. "Reduced Stress and Inflammatory Responsiveness in Experienced Meditators Compared to a Matched Healthy Control Group." *Psychoneuroendocrinology* 68 (June 2016): 117–125. doi: 10.1016/j.psyneuen.2016.02.013.

** Chapman, Fiscella, Kawachi, Duberstein, and Muennig. "Emotion Suppression."

Return with Inner Calm

You can strengthen your ability for inner calm, regardless of your circumstances. First, pay attention to when you're calm and when you're not. Next, notice the causes and conditions that promote calm and what stops you from being calm. By cultivating a habit of calming the mind and body, you'll develop the ability to access this place more quickly and easily. Create your own ways to return to mindfulness with inner calm by choosing from a combination of dedicated practices and daily reminders.

DEDICATED PRACTICE

All meditations that entail stopping and stabilizing the mind on a single point, like the breath, body, and feet while walking, or specific phrases, can develop inner calm. Just the act of stopping can help you see the ways you're feeding your restlessness and agitation. Stopping can also help you to relax and heal. If you struggle with sitting still, you can try mindful walking as a practice to instill inner calm. Walking in nature has its benefits, but all you need is a few feet of space to walk, and you can do this practice anywhere.

Return. Start by finding a quiet place to walk where you will not be interrupted.

1. Turn your attention inward to your body, standing tall, dropping your shoulders back and down.
2. Give your full care and attention to the sensations in your feet. When they're planted firmly on the ground, and as you lift one foot and place it in front of the other, notice sensations of touch, pressure, balance, gravity, weight, lightness, and anything else you experience.
3. When you reach the end of your space, with intention, turn around and walk back to where you started.

Do this a couple of times and then check in with the quality of your breath, body, and mind.

Listen. Listen within to the wisdom of your body and your inner dialogue.

- *If you notice that your mind is rushing or reactive, ask yourself the question I heard mindfulness teacher Gil Fronsdal offer in a live session: "What is so important that I have to sacrifice my ease?"* This reminder is also helpful when you're on the go and filling your cup with small agitations all day long. For example, when you're stuck in traffic, your computer freezes, you can't find your glasses, your favorite cup breaks, or you experience other routine irritants in your day, stop and ask yourself, Is this important enough for me to sacrifice my ease?

- *What are the causes and conditions that promote inner calm and what gets in the way of inner calm so that you can skillfully address the cause?*

- *What is your intention for inner calm before you begin your projects or meetings? If it's helpful, check in with what you can let go of in order to proceed with ease and clarity.*

Begin. Before you begin a meeting or project, return to your insights and intentions related to inner calm. You can proactively replace your habit of reacting to "tigers" with habits of acting with reverence, inquiry, silence, moving mindfully, guarding your senses, and cultivating friendships (that support you in living and leading with inner calm and clarity).

Take time in your day, several times a day, if possible, to empty your cup and make space for ideas and inspiration. Practice and play with the daily mantras to strengthen your habit of inner calm. Also, deploy the reminders to bring a lens of inner calm to return to mindfulness throughout your day.

DAILY MANTRAS TO RETURN WITH INNER CALM

Practice and play with the chosen reminders for the day with the following intentions in mind: challenging your default habit of clinging to attachments that are getting in the way of living and leading successfully, taking the time to rest, and bringing the lens of inner calm to enhance clarity when making decisions that lead to personal fulfillment, effective leadership, and meaningful impact in your community.

I. Mantra for the Day: The Art of Stopping
Calming the momentum of habits

> A horse is galloping quickly on a village road. The man riding it
> seems to be in a hurry to get to somewhere important. A curious
> villager standing alongside the road shouts, "Where are you
> going?" The rider replies, "I don't know! Ask the horse!"
> —Thich Nhat Hanh[49]

The horse is symbolic of our habits that are a powerful force, often guiding us in directions we may not want to go. If we stop and ask ourselves what we're doing and why, we may be surprised by the extent to which our behaviors are driven by our habits. Even when we know that's the case, it's hard to stop that horse.

Left unchecked, our habits can take us away from what we care about. Silently repeating the mantra, especially in moments of transition, can help stop your default thinking, talking, and behaviors. Return to this reminder to stop, listen, and let go during transitions in your day or whenever you feel like your mind is spinning out of control, like when you're trying to sleep or find clarity in a complex situation.

Return. At this moment, just *stop*. Without judging, notice the momentum of your thoughts, actions, or emotions. Take three deep breaths intentionally.

Listen. Take a few moments to notice your default habits of rushing and reacting. Once you're still, listen within. What can you let go of that is getting in the way of your inner calm and clarity?

Begin. Once you are able to soften the grip of your habitual reactions, begin your response or activity with inner calm.

---

49 Thich Nhat Hanh. *The Heart of the Buddha's Teaching: Transforming Suffering into Peace, Joy, and Liberation* (New York: Broadway Books, 1998).

Practice the art of stopping as you transition from one activity to another or whenever you need it. Proceed with calm and clarity.

II. Mantra for the Day: One-Minute Rest
Time to empty the cup

> Rested, we care again for the right things and
> the right people in the right way.
> —David Whyte[50]

Take time in your day, several times a day, if possible, to empty your cup and make space for what matters. You can do this very quickly by checking in with your body. Any tension or tightness in the body is a clue that you're holding on to something that needs your loving attention. You can't let go without knowing what it is you're trying to let go. Just turning your attention to places you're holding tension can help you uncover the emotions and thoughts associated with that tension.

Once you can see the cause of your tension, you can figure out the solution. It's also clarifying to realign with your intentions as you're emptying your cup—what is it you're clearing the space for?

Return. Take a one-minute rest and return to your body. Rub the palms of your hand and place them on your eyes, allowing them to rest. Move your hands to your jawline, neck, shoulders, chest, or wherever feels good in your body.

Listen. Listen within. What can you let go of at this moment to make room for what matters?

---

50 David Whyte. *Consolations: The Solace, Nourishment and Underlying Meaning of Everyday Words* (Langley, WA: Many Rivers Press, 2021).

Begin. Begin your activities with a relaxed body and mind aligned with what matters.

Try practicing and playing with this reminder with your family, with team members, and in your community before beginning a meeting or activity together.

III. Mantra for the Day: Soften All that Is Rigid
Letting go of tension and resistance

Discomfort is inevitable, but resistance can be optional. In your day, you may experience ups and downs over which you have no control. However, you do have control over your response. Instead of letting the energy of habits overcome your reaction, remind yourself to *soften all that is rigid*—to relax any tension you're holding in the body and let go of any resistance to your present-moment experience. This creates space to see clearly and act intentionally. Silently repeat the mantra whenever you feel triggered or regularly throughout your day. This helps you let go of any tension or resistance you're unconsciously holding in your body.

Return. Return to your body, sitting or standing. Scan and relax any tension you may be holding in your body: eyes, jaw, shoulders, or anywhere else in the body.

Listen. Listen within. Is there a thought, belief, or emotion that needs attention? What are your intentions for this situation?

Begin. Before you begin any action or interaction, check in to see if you're holding any tension or resistance. Soften all that is rigid within you. Begin your activity or interaction with intention and insight.

Turn to this gentle reminder when you're unsettled by unanticipated events, such as traffic jams and road rage, or when you seek to release the ongoing stress of racing through life and the constant evolution of technology.

IV. Mantra for the Day: Inner Calm, Outer Calm
Inner calm in interpersonal relationships

Inner calm empowers us to be both authentic and in harmony with others. Authentic means that our inner thoughts, feelings, and beliefs are in alignment with what we're saying and doing. Our authentic presence builds trust and supports harmony despite our differences.

This is a perfect reminder to cultivate inner calm in general or to bring a clarifying lens to a situation involving others. Repeat the mantra silently throughout your day or when you need a reminder to show up authentically in difficult situations.

Return. Take three deep breaths to return to your body. Release any tension you don't need to hold.

Listen. Reconnect to what really matters to you in this situation. Listen within:

- *What is getting in the way of your inner calm—what need is not being met, or what in you is being threatened?*
- *What do you care about?*
- *What do others care about in this situation?*

Begin. Act from this place of care. Carry your calm and clarity into the world.

Repeat the mantra silently throughout your day or when you need a reminder to show up authentically in difficult situations. If we're looking to promote peace in our relationships and our communities, we have to start within—inner calm, outer calm.

V. Mantra for the Day: Keep It Simple
A calm and clear mind

Muddy water, let stand, becomes clear.
—Lao Tzu

Remind yourself that sometimes less really is more. Take a few moments to pause, reflect, and connect with what matters the most. This will lead you on your way to taking simple steps toward what's truly important—setting an intention for effortless progress.

Whether you're starting a project, writing a blog post, or planning an event, this is a reminder for people like me (who like to make everything more complex than it needs to be)—to keep it simple.

Return. Inhale. Exhale. Return to your breath moving in and out of your body. Feel the spaciousness in your mind and body. Visualize your thoughts settling like mud, the mind like clear water. Let go of default ways to approach the task at hand. Invite simplicity and clarity.

Listen. Connect to what's important. What's one simple step to move forward with ease?

Begin. Begin your task with intention, trusting in the wisdom of simplicity.

VI. Mantra for the Day: Discomfort Is a Guide
Discovering the gift in discomfort

Discomfort often arises when our beliefs or expectations clash with reality. Instead of simply resisting the pain or avoiding it altogether, approach these moments with greater attention and intention. Recall from Chapter 3, *what gets in the way is the way.*

When triggered, soften around your body, breath, and emotions. Notice any judgments and rigidity that you're holding within. Soften the grip of any expectations you may have for that situation. Open up to what discomfort might be guiding you toward—it could hold great gifts! Mary Oliver's poem "The Uses of Sorrow" encourages us to recognize the gift even in a "box full of darkness" given to us by someone we love, despite it not being obvious initially.

Return to this mantra in moments of discomfort in your day. View everyday triggers such as being stuck in traffic, losing your keys, or experiencing technology breakdowns as opportunities to explore with kindness the expectations or beliefs that keep you trapped in reactive responses.

Return. In moments of discomfort, choose a mindfulness practice that brings you ease—awareness of breath, a body scan, mindful walking, or mindful eating. Practice for a few minutes or until your mind settles down. Notice what you're feeling and the underlying thoughts, with kindness to yourself.

Listen. Once your mind, body, and heart are settled, listen within:

- *What are your beliefs and expectations underlying your discomfort?*
- *Can you step back to see a bigger picture of what else is possible beyond your immediate thoughts and beliefs?*
- *In that clearer seeing, are you able to also see gifts or opportunities to grow and connect?*

Begin. Integrate the insights and gifts of clarity into your day.

Take a Moment to Celebrate!

Savor the moments of inner calm in your day. Celebrate the steps you're taking to rest and empty your cup. Every time you let go of what's not serving you, you make room for what matters to you. And that is exactly what the next chapter on focus is about—discerning what is important and giving it your full attention. When you feel ready, proceed to focus.

Mindful Focus: noun

The capacity to zero in on what matters most with a sense of ease.

Focus disrupts our tendency to be distracted by returning to what's important in any given moment.

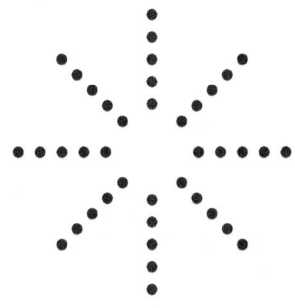

Skill Chapter 7

Focus

CHOOSE WHICH WOLF TO FEED

The power of presence means we are able to bring all four intelligences forward: mental, emotional, spiritual, and physical. Some individuals carry such presence that we identify them as charismatic or magnetic personalities. . . . When we choose to "show up" energetically, with all four intelligences, we express the power of presence.

—Angeles Arrien, *The Four-Fold Way: Walking* the *Paths of the Warrior, Teacher, Healer, and Visionary*

Before You Begin

Placing your hand on your chest, take a few breaths to invite your mind to be here with your body.

Reconnect with your intention for fostering focus in your life.

As you read this chapter, practice and play with the idea of being present with your four intelligences—mental, physical, emotional, and spiritual. Trust yourself to understand the significance of each of these, as we will explore them in greater detail later in the chapter.

As you read these words, your brain is inundated with a multitude of sensory stimuli, thought processes, and emotions. You're hearing sounds in your environment and within you. You're feeling the touch of your clothes on your skin and patterns of pressure where your body's making contact with the surface you're standing or sitting on. There's perhaps the taste of the last sip of coffee or bite from lunch lingering in your mouth. You're not only seeing the words on this page but also the spaces in between in the peripheral vision of things in your environment. As you swim in this sensory ocean, you're also making sense of these words and deciding how you feel about them. It's an endless stream of information that can easily overwhelm you if you were to process all of it at once.

Welcome to the seventh mindfulness skill: focus! Given the multitude of ways we can be pulled away from our present-moment experience, mindful focus is essential. It helps us stabilize our restless and distracted minds so we can return to mindfulness even in the middle of our busy lives. Focus dissolves our distractions, enabling us to attend to what's important—aligned with our values and intentions.

But our environments are bursting with information and stimulation; have you ever considered how your brain cleverly discerns what deserves your attention? Why do certain sights, sounds, or sensations pull us in?

This is where selective attention comes into play. I'm going to get a little geeky about this, but understanding how your brain prioritizes stimuli can empower you to regain control over your attention.

Selective Attention

Selective attention is the ability to prioritize and process specific information and block out the noise. This ability allows us, for instance, to focus on these words while suppressing other distracting sounds, sensations, and thoughts. This fundamental ability is linked to various cognitive skills—such as learning, working memory, and nonverbal intelligence—and academic achievement.[51] There are three well-known factors that the brain uses to prioritize what to focus on: (1) our goals, (2) salient environmental stimuli, and (3) selection and reward history.[52]

We consciously choose to focus on some things because they're aligned with our goals. For instance, reading this book cover to cover to strengthen mindful habits is a goal that signals the brain to focus on these words. However, there are times when our focus is interrupted without us actively choosing it—like when a loud crash interrupts us mid-thought. This category includes salient stimuli in our environment that hijack our attention because of the properties intrinsic to the stimuli—such as loud sound, sudden movement, a red item among green ones—and not our internal mental processes.

A third influence on the brain's decision to focus on certain information—that's unrelated to our current goals or the stimulus in our environment—is driven by the lingering effects of past selection episodes. For example, in the middle of reading this book, the thought of chocolate lava cake in your fridge might draw you away (which, FYI, I'd completely

---

51 Elif Isbell, Courtney Stevens, Eric Pakulak, Amanda Hampton Wray, Theodore A. Bell, and Helen J. Neville. "Neuroplasticity of Selective Attention: Research Foundations and Preliminary Evidence for a Gene by Intervention Interaction." *Proceedings of the National Academy of Sciences* 114, no. 35 (August 17, 2017): 9247–9254. doi: 10.1073/pnas.1707241114.

52 Edward Awh, Artem V. Belopolsky, and Jan Theeuwes. "Top-Down versus Bottom-Up Attentional Control: A Failed Theoretical Dichotomy." *Trends in Cognitive Sciences* 16, no. 8 (August 2012): 437–443. doi: 10.1016/j.tics.2012.06.010.

understand and not take personally). The driver of your attention, in this case, wouldn't be your current goals or salient stimuli in your immediate environment, but your memory of chocolate cake that was rewarding the last couple of times you ate it. If you choose to stay with reading instead of taking a break for cake (or any other distraction) what's the effort required to stay focused? Are you using willpower to keep the tantalizing thoughts of the cake at bay? What's the quality of your breath and body posture when you focus despite distractions?

When we focus, we tend to tighten our muscles or forehead and use up our limited cognitive resources to muster the willpower to stay focused. All of this can leave us depleted. Focus as a mindfulness skill is not just about paying attention but also intentionally choosing what to pay attention to and how to do so with minimal effort. Let's take a closer look.

Mindful Focus: The Power of Presence

Mindful focus is our innate capacity to zero in on what matters most with a sense of ease. Think of it as a superpower—you can direct your one-pointed attention to what's important in the middle of distractions. During meditation, we rest our attention on the breath, body sensations, or other selected objects of attention; this settling of the mind on a chosen object creates ease in the mind. The inner spaciousness makes room for what's important to be known and what's causing agitation also to be known—without needing to grasp or resist.

We can train our minds to evoke this quality of effortless focus throughout the day. However, what may feel relatively easy and even enjoyable during meditation may be quite daunting in our day. I can attest to that! I love the work that I do—creating customized mindfulness-based solutions for diverse clients, research projects to study mindfulness in marketing, and addressing my community's concerns as a town councilor. I also make time to meditate (of course), exercise, call my parents daily, and explore new experiences with my husband. It sounds like a perfect life on paper—and it is in so many ways for which I'm grateful—but this is only half the story.

The other half of the story that's taking place in my mind can get quite chaotic. My mind is always on: It likes to juggle between the ten open windows on my laptop as I rush to meet looming deadlines, while fighting the urge to resolve issues residents are complaining about but are beyond my town council responsibilities, and sporadically checking my Instagram for relief. Inviting mindful focus during my day is more than just giving my full attention to each activity. It is a challenge to maintain focus amid the busyness of everyday life, and it is also important to know what it entails.

THE FOUR INTELLIGENCES

Anthropologist Angeles Arrien describes the power of presence as an essential ability, especially in leaders. Angeles describes this as bringing all four intelligences forward—mental, emotional, spiritual, and physical.[53] When we show up in a way that what we're saying or doing matches our emotional tone, body language, and deepest aspirations and values, the outcome is fulfilling for all involved.

We recognize people who show up with their four intelligences unified as charismatic and captivating. On the flip side, when any of these four qualities are missing from how we show up, we are distracted, reactive, uncaring, and restless—qualities that don't inspire trust or loyalty in relationships.

For me, evoking the power of presence in my workday can look something like this: Even though my mind wants to rush forward to the next task, I take a momentary pause before beginning my next activity to return to my body, adjust my posture to how I want to show up, check in with the quality of my mind and realign with my intentions, listen within for anything that my busy mind may have missed, and then begin. On some days, I need to hit pause again and again. My mind is racing to juggle multiple responsibilities, and stopping to take a conscious breath and prioritize is very helpful.

When I approach my work—be it deskwork, meetings, or presentations—with the power of presence, I am at ease and effective. People hear me better, and I hear them. I'm able to stay with the ebbs and flows at

---

53 Angeles Arrien. *The Four-Fold Way: Walking the Paths of the Warrior, Teacher, Healer, and Visionary* (San Francisco: HarperOne, 1993).

work without losing focus on what's important. If you like, take a moment to see for yourself how the presence of the four intelligences impacts your present-moment experience. Besides bringing forth the four intelligences, mindful focus requires the right balance of effort and ease.

See for Yourself

Take a breath and exhale slowly, inviting your mind to be with your body. As you read these words, check in with yourself to see which intelligences you are bringing forward:

- Are you mentally present or distracted?
- Do you have physical composure, or is your body restless?
- What's the emotional quality of your presence—engaged, apathetic, or resistant?
- Are you reading this because you want to or because you feel you should?

Each of these four intelligences may be present in varying degrees at this moment. When you pay attention to them, you may also notice how the presence or absence of the four intelligences impacts your experience. Chances are, the more present you are in all four areas, the more fulfilling your experience will be, and the more effectively you'll be able to handle your responsibilities.

BALANCING EFFORT AND EASE

The word *focus* can conjure up an image of a cubicle worker with eyes glued to a computer screen and hunched over a keyboard that miraculously stays operational despite its user's ferocious one-hundred-words-a-minute typing rate. Perhaps you're picturing a basketball player on the free throw line, one swoosh away from sealing a championship game in overtime. But focus does not need to be this rigid or stressful. In fact, if you focus too hard, you may just hit the back of the rim on that championship-winning free throw. Focus too little, and you're thrown off by the cheering crowds. We need the right balance of effort and ease to hold something in focus.

Meditation isn't always easy. We know this. Our mind is so used to being stimulated that it can be uncomfortable to simply sit without the usual distractions. Additionally, our judgments and striving to still the mind can make it harder to focus. However, cultivating inner calm supports focus by strengthening our ability to let go of distractions and unnecessary striving. The invitation is to acknowledge when our minds are busy and gently return to what's important, as many times as necessary. While maintaining inner calm and focus does require practice, start small—just showing up in a posture that's easeful and alert is a good way to begin.

The next time you're meditating or concentrating at work, check in with your body. We often tense up when we focus—with furrowed brows, tight shoulders, and shallow breaths—without realizing it. Focusing with tension in our bodies is not sustainable. We can learn how to focus with greater ease instead of building up this unnecessary strain on ourselves. With training and practice, we can learn to focus with ease in the mind and body, even on shaky ground!

A STEADY MIND ON SHAKY GROUND

We can train ourselves to steady the mind and body, even when standing on shaky ground. I learned just how crucial this training is from an exhilarating experience at one of China's most iconic landmarks. Our guide decided that we were up for an adventure and took us off the beaten path to the Huanghuacheng section of the Great Wall—which was less restored than other parts but promised unique views. Navigating the unrestored parts of the Great Wall challenged my steadiness.

Without any warning, we found ourselves on a neglected part of the wall (generally recommended for experienced and sure-footed hikers, which I am not). Confronted with the steep and weathered narrow stairs—with four inches of width in some areas—I didn't think that I had much choice. I didn't want to be the only one staying back. I took a few deep breaths to calm my mind, which was freaking out (you can appreciate why we covered inner calm before focus). I then started my perilous journey with a laser-like focus as I traversed over loose rocks cascading down steep steps.

It felt like my life depended on every step—because it really did. In this way, I made it all the way up. I didn't look behind me even once. Coming down was a different kind of challenge, but by then, I had mastered my fear, using my breath to calm down and stay focused. In this experience, I clearly saw the value of a calm and concentrated mind in accomplishing goals, especially when walking on shaky ground.

Discern Which Wolf to Feed

My experience is what I agree to attend to.
—William James, *The Principles of Psychology*, 1890

The legendary psychologist William James said it more than a century ago: What we focus on becomes our reality. Our focus determines our experience, which influences what we feel, think, and choose to do or not do. The choices we make shape our lives. One could conclude the following:

Our Focus ⟶ The Life We Lead

This may be a simplistic conclusion because, in reality, there are many variables at play that impact our lives, but it doesn't take away from the fact that our focus matters more than we realize. The agency to choose what we pay attention to is essential to our well-being and accomplishment. However, our (over-)reliance on technology to meet all our needs—work, study, connect, shop, and entertain—has compromised our ability to focus on what is fulfilling. Rather than letting our history and environmental cues make decisions for us, we can regain our agency to focus on what's aligned with our intentions.

Have you heard the story of two wolves?[54] An old Cherokee chief told it to his grandson, and within this parable lies a valuable lesson about how we can take control of our lives. When we spend time focusing on thoughts or experiences that cause stress and suffering, they get ingrained in our minds; as such, they're more likely to color our experiences and be acted upon—ultimately promoting behaviors that aren't helpful for ourselves or those around us. Alternatively, when we focus on what promotes well-being for all involved, that becomes the inclination of the mind, and we're more likely to notice opportunities and act on them to promote well-being for all involved.

STORY

Which Wolf Are You Feeding?

An old Cherokee chief was teaching his grandson about life.

"A fight is going on inside me," he told the young boy. "A fight between two wolves.

"One is evil—full of anger, sorrow, regret, greed, self-pity, and false pride."

"The other is good—full of joy, peace, love, humility, kindness, and faith."

"This same fight is going on inside of you, grandson . . . and inside of every other person on the face of this earth."

The grandson ponders this for a moment and then asks, "Grandfather, which wolf will win?"

The old man smiled and simply said, "The one you feed."

In essence, the wisdom of the Cherokee chief, the Buddha, and distinguished psychologists like William James converge on a shared premise:

54 "Story of Two Wolves." Two Wolves Group, accessed 2023. http://www.twowolvesgroup.com /story-of-two-wolves/.

What we pay attention to grows stronger within us. We all have thoughts, memories, and experiences that leave us feeling hopeless, as well as those that are motivating and uplifting. We have limited brain resources for attention and action. What we choose to focus on determines our mindset, actions, and, indeed, our very lives.

This doesn't mean that if uncomfortable thoughts and emotions are emerging, we should not attend to them. Rather, the invitation is to approach our thoughts and experiences with compassion and curiosity, to uncover the root causes of our discomfort so we can address them. But if we observe that we tend to ruminate or let our emotions take over our experiences, we can learn to disrupt our defaults and incline the mind toward qualities that are skillful. Per the old Cherokee story, mindful focus helps us discern which wolf to feed by attending to the thoughts, people, and priorities that are fulfilling.

We all have within us two very different wolves: the critical one, which likes to remind us of our shortcomings and weaknesses, and the mindful one, which puts things in perspective and empowers us to make intentional choices. On days when I'm feeling tired or overwhelmed, my critical wolf will try to get a foothold and remind me that English is not my first language and that my schooling in an Indian system didn't adequately equip me with the tools to write creatively. When I allow this critical wolf to take over, it can send me down a rabbit hole where I start believing what it says: "You know you're not good! Not your fault—but here you are five years later, still trying to finish the book. Even if you do finish, who's going to read it?"

But thankfully, there's another wolf inside of us—the mindful one, which reminds us to step back and see the big picture, which also includes our intentions and strengths. This wolf sometimes speaks more quietly than its counterpart, but it carries with it our strengths of inner knowledge, perseverance, imagination, creativity, talents, and abilities: all the things that are needed to reach our goals.

The mindful wolf reminds me that while I may not have grown up with strong writing skills, a top marketing journal did publish my dissertation and a paper on mindfulness for which I was the lead author. The latter even received the American Marketing Association's best paper award in the public policy and marketing journal for its impact over three years. My writing is already making a difference in deepening my understanding of how I practice and teach mindfulness. My family and friends, my clients, and I are already better off because of this writing. Perhaps most importantly, I care about what I do, and it is in service of the greater good.

When I feed the mindful wolf, I am in touch with a lively stillness within me; I can approach writing with more ease and joy. I get more done on those days. During the writing of this book, I've had both wolves show up frequently. Now I recognize the wolves as they show up and only feed the mindful one. By focusing on my inner needs and priorities, I don't go down the rabbit hole of doubt and self-sabotage. Instead, I return to my inner knowing to discern what I need to support my writing—reaching out for help or focusing on my writing or something else.

You may recognize these two wolves in yourself and discover that one is more active than the other in different situations. Depending on which wolf you're feeding, you'll focus on different pieces of information that will push you to react in a particular way. For example, let's say you have a challenging encounter with a client. At that moment, if you feed the wolf that's angry and frustrated, you're more likely to notice all that's wrong with the client (not only what you experienced in the present encounter but also drawn from only those memories that support your narrative about the client).

If you instead choose to feed the mindful wolf, you may acknowledge your frustration but also stay open to what might be going on for the client to act in a disagreeable way. When you bring a lens of empathy and curiosity to your current encounter, you're more likely to pick up on pieces of information that completely shift your experience. You may realize that the client is not being dismissive or condescending but is concerned about her investment, or she is overwhelmed and reacting from a place of desperation. What you choose to focus on becomes your experience with the client, just as William James suggested.

To summarize the essence of mindful focus in world-renowned psychologist Amishi Jha's words from her 2021 book *Peak Mind*, "Attention is powerful. Attention is vulnerable. Attention is trainable." Before we go into looking at ways to strengthen focus, take a moment to contemplate your tendencies along the continuum for focus.

Where Are You on the Mindful Focus Continuum?

If you got a high score on the mindfulness assessment, it means you can give your full attention to the activity you're engaged in. When misappropriated, focus can mean you get myopic or obsessive, which leaves little room for new perspectives and possibilities. Excessive focus can also manifest in the body in the form of tightness, tension, and rigidity. For instance, you may notice that when you're focusing, you scrunch your forehead, lean forward, and tighten your chest or abdomen. Balance excessive focus with more open awareness and any of the energizing mindfulness skills: curiosity, energy, or appreciative joy.

GEEK OUT!

Shocking Facts About Focus!

- Sixty-seven percent of men and 25 percent of women chose to give themselves a mild electric shock[55] rather than sit quietly without any devices and distractions.
- Almost 50 percent of the time, the mind wanders away from the task at hand.
- Mindfulness practitioners use up fewer brain resources in performing attentional tasks.

A low level of focus means you may find it hard to pay attention to what you're doing and probably enjoy multitasking, which impacts productivity.[56] Every time we switch from one task to another, we lose our momentum and efficiency. However, you know yourself best. As with everything else, the practice of returning is not dogmatic. Neither is it

---

55 Nadia Whitehead. "People Would Rather Be Electrically Shocked than Left Alone with Their Thoughts." Science.org, July 3, 2014. https://www.science.org/content/article/people-would -rather-be-electrically-shocked-left-alone-their-thoughts-rev2.

56 American Psychological Association. "Multitasking," March 20, 2006.

suggesting that you never multitask. Rather, the invitation is to see for yourself whether you've relinquished your attention to the seductive powers of technology and other distractions. Or are you willfully choosing where your attention goes?

The important thing is that you have agency when it comes to the quality of your mind. Use the following daily practices and reminders to see what helps you regain control over your attention to focus on your priorities with spaciousness and ease.

Use the following table to recognize where you stand on the continuum for focus.

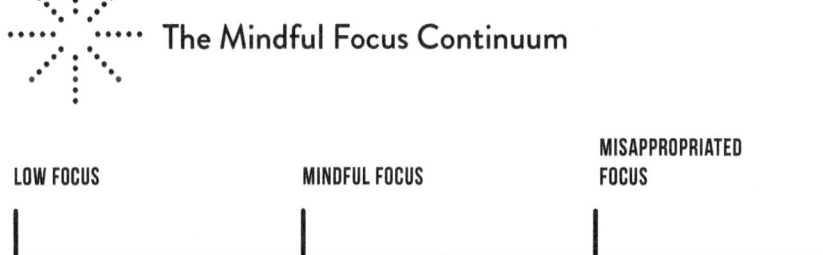 The Mindful Focus Continuum

LOW FOCUS	MINDFUL FOCUS	MISAPPROPRIATED FOCUS
Tendency to:	Tendency to:	Tendency to:
• Be distracted	• Be able to pay attention to what matters	• Be myopic
• Put in too little effort to focus	• Focus in a relaxed way	• Put in too much effort to focus
• Use up more brain resources to control a distracted mind than mindful focus	• Use up less brain resources to pay attention	• Use more brain resources than mindful focus
• Lack one or more intelligences	• Bring forward four intelligences: mental, emotional, physical, and spiritual	• Mostly bring forward mental intelligence

Return with Focus

The general instructions for returning to mindfulness with focus are to notice when you are focused and when you're not. When not focused, contemplate causes and conditions for lack of focus and what's necessary to be focused. When focused, contemplate how to continue to strengthen it.

The key to staying focused on what matters in the real world is *Sila*—a Pali (the local language in which the Buddha taught) term for skillful habits or discipline over our thoughts, speech, and actions. What we do in our lives affects our state of mind. For example, when we are unskillful in our speech or actions, we may experience guilt, shame, or remorse. A mind that is occupied with remorse cannot focus on the present moment. On the other hand, when we engage in skillful actions—those that don't cause harm and promote well-being—we feel at ease. When our minds and hearts are composed, it is easier to develop focus.

Find your own way to strengthen your ability to be present for what matters most with a combination of the dedicated practices and mantras.

DEDICATED PRACTICE

Focus can be developed by training the mind to settle on a single object like breath, body, or wholesome qualities such as loving-kindness, compassion, appreciative joy, and equanimity. And that same focused attention can be applied in moments of change—maybe it's the arising and dissolving sounds or thoughts—so you may gain insight from them too.

Return. As you practice this way of being mindful of objects, both stationary and changing alike, you can open yourself up to profound insights. Let's say you choose to focus on sounds in your environment. If you're in a relatively quiet room, at first, you may not hear anything. Or if you're in a noisy environment, your attention may be drawn to the louder sounds of the cars driving on the road, people talking, or the television playing in another room.

Once you stabilize your attention, you will start to notice many more sounds—a clock ticking, the quiet humming of the refrigerator or cooling system, the wind blowing, your heartbeat, and so on. As you continue to focus, you may start to notice the arising, changing, and dissolving of sounds. With deeper observation, without pushing, pulling, or running in circles, you can experience for yourself the truth about impermanence—nothing lasts forever.

Listen. The observation of changing sounds can lead to insights into your relationship with change—do you resist change, especially when it threatens your desired status quo? Are you striving for change that will lead to a desirable outcome?

This exercise is one example of pausing not only to observe but also to gain insight into patterns emerging from how you think and respond when faced with both desirable and undesirable changes alike.

Begin. Before you begin activities or interactions today, invite the power of your presence that is steady in an unsteady world.

You can practice with any object to focus on. And just as importantly, repeat the daily mantras throughout your day based on what you need most, or pick one randomly and trust that that's the mindful focus you need to bring to your situation.

 **DAILY MANTRAS TO RETURN WITH FOCUS**

Practice and play with the chosen reminders for the day with the following intentions in mind: disrupting your default habit of living and leading with a distracted mind, bringing the power of your presence in all actions and interactions, and discerning what's most important for personal fulfillment, aligned with your values and priorities as a leader, and essential to work together for the greater good.

I. Mantra for the Day: The Power of Presence
Aligning the four intelligences

Our presence is palpable when our four intelligences—physical, emotional, mental, and spiritual—are aligned. Attending to your work and relationships with the four intelligences will not only allow you to get more done with ease but also inspire an environment of calm focus and creativity. On the other hand, a frenzied mind can have rippling effects, including chaos and lack of trust, and can become completely overwhelming.

Pause before commencing work and interactions to unify the four intelligences.

Return. Bring attention to your physical body sitting or standing, tall and relaxed. Connect with what's important right now. Allow your whole heart and mind to align with your body and intentions.

Listen. Pause and listen within:

- *Is my body relaxed and alert?*
- *Am I mentally present?*
- *What's the quality of my emotions?*
- *Am I aligned with what matters to me?*

Begin. Bring the power of your full presence into your next action or interaction.

Return to this mantra throughout your day, particularly when it matters, like before a presentation, solving a problem, starting a new habit, and attending a networking event.

II. Mantra for the Day: What You Focus on Grows
Shift focus to see opportunities

> My experience is what I agree to attend to.
> —William James

It can be so easy to get swept up by our default habits, despite our innate ability to be mindful. It's like a tug-of-war between two wolves inside us—one represents fear and reactivity, while the other stands for clarity and choice. Remembering this story, especially when you find yourself being triggered, serves as an invitation back to presence. Mindful focus provides clarity to make conscious choices that align more deeply with what is most essential.

This doesn't mean that you're avoiding looking at your unpleasant thoughts and feelings. Rather, the invitation is to approach each situation—pleasant, unpleasant, or neutral—through the lens of the mindful wolf and not feed the wolf that distorts your understanding and keeps you stuck in old patterns of reactivity.

Return. Notice something uncomfortable in the present moment. How does it affect your mind and body? Now, shift the lens you use to focus. Can you see a positive or an opportunity in the same situation?

Listen. Take a few moments to listen within.

- *What are the unmet needs underlying your reactivity?*
- *What is possible when you shift focus to see what's positive in this situation or use a more objective lens to view the situation?*
- *What are your values and intentions?*

Begin. Invite a mindful lens to align your thoughts, speech, and actions before you begin any action or interaction.

Before you begin conversations or activities today, notice opportunities to shift your focus to invite a mindful lens to view the situation. You can also practice and play with this reminder throughout your day to check in with your unconscious tendencies to feed the reactive wolf and instead feed your mindful wolf.

III. Mantra for the Day: Unclench the Mind
Focus with ease

Striving may feel productive, but we are more effective when we pursue our goals with a relaxed presence. When we let go of our attachment to possessions and opinions, it can help us become more effective by fostering a relaxed presence.

Unclench that mental fist and release all distractions and strivings so you can focus with ease. Return to this reminder when you feel restless, like before going to sleep or making an important decision. If you frequently experience mental tension and headaches, it's beneficial to revisit this reminder at regular intervals throughout your day.

Return. Inhale and tighten your hands into fists. As you exhale, release the fists intentionally and relax tension in the mind and body. Return to an upright and easeful posture. Repeat this a couple of times till you feel like you've released tension you don't need to hold on to in your mind and body.

Listen. Listen within. Are you holding on to anything that's preventing you from being present with ease?

Begin. Carry forward a relaxed focus into your next project or activity.

IV. Mantra for the Day: Give the Gift of Presence
Undivided attention in interactions

In this world of constant disruption and noise, your undivided and unconditional attention is a precious gift to the recipient of your attention. Being present in this way builds trust while also strengthening the connection you have with others. Remember this mantra when engaging meaningfully with both friends and colleagues alike!

Return. Breathe in, breathe out, intentionally. Soften your body and relax your mind. Align with the four intelligences—physical, mental, emotional, and spiritual. Then, give your full care and attention to the words, feelings, and body language of the person you're interacting with. Gently notice how it feels to give your attention to someone else. Can you also stay connected and be kind to yourself?

Listen. What do you notice when you give your undivided and unconditional attention to what's being said and to the nonverbal cues, like subtle shifts in body language or an emotional tone that transcends words? Trust yourself to listen and speak from a deeper place of inner knowing.

Begin. Before you begin interacting with others, remind yourself to give the gift of your full presence to the people you're interacting with.

V. Mantra for the Day: Just Three Breaths
Focus on what's important

When life feels like it's spinning out of control, use the power of your breath to ground and center yourself in this moment. With three intentional breaths, reconnect with what's most essential now—letting go of anything that stands in its way. This practice is particularly beneficial during moments of overwhelming stress or anxiety, helping you to prioritize your ever-growing list of tasks and responsibilities.

Return. Come to a relaxed and alert posture.

1. With the first breath, relax the body.
2. With the second breath, soften any tension in the mind.
3. With the third breath, ask yourself, "What is most important right now?"

Listen. Once the mind is stabilized, stay with the question "What is most important right now?" Listen within to answers that emerge. Listen within to your intentions, priorities, and possibilities to move forward with ease. Trust yourself. You will know what you need to focus on in the present moment. If you still feel like your mind is running in circles, jot down all the tasks and prioritize them based on your intentions and goals.

Begin. Proceed with trust and intentionality, returning to the breath to anchor in the present moment.

Prioritizing the items on your to-do list when they start to feel overwhelming is a great practice. Writing down what you need to accomplish and then practicing with the three breaths can help you disrupt the inner turmoil and see clearly what is important, urgent, and most aligned with your intentions and values.

VI. Mantra for the Day: Foster Focus
Strengthen focus with practice

Our ability to stay focused is like a muscle—it requires training and care in order to develop. The more you return to mindful focus in noncritical situations, the stronger your focus will become when facing important tasks or decisions. Through daily practices and reminders to practice throughout your day, you can train yourself to focus easily—allowing for an increased concentration level no matter what comes your way.

Return. Bring attention to your body sitting, standing, or walking. Settle into your body. Choose to stabilize your attention on your breath, a body sensation, or patterns of pressure in your feet.

Listen. Once your attention is stabilized, take a moment to assess the thoughts occupying your mind. Without judgment, discern what is urgent and what is a distraction. If the distracting thoughts aren't crucial, allow them to pass and refocus on your current task. If a distraction holds importance but isn't pressing, make a note of it for future reference. Invite your undivided attention to one task at a time.

Begin. Rinse and repeat three times today to foster focus on what's important.

Take a Moment to Celebrate!

I invite you to be present with your four intelligences—mental, physical, emotional, and spiritual—and congratulate yourself for being present for yourself and others in this precious life! Now you are ready to ride the waves of change with grace.

Equanimity: noun

The ability to discern which mindfulness skills are needed to accurately perceive our reality, thereby empowering us to act intentionally.

Equanimity disrupts our impulsivity by determining the necessary mindfulness skills to apply in any given situation.

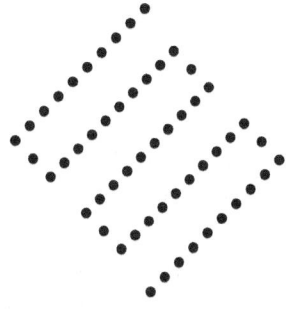

Skill Chapter 8

Equanimity

RIDE THE WAVES OF CHANGE WITH GRACE

When we are mindful, we are consciously aware of what is happening in our experience. Equanimity allows that awareness to be even and unbiased, so that we can make wise and loving choices.

—Mirabai Bush, from her memoir

Before You Begin

Congratulations on making it to the last chapter! Before you begin, take a few moments to return to your breath moving in and out of your chest, place a hand there, and connect with your intention for cultivating mindfulness skills.

As you read this chapter, the invitation is to be present to the words, listen within to what the words bring up for you, and stay open to any insights or steps you can take to be mindful in the real world.

Mindfulness is our innate capacity to see clearly and act intentionally. In moments that we let go of our distractions, resistance, and strivings, we automatically return to the lively stillness within us. However, it's normal to feel overwhelmed and discouraged when faced with the unexpected. That doesn't mean you've failed at being mindful. Experiencing difficult emotions, not knowing what's the correct course of action, yet still engaging with the situation without resisting or striving—this is mindfulness. What can help us ride the waves of change and challenges with grace is training in the last mindfulness skill: equanimity.

Imagine, for instance, a scenario where an unexpected mechanical delay on your flight threatens to derail a major meeting (feel free to replace this scenario with any other triggering situation). As you hear this, you immediately tense up, your heart starts to race, and you get angry. Frantic thoughts begin to circulate through your mind: *How could this happen? What an incompetent airline! I should have flown Delta! I'm going to miss the meeting! I'll let everyone down.*

Of course, because of your mindfulness training, your awareness kicks in, and you notice these thoughts. With a few breaths, you regain a sense of inner calm as you wait patiently to speak with the airline staff. However, within a few minutes, your mind veers off into the realm of worst-case scenarios: *The plane is indefinitely delayed. I'm gonna miss the meeting!* You quit the long line of people before the airline counter and find yourself pacing, having returned to the pattern of frustrated and frantic thinking.

In this scenario, you clearly tried to be mindful by bringing awareness to your experience and taking a few deep breaths to calm down, but the anxiety of missing one of the most important meetings of your life is overwhelming. Now this is a critical moment in being mindful in the real world. Most people at this point may conclude that mindfulness isn't working because they're still feeling anxious and can't see a solution in sight. Or they may settle for mindfulness to mean taking a few deep breaths to calm down. What they may not realize is that being with the discomfort of not knowing is also mindfulness; being with the messiness of your emotions is mindfulness. Don't stop now! In the middle of uncertainty and chaos, you can return to mindfulness with equanimity. Let's take a look at what equanimity looks like in everyday life.

Equanimity: Disrupt Impulsivity with Discernment

Equanimity is the ability to discern which mindfulness skills are needed to accurately perceive our reality, thereby empowering us to act intentionally. In any given situation, equanimity has the power to disrupt our biased impulsivity and infuse our awareness with the right combination of mindfulness skills to approach the situation with courage and care. Indeed, returning to mindfulness in the real world encompasses a range of skills—awareness, compassion, curiosity, energy, appreciative joy, inner calm, focus, and, ultimately, equanimity. In other words, for us to show up with equanimity under different circumstances, we need to strengthen the other seven mindfulness skills.

Joseph Goldstein defined equanimity at one of his talks as an evenness of mind or unshakable balance of mind. It seeks to prevent excess and deficiency of other mindfulness skills. In one of her talks, Rebecca Bradshaw—a mindfulness teacher also at the Insight Meditation Society in Barre—described equanimity in terms of poise and gracefulness in a world of change. She evokes the image of a mountain with its stability and ability to support so much weight. It is training the heart and mind to be so large that it can take everything with grace and balance. It enables us to stay in touch with reality and not be bound by it.

While equanimity is still and stable like the mountain, it is also flexible like bamboo. In fact, bamboo's strength lies in its flexibility. When confronted with challenges, we rigidly hold on to our default tendencies when acceptance and agility would serve us better. This is very similar to the serenity prayer: "May I have the serenity to accept the things I cannot change, the courage to change the things I can, and the wisdom to know the difference."

Returning to the scene of your delayed flight, let's take a look at what returning to your experience with equanimity might look like: You stabilize your mind with awareness of your breath and then shift your attention to sensations in your body, sounds in the airport, and your thoughts. You see your internal struggle caused by the rising emotions with self-compassion; you recognize this isn't your fault. *Sh*t happens!* You invite inner calm and see there are no real tigers. You don't have to fight your emotions. It's natural to feel stressed. Once you accept that, you can invite curiosity about the options available to you: What if there are other flights you could take? If you take another flight, would this airline give you a refund for their mistake? Can you Zoom into the meeting if there's no way to make it on time? Can you share your presentation and points with a colleague who can step in on your behalf? With a calm and clear mind, you can look at the options and choose what is most aligned with your intentions for that situation.

To return to the situation in a mindful way, every time your mind wants to revert to default reactions, you will need mindful energy. You may also invite some appreciative joy by acknowledging all that is going well, even in the middle of this difficult situation: Maybe a colleague steps in to present on your behalf, an airline employee figures out the right connection for you, even the fact that you're alive.

Equanimity allows you to remain unshaken by your circumstances and to invite the appropriate mindful lens to navigate the situation more skillfully. With equanimity, you can move through the frustration and panic stage and go right to seeing: what is present, what's possible, and what actions will be most helpful for everyone.

Again, reality may not be as straightforward as described in this example. Life can be messy, with high stakes and competing needs of those involved. It can feel excruciatingly uncomfortable to stay with the uncertainty of not knowing the right path forward. It's easy to settle for the familiar, even when it isn't what's best for us. But with equanimity, we are able to care deeply while still not being consumed by our hopes and fears. T. S. Eliot reminds us in his poignant poem "Ash Wednesday" that we need to learn to care and not care.

Unhook from Hopes and Fears

You may have heard this quote: "Train yourself to let go of everything you fear to lose." This isn't a quote from Buddha but from Yoda, the legendary Jedi Master from *Star Wars*. Arguably, the makers of this series were inspired by Buddhist teachings. Nevertheless, it may seem cooler to receive mindfulness teaching from a fictional green guru from *Star Wars* than an Indian philosopher who lived 2,500 years ago. The training that Yoda is referring to is the last mindfulness skill—equanimity.

Equanimity is the ability to ride the waves of change without attachment to what we hope for and what we fear. A useful taxonomy to examine our hopes and fears is found in the mindfulness teachings of the *eight worldly winds*: praise and blame, success and failure, pleasure and pain, and fame and disrepute.

We encounter stress and suffering when we get hooked or attached to our hopes and fears. Take our hopes for success and praise, for example. Success makes us feel good. We want to be successful at what we do. There's nothing wrong with that. However, success can also give rise to qualities—like arrogance, attachments, and expectations—that can impede our progress. Worse, they can derail us from our goals and lead us down paths we never intended to take.

Reflecting on my campaign for town council provides a valuable lesson for us all: If we're not vigilant, the energy of our hopes and fears can derail us from our values and intentions. My candidacy was one of high aspirations; I intended to use my mindfulness and research skills to create an environment where all members of our community could work together despite differences. People responded well to the opportunities I created for residents from across the political spectrum to meet all the candidates—I did this against the conventional wisdom of promoting only myself.

However, a few months in, as pressure increased leading up to Election Day, unbeknownst to me, winning elections started to take precedence over being service-oriented; anxiety began clouding my judgment. I noticed I was getting more easily triggered and reacting rather than responding intentionally. It was then that I stopped to return to mindfulness and saw the cause for my anxiety—I didn't want to lose. . . . I had invested so much time and energy into the campaign; I had to win! Thankfully, by pausing to reflect on my reactivity before making important decisions for the future, I got back on track. I realigned my thinking, speech, and decisions with the intentions and values that drove me to run for town council in the first place.

Similarly, fear of failure can also be a deterrent to our goals. We know that everyone goes through failure in life, yet most of us—consciously or unconsciously—fear failure. When we're trying to avoid failure, we're not fully present or giving 100 percent because a part of us is occupied by aversion to failure. When we over-identify with failure, we create feelings of self-doubt, inadequacies, and avoidances—all of which prevent us from seeing and seizing opportunities right in front of us.

Our hope for pleasure and fear of pain also lead to suffering. We know that all situations are impermanent. Yet, we get attached to pleasant events and want them to last longer—if not forever. I've often caught myself not enjoying what's happening—like eating my favorite dessert (you may have guessed it—chocolate lava cake!), a head massage, time with family in India, or a fun vacation—because I'm already anticipating its ending. It's worse when something bad happens, and we feel how unfair life is. Even something seemingly trivial, such as a flat tire at the end of the day, can feel so unfortunate. We resist reality. It's clearly happening, but we can hear ourselves saying, *No, this cannot be happening.* The mind is quite irrational at times.

The training to let go of everything you fear to lose begins with recognizing the presence of the eight worldly winds in any given situation. Sometimes, just seeing our hopes and fears weakens their grip on us, allowing us to return to mindfulness. But often, our attachment is too great to just let go. Consequently, we need to cultivate wisdom.

The Wisdom of Seeing that Sh*t Happens

Equanimity is the wisdom that comes from understanding that bad things just happen sometimes. As much as we may want to control every single aspect of our life, sometimes sh*t happens! But what makes us resilient in the face of such adversity is equanimity—the ability to pause, recognize our biases or preferences, and observe reality with a clear mind that is able to see the good and bad in every situation.

I had the opportunity to practice this teaching as I was writing this chapter. I'd left my family and friends in the United States to be with my aging parents in India over Christmas break. At the time, I was trying to meet a deadline to complete this book, and I got sick. First, it was some kind of viral flu, and then conjunctivitis (pink eye). Besides dealing with a headache and swollen eyes while trying to finish this chapter, I missed out on the season's festivities with my parents. I also couldn't spend much time with them for fear of transmitting the infection to them.

Remember the two wolves from Skill Chapter 7? If I focused on the negative wolf in me, I'd go into a spiral of self-pity—*I can't believe this is happening to my parents and me*—and that wouldn't have been helpful to me. My parents were already feeling terrible for me. The fact is that reality was bigger than my sickness at that moment. When I fed my mindful wolf, I was able to gain a bigger, more spacious view: *I'm able to travel to be with my parents, enjoy home-cooked meals, and write about stuff that I enjoy—while listening to epic music.* Life is so much better through the lens of equanimity.

Equanimity is the ability to see the reality of our experience in a deep and profound way. What weakens the grip of our hopes and fears is the wisdom that emerges from seeing the unreliability and "unsatisfactoriness" of all transient phenomena. When we recognize the constant flux of everything in our lives—including ourselves—we begin to see the point-lessness of depending on fleeting experiences for happiness. Our freedom and fulfillment lie in being able to live through every moment with an open heart—appreciating but not clinging to ephemeral pleasures such as tasty meals, time with friends, or success at work.

According to my teacher Joseph Goldstein, there are many stories in the Buddhist texts of people getting enlightened by hearing just this one teaching: "Whatever has the nature to arise will also pass away."[57] If our understanding of this teaching were complete, we would let go of all attachments automatically.

Tapping into appreciative joy also supports this teaching—our innate sense of well-being that is independent of the wavering worldly winds. Our deepest happiness lies in an unconditional acceptance of our changing circumstances.

Unexpected change causes resistance in most of us, even when it's minor—like having to take a new route because of a closed road, being forced to try a new breakfast cereal because your favorite cereal is out of stock or friends you wanted to meet at a networking event not showing up.

What if the unexpected change opened up new opportunities for joy, learning, and growth? Maybe you'd discover a more scenic route than your usual one, a tastier and healthier cereal than the one you grew up eating, and new opportunities you'd have missed out on if you stayed with your friends.

STORY
Good Luck, Bad Luck

In a small village lived an elderly farmer who owned a magnificent horse. This beast was not only the pride of his family but also their primary source of income. One day, in an unforeseen turn of events, the horse disappeared. Fellow villagers came to the elderly man, expressing their sympathy for this unfortunate incident that had befallen him. After all, the loss of the horse was a severe financial hit.

"Good luck, bad luck; who can tell?" was the man's calm response. "All I know is that my horse is no longer here."

The villagers, taken aback by his stoic acceptance of the apparent disaster, went back to their routines. Days later, the villagers were astounded to see the man's horse return, leading a group of twelve wild horses. They rushed to congratulate the man on his incredible fortune. He now had twelve additional horses, which could potentially multiply his income twelvefold!

57 Sounds True. "Deeper Dimensions of Mindfulness—Part 1," accessed 2023. https://www
    .resources.soundstrue.com/transcript/deeper-dimensions-of-mindfulness-part-1/.

"Good luck, bad luck; who can tell?" the elderly man echoed his previous sentiment. "What I see is that twelve additional horses have arrived."

The following week, as the elderly man's son was attempting to tame one of the new horses, he was thrown off and ended up with both his legs broken. The villagers gasped at the misfortune, wondering how the work would get done now that the son was incapacitated and the elderly man too aged to shoulder the burden alone.

"Good luck, bad luck; who can tell?" came the now familiar yet still perplexing reply from the elderly man. "What I know is that my son has broken his legs."

Not long after, the government forcefully evacuated all the able-bodied men from the village due to an outbreak of war. However, the elderly man's son was exempted from this fate due to his broken legs. Good luck, bad luck; who can tell?

The parable also illustrates the wisdom of knowing that we don't always know the big picture. How many of us can say that we'd have responded to the winds of change with equanimity, like the farmer?

See for Yourself

Take a moment to sit in an upright posture, allowing your body to relax into a comfortable position. Now, fold your arms in front of you in a natural way, paying attention to how this feels.

Once you get comfortable in this posture, slowly unfold your arms and then refold them, but this time in the opposite way. Notice any differences or sensations that arise. Does it feel unfamiliar or slightly uncomfortable? If yes, notice your resistance to this subtle change and your automatic reaction to discomfort.

continued

In my workshop, most people have a strong preference for one way of folding arms over the other. Even though this is such a minor change, it reveals to us the stickiness in our minds for what's familiar.

Remember, embracing change is not always easy, but by acknowledging our resistance and automatic reactions, we can cultivate a mindset that is more open and adaptable. So next time you encounter a change, big or small, take a moment to reflect on this exercise and remind yourself of the opportunities that lie beyond your comfort zone.

Participants in my workshop get to see for themselves how they respond to change with a simple exercise. Feel free to try this for yourself.

How did you respond to the shift? Perhaps the change requested in the exercise was manageable, and you adapted with ease. Now, can you recall a time when you faced more significant changes in your life or within your organization? Instances where difficult yet crucial transformations were required? Perhaps you were at the helm of this transformation? Could you or those you led manage to let go of deeply ingrained habits, traditional work methods, and loyalties? In the absence of awareness, it is easy to acquiesce to the many good reasons not to change that our minds will come up with, as our natural tendency is to resist unwanted change.

Conversely, when desired changes don't materialize as expected, it's natural to feel disappointed. Often, we're unable to let go of this disappointment, which then morphs into resentment or regret. However, staying level-headed and present in every situation can lead to unexpected opportunities—enabling us to discover something even better than what was originally planned. I'm reminded of my own story: Many years ago, after getting married, I quit my job and moved to a different state to be with my husband. I'd hoped that I'd get a similar academic position to the one I'd left behind, but I didn't. I spent a lot of time repenting my loss of academic identity and feared I'd never find a comparable job in the small college town I'd moved to.

It took me four years to stop and take a fresh look at my situation. On my forty-fourth birthday, I was driving on a sunny New England summer day when I returned to my inner wisdom with a question—what can I do with all my degrees when there are no jobs in the area? In response, my inner voice posed another question: *If you could do anything in the world, what would it be?* Though the question may sound like a well-worn cliché, the place it came from cracked open something in me, and I immediately knew the answer—mindfulness. In that instant, it became crystal clear that I wanted to teach mindfulness, not marketing. My inner voice responded, *Then go and do that!*

Letting go of my attachment to being only a business professor allowed space for new possibilities to pursue what was truly meaningful to me. My personal mindfulness practice had been deeply transformative for me, and I now wanted to share it with the world—specifically in business and education, as those were my areas of expertise. And just like that, returning to myself and listening within opened the most incredible path for me, which I am now sharing with you!

Equanimity in Relationships

Equanimity also cultivates our ability to be impartial and hold all equally—those who blame us and those who praise us. This is an important quality (especially for leaders) to create environments that feel safe and inclusive for everyone—even those who are hostile toward us. As you can imagine, this is not easy in the face of conflict and crisis. But by training in the different mindfulness skills, we can strengthen equanimity in relationships: Compassion teaches us to seek understanding and see our interbeing, curiosity nurtures friendliness and patience, appreciative joy invites us to see the good in everyone, inner calm trains us in letting go of our strong views, and with focus, we can zero in on what's most important and not get distracted by the drama—either our own or that of others.

Equanimity also applies to the people we care about. We want the best for them, and in the process, we can become controlling and demanding. A balanced mind recognizes that as much as we care about certain people, they have their own lives to lead. It is also about creating clear boundaries to not allow our agendas to control others' lives and to honor each person's individual journey as they deem best.

We can deeply love others and offer them assistance,
but in the end they must learn for themselves.
—Jack Kornfield[58]

Equanimity is a commitment to cultivate an accurate understanding of the situation and take skillful actions that are fair and equitable. Before you explore the daily practices and mantras, do you know where you stand on the equanimity continuum?

Where Are You on the Equanimity Continuum?

If you scored high on this skill in the mindfulness assessment, you are likely to be thoughtful and take your time before making decisions. A high equanimity score could also be indifference in disguise. When we speak of evenness of mind, it could be the result of not caring or withdrawal from difficult emotions. However, equanimity involves staying intimately connected with our emotions while not letting them take over. In difficult situations, equanimity is enhanced by other mindfulness skills—particularly awareness accompanied by compassion, curiosity, energy, appreciative joy, and inner calm.

If you scored low on this mindfulness skill, use the daily practices and mantras this week to stabilize the mind and create space around your decisions and interactions. The Equanimity Continuum table depicts a few of the tendencies related to equanimity when it is present and when it is low or misappropriated.

---

58 Jack Kornfield. "Meditation on Equanimity." JackKornfield.com, August 6, 2017. https://jack kornfield.com/meditation-equanimity/.

The Equanimity Continuum

LOW EQUANIMITY	EQUANIMITY	MISAPPROPRIATED EQUANIMITY

Tendency to:

- Be low on some or all mindfulness skills
- Be overly attached or controlling, indifferent, or hostile
- Experience extreme highs and lows and burnout

Tendency to:

- Discern which and how much of each mindfulness skill is needed
- Be balanced and fair in relationships
- Feel resilient and fulfilled

Tendency to:

- Have mindfulness skills misappropriated, like inner calm misappropriated by indifference
- Be indifferent or avoidant of difficult interactions
- Feel disconnected and depressed

Return with Equanimity

Equanimity is strengthened by fostering the other seven mindful habits. The following dedicated practices and mantras are based on the earlier practices. However, one practice unique to equanimity is described in more detail.

DEDICATED PRACTICE

Pick a dedicated practice to strengthen any of the mindfulness skills, aiming to restore your unshakeable and balanced mindset. There is one practice that is unique to bringing equanimity to relationships. This involves an impartial holding of all people equally. It can be cultivated with the practice of repeating the following phrases (or any other phrases that resonate with you personally) to see the wisdom in letting go of attachments and a desire to control other people's lives. This practice acknowledges that every individual is accountable for their own actions, and their happiness hinges on their deeds and actions.

Return. Steady your mind and body by directing your attention to your body, breath, and mind.

1. Return to your body, sitting or standing—stable and strong like a mountain.
2. Return to your breath—moving naturally and effortlessly like the wind.
3. Return to your mind—where thoughts come and go like clouds in a vast sky.

After stabilizing the mind, offer these or other phrases to people in your life as you feel appropriate, like we did for our compassion practice. You can start with a neutral person, a person you have difficulty with, people whom you care for, and beyond to individuals and groups you don't know. You can even offer these phrases to yourself to return to the present moment with equanimity. Silently repeat these phrases with kindness:

1. Your happiness and suffering depend on your thoughts and actions and not my wishes for you.
2. May you have the awareness to see the arising and passing of all things with equanimity.
3. May you have balance and ease in your life.

Listen. After repeating the phrases a couple of times, take a few minutes to listen to what's arising within you. Notice how offering these phrases to different people evokes different experiences within you. Here are suggested questions for reflection:

- *What supports you in being impartial and fair toward all people?*
- *What gets in the way of showing up with unconditional acceptance for people who praise you and blame you?*

- *What are you holding on to that prevents you from being balanced in relationships?*

Begin. Before you enter any interaction or in the middle of difficult conversations, return to the present moment with equanimity. Repeat this mantra to separate yourself from your emotions: *You are the heir of your actions. Your happiness and suffering depend on your thoughts and actions and not my wishes for you.* Proceed with equanimity . . .

DAILY MANTRAS TO RETURN WITH EQUANIMITY

Practice and play with the chosen reminders for the day with the following intentions in mind: disrupting your default habit of living and leading with impulsivity, returning to the unshakable quality of your mind, meeting the waves of change with grace, and discerning which mindfulness skills you need to make decisions that promote personal fulfillment, effective leadership, and global impact.

I. Mantra for the Day: Steady as a Mountain
Return to the unshakable quality of your mind

Things are always changing. With practice, your steady awareness can become a refuge. You can return to this mantra just to strengthen the unshakable quality of your mind or when you find yourself in a difficult situation. You could play with this mantra during a happy situation as well. This is a great reminder to return to the unchanging and resilient qualities of your mind that can offer stability in the middle of uncertainty and change.

Return. Observe a changing phenomenon: breath, sensation, sounds, and so on. Notice the changes present at the beginning, middle, and end of the experience. As feelings and thoughts come and go, rest in the steadiness of your awareness, which is unchanging, stable, and timeless like a mountain.

Listen. Once your mind is stabilized, apply the lens of equanimity to view your situation.

- *What do you see when your mind is able to be present with an unwavering quality?*
- *What can you let go of, even if only for a moment, to return to a steady mind?*
- *How does your reality shift when you bring a steady mind to see the big picture?*

Begin. Align your thoughts, speech, and actions with a steady mind before responding or taking any action.

Return to this steadiness before you begin any action or interaction in your day.

II. Mantra for the Day: Sh∗t Happens!
Moving from resistance to acceptance and action

Resistance and denial are natural responses to change. With practice, we can train the mind to move through our resistance and frustration toward acceptance and action. Return to this mantra when you meet obstacles or things don't go as you expected.

Return. Take three breaths to return to your body. Stabilize your mind on your breath, moving effortlessly in and out of your body. Acknowledge any resistance and remind yourself, *Sh*t happens!*

Listen. Listen to what's emerging in you. Then ask yourself these questions:

- *What's here?*
- *What's important?*
- *What's possible?*

Begin. Let the clarity of seeing things as they are, creative possibilities, and your intentions guide your next step. Be kind to yourself—the more you practice, the easier it becomes!

Return to the wisdom of seeing that sh*t happens. It is unrealistic to expect that life will always unfold exactly the way we'd like it to. Instead, connect with what's important, what's possible, and what's one small step you can take that's aligned with your intentions and values.

III. Mantra for the Day: The Third Way!
Make room for creative thinking

When things seem black and white, there is usually room for gray. What's the third way? Practice and play with this mantra in noncritical situations so you're able to access creative ease in difficult situations. Return to this mantra when you feel stuck in an either-or situation or intentionally bring to mind an either-or situation. For example, for breakfast, should I eat oatmeal or eggs? Should I skip the party or go, even though I don't want to? An example from Skill Chapter 3 on curiosity—should the town council impose a moratorium on large-scale solar or not? The practice is to let go of your assumptions and impulsivity and make room for many imperfect ideas and possibilities.

Return. Breathe in and make a tight fist. As you exhale, unclench your fist. Repeat this a couple of times until you feel your mind and body are spacious.

Listen. Consider both possibilities without resisting or grasping. Listen within for the third way! Make a list of all other possibilities emerging in that space of nonattachment. Don't limit yourself to only "good" ideas. Play with ideas and give yourself permission to include all kinds of solutions that could be a third way of resolving the solution. (Go back to the solar example in Skill Chapter 3 for the third way.) Trust yourself, and don't take yourself too seriously.

Begin. Based on your reflections, trust your inner knowing and begin— even if it's one small step in a direction that's aligned with your intentions.

IV. Mantra for the Day: Each on Our Own Path
Equanimity in interpersonal relationships

We can't control other people's happiness and destinies, but we can show up to support them. Return to this mantra when you want equanimity in relationships. This is a good reminder to return to an even mind that is unbiased toward those who praise and blame us.

Return. Place your hand on your chest to feel your beating heart. Once your mind is stabilized, bring to mind the person for whom you want to show up in a balanced way. Repeat the mantra: "You are accountable for your actions. Your happiness and suffering depend on your thoughts and actions and not my wishes for you."

Listen. Listen within:

- *What does the mantra bring up for you? Make space for thoughts and emotions to arise.*
- *Can you extend understanding and support while respecting their choices and unique journey?*
- *What are your intentions with respect to this person?*

Begin. Show up wholeheartedly for this person. Return to the wisdom of the mantra "each on their own path," and let it open new ways of interacting that are caring and carefree.

V. Mantra for the Day: Unhook Yourself
Get free from the things that control you

Train yourself to let go of everything you fear to lose.
—Yoda

It's easy to get hooked by the eight worldly winds: (a) praise or blame, (b) success or failure, (c) pleasure or pain, and (d) fame or disrepute. But inviting equanimity helps us recognize impermanence. Return to this mantra when you notice you're hooked by one of the worldly winds, or you can also return to it regularly to check in with the subtle ways that your hopes and fears are keeping you trapped.

Letting go of our hopes can feel scary and rudderless. As you consider letting go of the attachment to your hopes, align with your intentions and values. Your intentions can provide the inner compass even as you let go of all attachments. Let what you love and care about guide your actions and interactions.

Return. Give full care and attention to the sensations of your breathing body. Notice the impermanence of each breath. Check in; are you holding on to any of the eight worldly winds, (a) praise or blame, (b) success or failure, (c) pleasure or pain, or (d) fame or disrepute? See the impermanence of all phenomena.

Listen. Listen within to what remains after you let go of your hopes and fears. Are there opportunities for learning and growth?

Begin. Return to this wisdom before you begin any action and interaction to show up in a free and fearless way that is grounded by your intentions and values.

VI. Mantra for the Day: Vast as the Ocean
Begin all activities with a spacious mind

Waves come and go on the surface of the ocean. Its depths remain undisturbed. Return to this vast quality of mind, whether experiencing difficulty or ease.

Return. Rest in a mind that is vast, like the ocean. Let any thoughts and feelings arise and fall like ocean waves without disturbing the depth of your being.

Listen. How does touching this awareness change your experience? Listen within.

Begin. Return to the stillness and spaciousness of your mind—vast as the ocean—before you begin any activity today.

Take a Moment to Celebrate!

Congratulations on completing the magical and important journey of practicing and playing with the eight skills to return to mindfulness! The eight skills empower us to live, love, and lead with clarity and care. If we're looking for real-world change in and around us, the shift begins within. The eight mindfulness skills create a reliable and joyful path to return to the inner knowing that enables us to see clearly and act intentionally, regardless of the circumstances we find ourselves in. From this place of inner knowing, we can recognize ourselves and others as integral parts of an interconnected world, and collaborate for our mutual well-being. If this sounds too audacious of a goal, just know that every action you take to care for your mind, body, and spirit is already making the world better.

Take a few moments to acknowledge your commitment: You showed up to reading this book, didn't give up, and trusted yourself! This is a life-long practice. Feel free to revisit the dedicated practices and mantras or select the ones you wish to incorporate into your day. Or simply remind yourself to return, listen, and begin . . .

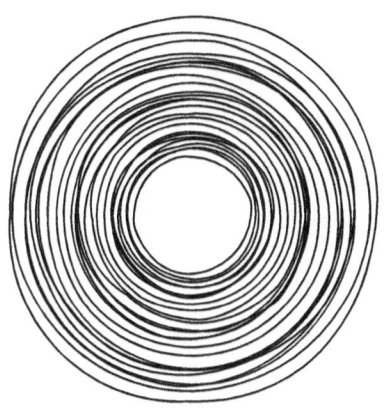

Part III

Acknowledgments and Resources

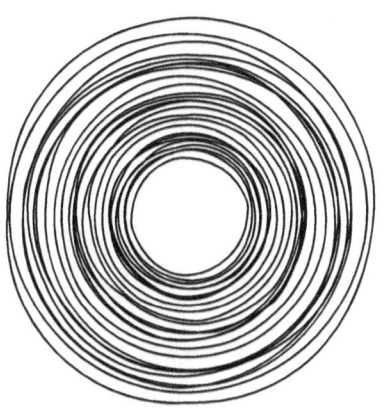

References

Part I
Chapter 1: A Wake-Up Call!

American Psychological Association. "Stress in America™ 2020: A National Mental Health Crisis." American Psychological Association, retrieved March 17, 2023. https://www.apa.org/news/press/releases/stress/2020/report-october.

Bahl, S., and G.R. Milne. "Talking to Ourselves: A Dialogical Exploration of Consumption Experiences." *Journal of Consumer Research* 37, no. 1 (2010): 176–195. https://doi.org/10.1086/650000.

Guterres, A. "Global Wake-Up Call," 2020. https://www.un.org/en/coronavirus/global-wake-call.

Michelman, P. "Can We End the Crisis of Agency?" *MIT Sloan Management Review*, September 18, 2019. https://sloanreview.mit.edu/article/can-we-end-the-crisis-of-agency/.

Reeves, Martin, and Lisanne Püschel. "Die Another Day: What Leaders Can Do About the Shrinking Life Expectancy of Corporations." Boston Consulting Group, December 2, 2015. https://www.bcg.com/publications/2015/strategy-die-another-day-what-leaders-can-do-about-the-shrinking-life-expectancy-of-corporations.

Shantideva, translated by Padmakara Translation Group. *The Way of the Bodhisattva* (Boston: Shambhala Publications, 2006). https://www.shambhala.com/the-way-of-the-bodhisattva-1660.html.

Welzel, C., and R. Inglehart. "Agency, Values, and Well-Being: A Human Development Model." *Social Indicators Research* 97 (2010): 43–63.

Zhexembayeva, N. "3 Things You're Getting Wrong About Organizational Change." *Harvard Business Review,* June 9, 2020.

Chapter 2: Mindfulness Is Easier than You Think

Bargh, J.A., and T.L. Chartrand. "The Unbearable Automaticity of Being." *American Psychologist* 54, no. 7 (1999): 462–479. https://doi.org/10.1037/0003-066X.54.7.462.

"Mind Wandering Is More than Just a Fault in the System." Max-Planck-Gesellschaft, April 12, 2017. https://www.mpg.de/11229713/mind-wandering.

Rumi, translated by Coleman Barks. *The Essential Rumi* (New York: HarperCollins, 2004).

Chapter 3: What Gets in the Way Is the Way

Chödrön, P. *When Things Fall Apart: Heart Advice for Difficult Times* (Boston: Shambhala Publications, 2000).

Chapter 4: A Roadmap for Real-World Mindfulness

Hesse, H., translated by Hilda Rosner. *Siddhartha: A Novel* (New York: Bantam, 1982).

Part II
Skill Chapter 1: Awareness

The Actualization Agent. "This Is Water! by David Foster Wallace." YouTube Video. December 15, 2013. https://www.youtube.com/watch?v=eC7xzavzEKY.

Arrien, A. Goodreads. https://www.goodreads.com/quotes/1204741-i-trust-the-mystery -i-trust-what-comes-in-silence.

Bargh, J.A., and T.L. Chartrand. "The Unbearable Automaticity of Being." *American Psychologist* 54, no. 7 (1999): 462–479. https://doi.org/10.1037/0003-066X.54.7.462.

Schooler, J.W., J. Smallwood, K. Christoff, T.C. Handy, E.D. Reichle, and M.A. Sayette. "Meta-Awareness, Perceptual Decoupling and the Wandering Mind." *Trends in Cognitive Sciences* 15, no. 7 (2011): 319–326. https://doi.org/10.1016/j.tics.2011.05.006.

Skill Chapter 2: Compassion

Klimecki, O.M., S. Leiberg, M. Ricard, and T. Singer. "Differential Pattern of Functional Brain Plasticity After Compassion and Empathy Training." *Social Cognitive and Affective Neuroscience* 9, no. 6 (2014): 873–879. https://doi.org/10.1093/scan/nst060.

Nhat Hanh, T. *Peace Is Every Step: The Path of Mindfulness in Everyday Life* (New York: Random House, 1995).

Nhat Hanh, T. "Please Call Me by My True Names." Plum Village: Thay's Poetry. https ://plumvillage.org/articles/please-call-me-by-my-true-names-song-poem/.

Strauss, C., B. Lever Taylor, J. Gu, W. Kuyken, R. Baer, F. Jones, and K. Cavanagh. "What Is Compassion and How Can We Measure It? A Review of Definitions and Measures." *Clinical Psychology Review* 47 (2016): 15–27. https://doi.org/10.1016/j.cpr.2016.05.004.

Travers, J. "Children, Ubuntu, and Interbeing." Parallax, 2016. https://www.parallax.org/mindfulnessbell/article/children-ubun-tu-and-interbeing/.

Vaughn, D.A., R.R. Savjani, M.S. Cohen, and D.M. Eagleman. "Empathic Neural Responses Predict Group Allegiance." *Frontiers in Human Neuroscience* 12 (2018): 302. https://doi.org/10.3389/fnhum.2018.00302.

Skill Chapter 3: Curiosity

Berger, W. "Why Curious People Are Destined for the C-Suite." *Harvard Business Review*, September 11, 2015. https://hbr.org/2015/09/why-curious-people-are-destined-for-the-c-suite.

Broockman, D., and J. Kalla. "Durably Reducing Transphobia: A Field Experiment on Door-to-Door Canvassing." *Science* 352, no. 6282 (2016): 220–224. https://doi.org/10.1126/science.aad9713.

Eurich, T. "What Self-Awareness Really Is (and How to Cultivate It)." *Harvard Business Review*, January 4, 2018. https://hbr.org/2018/01/what-self-awareness-really-is-and-how-to-cultivate-it.

Hsee, C.K., and B. Ruan. "The Pandora Effect: The Power and Peril of Curiosity." *Psychological Science* 27, no. 5 (2016): 659–666. https://doi.org/10.1177/0956797616631733.

Kidd, C., and B. Hayden. "The Psychology and Neuroscience of Curiosity." *Neuron* 88, no. 3 (2015): 449–460. https://doi.org/10.1016/j.neuron.2015.09.010.

People's Action. "How to Defeat Trump and Heal America." PeoplesAction.org, 2021. https://peoplesaction.org/wp-content/uploads/2020/09/PA-ReportDeepCanvassingResults09.14-FINAL.pdf.

Rilke, R. M., translated by M.D.H. Norton. *Letters to a Young Poet* (New York: Norton, 1993).

Roberts, J. "The Power of Patience: Teaching Students the Value of Deceleration and Immersive Attention." *Harvard Magazine*, 2013. https://www.harvardmagazine.com/2013/11/the-power-of-patience.

Rumi, translated by Coleman Barks. *The Illuminated Rumi* (New York: Harmony/Rodale, 1997).

Webster's 1913. "Curiosity." https://www.websters1913.com/words/Curiosity.

Skill Chapter 4: Energy

Baumeister, R.F., E. Bratslavsky, M. Muraven, and D.M. Tice. "Ego Depletion: Is the Active Self a Limited Resource?" *Journal of Personality and Social Psychology* 74, no. 5 (1998): 1252–1265. https://doi.org/10.1037/0022-3514.74.5.1252.

"Rumi." Goodreads. https://www.goodreads.com/author/show/875661.Rumi.

Ryan, R.M., and C. Frederick. "On Energy, Personality, and Health: Subjective Vitality as a Dynamic Reflection of Well-Being." *Journal of Personality* 65, no. 3 (1997): 529–565. https://doi.org/10.1111/j.1467-6494.1997.tb00326.x.

Seppälä, E. "Your High-Intensity Feelings May Be Tiring You Out." *Harvard Business Review*, February 1, 2016. https://hbr.org/2016/02/your-high-intensity-feelings-may-be-tiring-you-out.

Thayer, R. E. "Energy, Tiredness, and Tension Effects of a Sugar Snack versus Moderate Exercise." *Journal of Personality and Social Psychology* 52, no. 1 (1987): 119–125. https://doi.org/10.1037/0022-3514.52.1.119.

Thomson, P., and S.V. Jaque. *Creativity and the Performing Artist: Behind the Mask* (Cambridge, MA: Academic Press 2017).

Wedell-Wedellsborg, M. "How Women at the Top Can Renew Their Mental Energy." *Harvard Business Review*, April 16, 2018. https://hbr.org/2018/04/how-women-at-the-top-can-renew-their-mental-energy.

Skill Chapter 5: Appreciative Joy

Baumeister, R.F., E. Bratslavsky, C. Finkenauer, and K.D. Vohs. "Bad Is Stronger than Good." *Review of General Psychology* 5, no. 4 (2001): 323–370. https://doi.org/10.1037/1089-2680.5.4.323.

Bergeisen, M. "The Neuroscience of Happiness." *Greater Good Magazine*, September 22, 2010. https://greatergood.berkeley.edu/article/item/the_neuroscience_of_happiness.

Carter, K., and A. Hawkins. "Joy at Work: Creating a Culture of Resilience." *Nursing Management (Springhouse)* 50, no. 12 (December 2019). https://pubmed.ncbi.nlm.nih.gov/31764542/.

Cunningham, W.A., and T. Kirkland. "The Joyful, yet Balanced, Amygdala: Moderated Responses to Positive but Not Negative Stimuli in Trait Happiness." *Social Cognitive and Affective Neuroscience* 9, no. 6 (2013): 760–766. https://doi.org/10.1093/scan /nst045.

Eva, A. "How to Nurture Empathic Joy in Your Classroom." *Greater Good Magazine*, February 2, 2017. https://greatergood.berkeley.edu/article/item/how_to_nurture _empathic_joy_in_your_classroom.

Friedman, R. "Staying Motivated After a Major Achievement." *Harvard Business Review*, February 3, 2015. https://hbr.org/2015/02/staying-motivated-after-a-major -achievement.

Hanson, R. *Hardwiring Happiness: The New Brain Science of Contentment, Calm, and Confidence* (Beijing: China Machine Press, 2013).

Johnson, M.K. "Joy: a Review of the Literature and Suggestions for Future Directions." *The Journal of Positive Psychology* 15, no. 1 (2019): 5–24. https://doi.org/10.1080/1743 9760.2019.1685581.

Kimmerer, R.W. *Braiding Sweetgrass: Indigenous Wisdom, Scientific Knowledge and the Teachings of Plants* (Minneapolis: Milkweed Editions, 2015).

Lambert, C. "The Science of Happiness." *Harvard Magazine*, 2007. https://www .harvardmagazine.com/2007/01/the-science-of-happiness.html.

Liu, A. "Making Joy a Priority at Work." *Harvard Business Review*, July 17, 2019. https ://hbr.org/2019/07/making-joy-a-priority-at-work.

Lyubomirsky, S., L. King, and E. Diener. "The Benefits of Frequent Positive Affect: Does Happiness Lead to Success?" *Psychological Bulletin* 131, no. 6 (2005): 803–855. https ://doi.org/10.1037/0033-2909.131.6.803.

Moss, J. "When Passion Leads to Burnout." *Harvard Business Review*, July 1, 2019. https://hbr.org/2019/07/when-passion-leads-to-burnout.

Oliver, M. *Red Bird: Poems* (Boston: Beacon Press, 2009).

Pittinsky, T.L., and R.M. Montoya. "Empathic Joy in Positive Intergroup Relations." *Journal of Social Issues* 72, no. 3 (2016): 511–523. https://doi.org/10.1111/josi.12179.

Stokes, J., and O. Karihwatéhkwen. *Thanksgiving Address: Greetings to the Natural World* (Six Nations Indian Museum, 1993).

Tignor, S. "Naomi Osaka Isn't Enjoying Herself Even When She Wins—So You Can Understand Her Need for a Break from the Game." Tennis.com, September 4, 2021. https://www.tennis.com/news/articles/naomi-osaka-isn-t-enjoying-herself-even -when-she-wins-so-you-can-understand-her-.

Vaish, A., T. Grossmann, and A. Woodward. "Not All Emotions Are Created Equal: The Negativity Bias in Social-Emotional Development." *Psychological Bulletin* 134, no. 3 (2008): 383–403. https://doi.org/10.1037/0033-2909.134.3.383.

Skill Chapter 6: Inner Calm

Achor, S., and M. Gielan. "Resilience Is About How You Recharge, Not How You Endure." *Harvard Business Review*, June 24, 2016. https://hbr.org/2016/06/resilience -is-about-how-you-recharge-not-how-you-endure.

Chapman, B.P., K. Fiscella, I. Kawachi, P. Duberstein, and P. Muennig. "Emotion Suppression and Mortality Risk over a 12-Year Follow-Up." *Journal of Psychosomatic Research* 75, no. 4 (2013): 381–385. https://doi.org/10.1016/j.jpsychores.2013.07.014.

Nhat Hanh, T. *The Heart of the Buddha's Teaching: Transforming Suffering into Peace, Joy, and Liberation* (New York: Harmony, 1999).

Oliver, M. *Thirst: Poems* (Amsterdam University Press, 2006).

Rosenkranz, M.A., A. Lutz, D.M. Perlman, D.R. Bachhuber, B.S. Schuyler, D.G. MacCoon, and R.J. Davidson. "Reduced Stress and Inflammatory Responsiveness in Experienced Meditators Compared to a Matched Healthy Control Group." *Psychoneuroendocrinology* 68 (2016): 117–125. https://doi.org/10.1016/j.psyneuen .2016.02.013.

Taylor, J.B. *My Stroke of Insight: A Brain Scientist's Personal Journey* (New York: Penguin, 2009).

Whyte, D. *Consolations: The Solace, Nourishment, and Underlying Meaning of Everyday Words* (Langley, WA: Many Rivers Press, 2021).

Wikipedia. "Amygdala hijack." Wikipedia. Last modified December 14, 2022. https ://en.wikipedia.org/wiki/Amygdala_hijack.

Skill Chapter 7: Focus

American Psychological Association. "Multitasking: Switching Costs." American Psychological Association, March 2006. https://www.apa.org/topics/research /multitasking.

Arrien, A. *The Four-Fold Way: Walking the Paths of the Warrior, Teacher, Healer, and Visionary*. (San Francisco: HarperOne, 1993).

Awh, E., A.V. Belopolsky, and J. Theeuwes. "Top-Down versus Bottom-Up Attentional Control: A Failed Theoretical Dichotomy." *Trends in Cognitive Sciences* 16, no. 8 (2012): 437–443. https://doi.org/10.1016/j.tics.2012.06.010.

Isbell, E., C. Stevens, E. Pakulak, A. Hampton Wray, T.A. Bell, and H.J. Neville. "Neuroplasticity of Selective Attention: Research Foundations and Preliminary Evidence for a Gene by Intervention Interaction." *Proceedings of the National Academy of Sciences* 114, no. 35 (2017): 9247–9254. https://doi.org/10.1073/pnas.1707241114.

James, W. *The Principles of Psychology: Volumes 1 and 2* (New York: Henry Holt, 2021).

Jha, A.P. *Peak Mind* (New York: HarperCollins, 2021).

Killingsworth, M.A., and D.T. Gilbert. "A Wandering Mind Is an Unhappy Mind." *Science* 330, no. 6006 (2010): 932. https://doi.org/10.1126/science.1192439.

"Story of Two Wolves." Two Wolves Group. http://www.twowolvesgroup.com/story-of -two-wolves/.

Whitehead, N. "People Would Rather Be Electrically Shocked than Left Alone with Their Thoughts." Science.org, July 2014. https://www.science.org/content/article /people-would-rather-be-electrically-shocked-left-alone-their-thoughts-rev2.

Skill Chapter 8: Equanimity

Goldstein, J., "Deeper Dimensions of Mindfulness, Part 1." By T. Simon. Sounds True, February 2014. https://www.resources.soundstrue.com/transcript/deeper-dimensions -of-mindfulness-part-1/?print=print.

Goldstein, J. *Mindfulness: A Practical Guide to Awakening* (Sounds True, 2013).

Kornfield, J. "Audio: Meditation on Equanimity." Jack Kornfield, August 22, 2018). https://jackkornfield.com/meditation-equanimity/.

Lucas, G., director. *Star Wars: Revenge of the Sith*. 20th Century Fox Home Entertainment, 2013. 2 hr., 20 min.

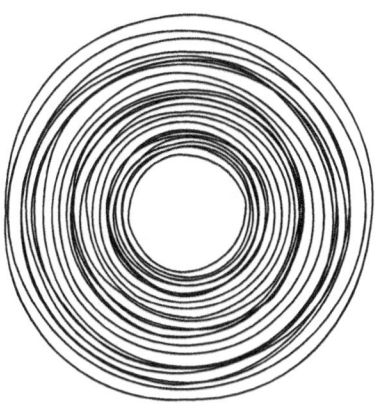

Resources

This is a partial list of books, websites, and other resources that I have benefited from.

Companion Resources for *Return to Mindfulness*

1. Take a free mindfulness assessment: https://knowyourmind.training/take-the-mindfulness-quiz/

2. The "return" mindfulness cards to go with this book: https://www.deckible.com/card-decks/1U-return-8-habits-to-be-mindful-in-real-world-shalini-bahl-ph-d-max-alaghband

3. Online eight-week programs with Shalini Bahl, Ph.D.: https://knowyourmind.training/start-here/

4. Take the online eight-week program to foster the eight mindful habits: https://knowyourmind.training/product/know-your-mind-online-training/

Books

1. *Mindfulness: A Practical Guide to Awakening* by Joseph Goldstein (Sounds True, 2013).

2. *Zen and the Art of Saving the Planet* by Thich Nhat Hanh (HarperCollins, 2022).

3. *The Book of Joy* by HH the Dalai Lama, Archbishop Desmond Tutu, and Douglas Carlton Abrams (Penguin Random House, 2016).

4. *Mastering the Core Teachings of the Buddha: An Unusually Hardcore Dharma Book* by Daniel Ingram (AEON Books, 2008).

5. *Compassion in Action* by Ram Dass and Mirabai Bush (Potter/Ten Speed /Harmony/Rodale, 1995).

6. *Seeking the Heart of Wisdom* by Joseph Goldstein and Jack Kornfield (Shambhala Publications, 1987).

7. *Contemplative Practices in Higher Education: Powerful Methods to Transform Teaching and Learning* by Daniel Barbezat and Mirabai Bush (Jossey-Bass, 2013).

8. *Comfortable with Uncertainty: 108 Teachings on Cultivating Fearlessness and Compassion* by Pema Chödrön (Shambhala Publications, 2003).

9. *Path to God* by Ram Dass (Harmony, 2005).

10. *Full Catastrophe Living* by Jon Kabat-Zinn (Delta Trade Paperbacks, 1990).

11. *Peak Mind* by Amishi P. Jha (HarperCollins, 2021).

12. *Insight Meditation* by Joseph Goldstein (Shambhala Publications, 1993).

13. *Letters to a Young Poet* by Rainer Maria Rilke, translated by Anita Barrows and Joanna Macy (Shambhala Publications, 2021).

14. *Walking Each Other Home: Conversations on Loving and Dying* by Ram Dass and Mirabai Bush (Sounds True, 2018).

15. *The Four-Fold Way: Walking the Paths of the Warrior, Teacher, Healer, and Visionary* by Angeles Arrien (HarperCollins, 1993).

16. *Cave in the Snow* by Vicki Mackenzie (Dharma Audiobooks, 2015).

17. *Walking the Walk* by Pema Chödrön (Sounds True, 2014).

18. *Rilke's Book of Hours, Love Poems to God* by Rainer Maria Rilke, translated by Anita Barrows and Joanna Macy (Riverhead Books, 1996).

19. *The Essential Rumi* by Rumi, translated by Coleman Banks (HarperCollins, 2004).

20. *Consolations* by David Whyte (Many Rivers Press, 2021).

21. *A Thousand Mornings* by Mary Oliver (Penguin, 2013).

Websites

1. Dharma Seed. https://dharmaseed.org

2. Mindful.org. https://www.mindful.org

3. On Being. https://onbeing.org

Retreat Centers

1. Vipassana Center in Shelburne Falls, MA. https://www.dhamma.org
2. Insight Meditation Society in Barre, MA. https://www.dharma.org
3. Barre Center for Buddhist Studies in Barre, MA. https://www.buddhistinquiry.org
4. Garrison Institute in Garrison, NY. https://www.garrisoninstitute.org

Apps

There are many apps out there, and I am only sharing the ones that I have used. Apps are great for sustaining your practice, but I highly recommend learning from a teacher the basics of mindfulness before using apps.

1. Dharma Seed
2. Insight Timer
3. Simple Habit App
4. Return to Mindfulness on Deckible
5. Ten Percent Happier

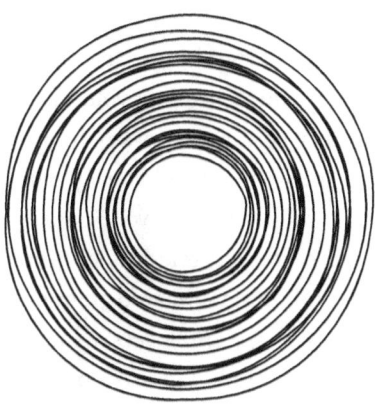

A Note of Gratitude

This book has been a labor of love shaped by the hearts, minds, and efforts of countless beings. I owe my deepest gratitude to the many who've made this book possible, starting with the Buddha and his lineage of teachers who've made the incredible teachings on mindfulness available to me. It's unrealistic to name everyone on my gratitude list, and if I did not mention you on these pages, please know that I am grateful for you in my life.

My professional journey to become a certified teacher began with the Mindfulness-Based Stress Reduction program, and for that, I am thankful to Jon Kabat-Zinn, Ph.D., the visionary behind the world-renowned program.

To Jon: You've been an embodiment of grace, wisdom, and humor, not only in your role as a teacher, but you've also shown me what it means to be mindful in the real world.

Jon provided the early foundation for my mindfulness journey, but it was Joseph Goldstein who guided me to its depths. Seeking deeper understanding after my big wake-up call, I stumbled upon Joseph's book *Mindfulness: A Practical Guide to Awakening*. His clear teachings introduced me to Buddha's genius framework for grasping how our minds work.

To Joseph: Your book and teachings have opened my heart and mind in unexpected ways. Every time I listen to you, I learn something new, even when I think you couldn't possibly have anything new to say. I love your laugh in the middle of meditations and your genuineness as a teacher and human being. A big bow of gratitude to you!

In my search for a corporate mindfulness program, I learned about Search Inside Yourself, a mindfulness-based emotional intelligence program that had been created for Google employees. Mirabai Bush, a creative force, not only co-created this program but is also a prolific writer with numerous books to her name. She introduced contemplative practices to companies way before it became mainstream—a true OG who traveled to India in the 1960s to learn from renowned teachers like Neem Karoli Baba and Goenka. I was intrigued by her, especially since there were so few women teachers in the mindfulness world at the time. I stalked her on Facebook and was surprised by her warm response and openness to meeting.

To Mirabai: I am blessed to have you as a role model, mentor, and teacher in my life. The mantra that you learned from your teacher Maharaj-ji, "love all, serve all," is a reminder that I keep close to my heart. Thank you for your big heart that makes room for so many people and all you do to make this world a better place for all beings.

Following Mirabai, I took my first Search Inside Yourself (SIY) class with her and Chade-Meng Tang, the co-founder of the program at Google. Soon after, I signed up to be in their first cohort of SIY teachers. It is here that I made many wonderful friends, including my pod members Julie Murphy and Vasco Gaspar and our cohort mentor Mark Coleman.

To Mark: Your guided meditations with bells are still my favorite! You taught me how to show up honestly in my role as a mindfulness teacher. Thank you for your lovely teachings to wake up in the wild and for helping me discover my gifts as a teacher.

Another badass teacher that I've been fortunate to learn from is Sharon Salzberg, who is also one of the OGs who traveled with Mirabai and Joseph to India. There are so many more teachers to thank—I am so in awe and full of gratitude for this whole group of teachers who've dedicated their lives to living and teaching mindfulness.

Shifting gears to the gang of editors and writing coaches who supported me on this journey. I started with a ten-week Bring Your Book to Life program with Lisa Tener, who is a brilliant teacher, editor, and one of the most resourceful people I've ever met. I completed the first draft of this book in the form of a handbook in her program to go along with the new eight-week program that I launched at the time.

To Lisa: Thank you for being such a positive, practical, and creative guide for me and so many new authors. I so appreciate your willingness to generously share your skills and resources to help us all succeed!

Thanks to Lisa's introduction, I met Kelly Malone—my incredibly talented and brave editor who undertook the herculean task of undoing my academic style of writing and helped me find my voice as a writer. I am still a work in progress, but I have come a long way since my first nerdy draft.

To Kelly: I am deeply grateful to you for your humor, spaciousness, and patience in working through several drafts of this book. A huge shout-out for your valuable insights and editing prowess while building my confidence as a writer. I appreciate your deep understanding of mindfulness and the bigger why for this book. Your big heart and masterful edits have enriched this book immensely.

In the middle of what might have been my third or fourth version of this book, I found myself plummeting to rock bottom. Enter Jena Schwartz, a writing coach offering "fierce encouragement for writing + life," which is exactly what I needed at the time. Fierce indeed—I rewrote fifteen chapters in fifteen weeks, all while navigating the pandemonium of a pandemic.

Jena, your poetic touch and structure rescued me from the depths of creative despair—so much gratitude.

Last but not least is the person who reminded me to return to my truth and set it free. Amy Thompson, a poet and master storyteller, came into my life to coach me for a TEDx talk over four weeks—a journey usually spanning six months. The TEDx talk was a miracle, further reinforcing the power of returning to my inner knowing (that you can read on Mindful.org).

To Amy: I am so in awe and beyond grateful to you for the magical ways in which you expanded my creative consciousness.

To the folks at Mindful.org, especially Amber Tucker and Ava Whitney-Coulter, who worked with me as editors, thank you for believing in me and building a platform where I can share insights about mindfulness in the real world with a global audience.

To Richard Fernandez: I admire your humble, honest, and mindful leadership at Search Inside Yourself and before that at Wisdom Labs. Your confidence in me made me a better teacher. Thank you for all you do to make this world a better place.

I would be remiss if I didn't acknowledge Max Alaghband for the many wonderful ways his partnership in creating the companion mindfulness cards to go with this book on Deckible.com transformed this book.

To Max: Your skills in human-centered design to understand what mindfulness practitioners are seeking in taking their practice into the world were invaluable. Moreover, I am grateful for your care, wisdom, and choice of words that brought spaciousness and clarity to the daily practices and reminders in the cards. Your mindful coffee-making and tea ceremonies were precious gifts to our creative process. Most of all, I am grateful for your mindful friendship.

Thank you also for introducing me to Laureen Andalib, whose beautiful design for the cards, using the eight icons for mindful habits originally designed by Jason Garvale, inspired the design for the inside of this book. A big shout-out to Uttara Nanda for her creative expression in the earlier renditions of the book cover and design.

Kudos to the incredible Farah Ameen, who proofread this book in record time! A big thank you also to Patrick Milne for the earlier edits to get the e-book up on my website.

Collaborating with Greenleaf Book Group has been one of the best decisions I made during my journey with this book. I want to extend my heartfelt gratitude to Sheila Parr for the exquisite cover design that is a visual reminder for readers to return again and again to mindfulness. The care with which you designed the different elements inside the book is remarkable. Furthermore, I am indebted to my editing team, particularly Sally Garland, whose thought-provoking questions have added a new level of clarity and structure to the book.

Two other people who've been an integral part of this journey with me are my son, Ankrish Bahl Milne, and my husband, George R. Milne.

Ankrish was stuck with us at home during the pandemic, and what a gift that turned out to be. He wrote stories for the book and the online program accompanying the book. He was also part of the OG team that worked on developing the companion product that eventually became the mindfulness cards on Deckible.com.

To Ankrish: I am grateful that I got to work with you in this capacity. Prior to this, I didn't fully appreciate your special gifts in writing, playful humor, and deep insights that were vital to the book and product development. I appreciated your scientific inquiry to ensure that the conclusions and connections I was making were sound. Your presence is one of the biggest blessings in my life.

George is not only my life partner and fellow seeker but also my biggest collaborator as a mindfulness researcher.

To George: Thank you for walking hundreds of miles with me, talking through the different versions of this book, titles, and insights. I so appreciate your mad research skills, without which I couldn't have come up with the mindfulness assessment tool to go with this book. Your playfulness, sense of adventure, and love for nature remind me to return and renew. Thank you for believing in me and being the biggest fan of my twenty-minute body scan on Insight Timer ☺.

I also want to thank all my clients whose practice keeps me going and my friends and family whose love nourishes me.

Finally, a deep bow of gratitude to my incredible parents—Suman Bahl and Kanwar C. Bahl—without whom this book wouldn't exist!

To Mummy and Daddy: Your unwavering love, lessons of hard work and integrity, and grace are the bedrock for this book and the work I do. You unconditionally supported me as I carved my unique path in life that many in our culture would've considered unconventional. I am grateful for your love and blessings.

Despite the love and support of so many people, writing can be a lonely journey. In my darkest hours, when I felt isolated, stuck, or doubtful, I knew I was never alone. I bow down to my ancestors who walk with me; Goddess Saraswati, who is a muse of creativity, music, science, and wisdom; and all beings who knowingly and unknowingly contributed to my journey as a seeker, writer, and teacher.

About the Author

SHALINI BAHL, PH.D., is a mindfulness consultant, an award-winning researcher, and certified mindfulness teacher. She has dedicated over 15 years researching and developing cross-disciplinary solutions to help businesses, educators, and political clients build essential mindfulness skills. Her mission is to empower individuals to disrupt default thinking and live with empowered choice for personal and collective fulfillment, creating a better world for all.

Certified at the Center for Mindfulness, UMass Medical School, and the Search Inside Yourself Leadership Institute that originated at Google, Dr. Bahl is the Founder of Know Your Mind LLC, a social business committed to making evidence-based mindfulness skills widely accessible. Her teachings are rooted in time-tested principles of mindfulness, backed by insights from neuroscience, psychology, and a human-centered approach.

As a former successful entrepreneur and business professor who has lived and worked in three countries—India, Kuwait, and the USA—Dr. Bahl has a deep appreciation of each client's unique journey and meets them where they are. She works with diverse audiences including CEOs and executives at Fortune 500 companies, educators, and students.

Beyond her professional achievements, Dr. Bahl is a TEDx speaker and has real-world experience of practicing mindfulness not only as a teacher but also as an elected municipal leader and academic.

Her pioneering work in this field has been published in premier marketing and public policy journals. One of the papers, a collaboration with other researchers, won the Best Research Paper Award from The American Marketing Association in 2019. Dr. Bahl's guided meditations and programs have had over 250,000 plays on the Insight Timer and Simple Habit app, making her resources accessible to all who seek them.

When she's not researching or teaching mindfulness, she loves to cook tasty and healthy vegetarian food, dance and make music, hike in nature with family and friends, and all kinds of creative projects. Her love for life and mindfulness is contagious, and she brings this infectious energy to every aspect of her work.